From Plough to Entrepreneurship:
A History of African Entrepreneurs in Evaton 1905-1960s

Vusumuzi R. Kumalo

Langaa Research & Publishing CIG
Mankon, Bamenda

Publisher
Langaa RPCIG
Langaa Research & Publishing Common Initiative Group
P.O. Box 902 Mankon
Bamenda
North West Region
Cameroon
Langaagrp@gmail.com
www.langaa-rpcig.net

Distributed in and outside N. America by African Books Collective
orders@africanbookscollective.com
www.africanbookscollective.com

ISBN-10: 9956-551-53-8

ISBN-13: 978-9956-551-53-8

© Vusumuzi R. Kumalo 2020

All rights reserved.
No part of this book may be reproduced or transmitted in any form or by any means, mechanical or electronic, including photocopying and recording, or be stored in any information storage or retrieval system, without written permission from the publisher

Table of Contents

Preface v

Introduction vii

Chapter 1

Introduction 1

Chapter 2

The origins and character
of Evaton 65

Chapter 3

Subsistence farming and
economic independence........................127

Chapter 4

Transition from unregulated
to regulated trade 205

Bibliography..209

Preface

In a sense, *From Plough to Entrepreneurship* is inspired by the work of South African historians who have contributed significantly to the transformation of South African history well beyond a liberal and conservative approach. During my pupillage at the University of the Witwatersrand, I benefitted greatly from exposure to the work of several historians whose interests have impinged on mine. One of the historians who inspired me was Timothy Keegan and his work on rural transformation in the Highveld. To disentangle the work of Keegan from this volume is impossible. What can be said with certainty is that Keegan's work provided the basis of this book. For his publication, oral testimonies constituted the prime source of information. During his research, Keegan spent valuable time interviewing African sharecroppers and independent farmers who could not be traced in government records. His main concern was on rural race relations and the historical dynamics of sharecropping enterprises in the Highveld. He conducted interviews on the sharecropper struggle for economic independence during the culmination of the proletarianisation process that took place after mineral discovery in South Africa in the nineteenth century. The larger proportion of families that Keegan interviewed later settled in Evaton, where they bought properties on an unprecedented scale from 1905 onwards.

As prosperous farmers displaced from white owned farms, the sharecroppers obtained small-holding plots in the freehold township of Evaton with the aim of re-establishing themselves as farmers, thereby sustaining their economic independence in an urban environment. After reading Keegan's work, I followed up on sharecropper's families that he interviewed and traced their family histories in Evaton. My aim was to trace whether these families managed to maintain their economic independence or not. My findings, presented in this volume, reveal that the larger proportion of these families altered their economic activities from plough to entrepreneurship. In Evaton they opened shops, butcheries, funeral parlours and other economic enterprises that serviced the people of the township.

This project could not have been carried out without the advice of numerous friends, academics and the people of Evaton that I interviewed, some of whom have passed away. It would be an indulgence to even try to enumerate them here. There are, however, few who should be mentioned. The Kekane brothers, Maisela and Tladi Kekane, the late Dwight Seremi, Alf Kumalo, Mr Qupe, to name a few. I should also like to thank the publisher for publishing this book.

Introduction

Evaton is one of the oldest remaining freehold locations in South Africa yet its history is less well-known compared to locations and townships that were established after it. The history of Evaton can be better understood within the broader context of economic and rural transformation that took place from the late nineteenth to the mid-twentieth century. This was a period that witnessed crucial developments that included industrialisation, the growth of urbanisation, the influx of Africans[1] who serviced the towns and manufacturing industries, as well as the movement of sharecroppers and labour tenants from white farms. For the Union government, all these historical dynamics created a new problem of control. This crisis was addressed by creating policies that aimed at controlling African people in urban areas, and isolating them by consigning them to urban locations. These locations were designed to be labour reserves that secured a supply of cheap labour for white businesses. In these residential spaces, opportunities for personal advancement and financial independence through trade were limited. Local white authorities in many cases denied Africans property rights and tightly monitored the access of African people to these locations.

Evaton was distinct from most other African settlements. One aspect that made it unique was its status as a freehold township. This status makes it a rarity, like freehold areas of Johannesburg such as Sophiatown and Alexandra. The other areas mentioned were, however, really part of the greater Johannesburg urban area. Despite the formal status of both Alexandra and Sophiatown as being outside the municipal boundary, these freehold settlements were labour reserves with, by the 1930s, a high population of wage labourers. Evaton, some miles distant from Johannesburg, was not. Officially some of these freehold localities were labelled as slums. The chief justification for labelling them as such was based on their overcrowdedness, poverty, and blighted physical appearance. Unlike Evaton, which was sparsely populated, Sophiatown suffered from an 'insalubrious environment [that] was marked by gutters, uncollected garbage ...inadequate filthy lavatories, and stench.'[2]

What distinguished Evaton from these areas was its economic history, self-sufficiency, demography, and geographical location. 'Evaton is one of the most orderly places I know of in the Transvaal,' said Sol Plaatjie, testifying to the Native Economic Commission.[3] Physically, the area had big yards which enabled residents to be relatively successful subsistence farmers for the first three decades of its development in the twentieth century. Subsistence farming allowed local residents to refrain from working for white industrialists. Another important aspect that made Evaton stand out was the presence of the Wilberforce Institute, the only African controlled school in the Transvaal. The main purpose of the Institute was to produce self-reliant citizens. In its motto 'African advancement', Wilberforce stressed the importance of providing students with industrial training as well as academic skills. The school was under the control of the African Methodist Episcopal Church, which African Americans established in the United States and attracted a group of educated Africans to settle in the area.

Even after the collapse of subsistence farming, the area provided opportunities for entrepreneurial growth and opportunities for Africans. These opportunities included enterprises such as grave digging and ambulance operations. In the freehold areas of Johannesburg, these services were under the control of the Johannesburg City Council. Due to its relative autonomy and opportunities, Evaton attracted Africans with means to buy properties and set up homes there. These Africans saw Evaton as an area where they could advance their social and economic life in an urban environment. Depending on individual interest, Evaton's freehold status and autonomy provided room for Africans who aspired to advance themselves in different spheres of life such as religion, the economy and education. The area also provided a refuge to Africans who sought to evade municipal control.

Evaton was established in 1905 and is situated thirteen miles from Vereeniging and twenty-eight miles from Johannesburg. As a thinly populated semi-agricultural centre in the Vaal, Evaton attracted displaced sharecroppers that were squeezed off the land around the Highveld[4] as well as educated Africans mostly from the Reef. There were also a few independent farmers from Natal and some *Oorlams* (indigenous people of Southern Africa familiar, as a result of long contact, with the customs, standards, and language of the Dutch colonists) families who came from the *Zuid Afrikaanse Republiek* and Orange Free State. Similar social, political, and economic forces caused these groups to move to Evaton. The urban educated group was deprived of the right to land ownership elsewhere where they could build schools and churches. They also suffered under pass laws that restricted their movements. Sharecroppers and a small number of *Oorlams* were displaced after the Anglo-Boer War (South African War) of 1899-1902, which together with technological developments forced them to seek land where they could continue with their farming enterprises. Independent farmers that enjoyed the privilege of owning land in colonial Natal were attracted by the freehold status of the area and the large stands that were available. For these groups, access to land and the right to land ownership contributed to their economic prosperity and educational and spiritual advancement as well as the right to use both physical and social resources. Some liquidated their livestock and assets and invested in entrepreneurial activities. Evaton was, therefore, salient and central to African economic independence and advancement.

Considering their rural entrepreneurial exposure, both former share-croppers and independent farmers moved to Evaton with the hope of re-establishing themselves as commercial farmers. The subdivision of land which reduced their size of land into small agricultural holdings did not, however, allow local residents to farm for commercial gain, but for subsistence purposes only.

The early phase of local development was characterised by the flourishing of the subsistence economy. During this period, the local economy was based on pre-colonial reciprocity that relied on a strong sense of sharing among local families. Monetary ties were minimal, and the local economy was characterised by a range of small-scale economic activities along with bartering that was integrated with social interactions. Under this economic system, there was a greater degree of local community participation in all local activities ranging from public works to home building. Evaton was then a small settlement, but its social and economic life was to be disturbed by the development of secondary industries in nearby Vereeniging.

The development of secondary industries in the late 1930s and 1940s triggered African employment in manufacturing to grow rapidly. Many workers that were drawn into the labour market were newly urbanised while others came from the farms where they had worked as farm workers. In urban municipalities, access was tightly controlled under the 1923 Urban Areas Act and there was a serious shortage of housing. This made it difficult for many Africans to settle freely in these areas without being subject to regulations. Life in urban municipal areas became difficult for African men and women who were restricted from settling in urban centres which were the only places where employment was available. African people were not permitted to settle without the necessary paperwork. These conditions pushed many African migrant workers to unregulated areas like Evaton which enjoyed freehold status. In Evaton, these workers rented rooms from local stand-holders and turned the locale into their urban home. Economically, this transformation led to the shift from subsistence farming to an open market monetary economy that depended on the growth of secondary industry. This new economic system gave birth to the emergence of local enterprises. These developments in Evaton happened at the same time as the coming to power of the National Party.[5] They drew the attention of the Nationalist government that implemented new measures of control which impacted negatively on the local autonomy of black people.

Notes

[1] The labels used to describe indigenous people of South Africa have undergone significant changes in the past years. In recent times, two labels have been used most often to describe indigenous people as 'black' and 'African', but it is not generally clear what the preferred term is from the perspective of the indigenous themselves. For this study the author will refer to them as Africans.

[2] D. Hart and G. Pirie, 'The Sight and Soul of Sophiatown,' *Geographical Review*, Vol 74, 1984, p. 40.

[3] Report of Native Economic Commission 1930-1932 UG, 22, Pretoria Government S. Plaatjie's testimony in the Printers, 1932.

[4] T. Keegan, 'Crisis and Catharsis in the Development of Capitalism in South African Agriculture,' *African Affairs*, 84, July 1985, p. 372.

[5] National Party was a political party in South Africa founded in 1914 and disbanded in 1997. The party was originally an Afrikaner ethnic nationalist party that promoted Afrikaner interests in South Africa. The NP was the governing party of South Africa from 1948 until 1994 and was disbanded in 2005. Its policies included apartheid, the establishment of a South African Republic, and the promotion of Afrikaner culture.

Chapter 1

The origins and character of Evaton

Introduction

The legal victory of Edward Tsewu permanently altered the face of African land-ownership in the Transvaal. Africans could buy land and register properties in their own names. All Africans wishing to begin a new life and make Evaton their home were welcome. By 1905, the settlement acquired a status of being a freehold settlement, and also became an important African educational and religious centre for Africans in the Transvaal. Evaton provided local resident's space as a defence mechanism against demands made on them by the Industrial Revolution and their struggle against increased dependency in wage labour affected the shape of the Evaton community over time. This chapter deals with the origins of Evaton and its distinct character. It reveals that the distinctiveness of Evaton lies in its social composition, the personality of the people who formed it, its economic history and the presence of the Wilberforce Institute. In addition, the idea of Ethiopianism attached to Evaton's origin makes it distinct in comparison to other freehold areas.

This chapter is divided into three parts. The first part deals with the origins of Evaton and the role of Ethiopianism in the founding of Evaton. The second section concentrates on the first wave of residents which comprised of sharecroppers and independent farmers from Natal as well as educated residents. The last section concentrates on the period after 1913. During this phase the Union government changed its political strategy towards African landowners which in turn changed the pattern of local purchases of stands in Evaton. This period experienced the arrival of the second wave of newcomers who had to follow a tedious process when buying properties. The final section of the chapter analyses local economic practices and the socio-cultural practice of reciprocity that bonded the local community together.

The origins of Evaton and the role of Ethiopianism

After the Anglo-Boer War, white colonists had acquired control of African land. They owned and controlled much of the best land in different territories of South Africa. The greater part of the African land occupied by white colonists was, therefore, acquired by the force of arms. In blunt terms, then, what took place during this period was the militaristic occupation and subjection of Africans to a colonial regime. This implies that the land issue was intimately bound up with the question of political control and power. The colonial political imposition was not, however, well received by Africans - it was often resisted bitterly in different parts of the country. In Zululand for instance, the defeat of amaZulu by the British was much longer and less obvious, and more a bloody process.[1] Both the Zulu and the BaPedi Kingdom became the vital obstacles to colonial control. In the Transvaal, the Pedi remained the 'stumbling block to effective British rule and a potent symbol of the possibility of continued African resistance to colonial claims to the land and demands for labour and tax.'[2] There were, of course, some land parcels that were occupied peacefully after the peaceful agreement with African chiefs, such as the Griqua chief Andries Waterboer who signed the treaty with Governor Sir Benjamin D'Urban in the 1830s.[3] For many African chiefs, these treaties guaranteed their orbit of colonists' trade. In some cases, white land invasion was easily achieved by exploiting chiefdom rivalry that was common among African chiefdom families. Among the BaTswana, the roles played by the Boers and the British in exploiting these polarisations led to the Barolong War.[4] These two Barolong branches, the Ratshidi and the Rapulana, were situated close to each other and were involved in a prolonged struggle for land. This Barolong War marked one of the factors that led to the establishment of the British Bechuanaland.[5] After the completion of the colonial conquest South Africa was now divided into four provinces under the political control of the Boers and British colonists. The Boers, who rebelled against the Cape British government and trekked to the interior, gained control of the Orange Free State and the Transvaal. The British colonists on the other hand-controlled Natal and the Cape Province. White Christian belief also presented another feature of colonialism. 'The missionaries wanted to prepare the Barolong for exploitation in the industries – something that would keep them poor and hungry to make them to become 'slaves' of the industrial world.'[6] White Christians felt morally superior to 'heathen Africans'. This notion of superiority was driven and reinforced by the theories of racial superiority which placed white people on the top of the hierarchy and Africans at the bottom.[7] The introduction of Christianity to Africans was considered by white missionaries as beneficial to Africans. The idea of racial superiority in Christian mission stations gave rise to new forms of African resistance to colonialism. In the Transvaal in particular, the new form of non-violent resistance was spearheaded by the group of African clergy who seceded from white mission stations, this group called themselves Ethiopianists.[8] These leaders of the independent churches added their intellectual fervour to political equation and, in most cases, became leaders of the political organisations. After the Anglo Boer War (1899-1902), they founded the Transvaal African freehold settlements in which they built African-controlled churches and schools.

As the nineteenth century progressed Boer Republics and British colonies introduced different laws to govern the colonies.

These laws provided the essential context in which social and economic changes took place in South Africa. They shaped up internal urban development that emanated from technological advancement and the discovery of minerals. The new laws brought radical change in the daily lives of African people and also introduced new means of landownership. In what could be called indigenous law that regulates African landownership, the chief was the sole administrator of land. He or she allocated land within his or her district and once the piece of land had been allocated the respective user who might be regarded in the western world as the owner had sole control over it.[9] Others wishing to use the land would need to approach the new owner for consent. Land was allocated in perpetuity and was inheritable from generation to generation. After the conquest the land was never transferred in ownership but was registered in the name of the Secretary of Native Affairs as trustee. This was never divulged to the `purchasers' in Natal and the Cape colony.[10]

In the Afrikaner-controlled Orange Free State and Transvaal, Article 159 of the Volksraad Resolution of 18 June 1855 explicitly stated that no African landownership was allowed.[11] At the same time, Africans were technically without any land and were dependent on the Afrikaner authorities to demarcate 'locations' for them.[12] Whites allowed Africans to live on the locations on condition of 'good behaviour', but did not allow them to own the land with title deeds. Some Africans lived on white farms on tenancy arrangements that were cemented by economic relations. After the collapse of extensive pastoralism and hunting, which served as the cornerstone of the Boer's economy. Many Boers in the Highveld depended on the sharecropping enterprise. In urban areas Africans were landless and overcrowded in slums, with public health as well as safety often seen in the light of class and ethnic differences. It is in this context that the origins of Evaton could be located. Like many freehold settlements, the establishment of Evaton must be understood, not only within the context of the post Anglo-Boer War African acquisition of private land, but from the broader understanding of a deeper colonial history of land dispossession and African Christian secession from white mainstream churches.

Evaton was subdivided from Weldebeesfontein Farm No. 12. It was located between two industrial towns, namely Johannesburg and Vereeniging. The farm was first bounded by the Golden Highway on the west and the railway line that links the afore-mentioned towns on the east. The farm was owned by Joshua François Joubert and François Jacobus Johannes Joubert under a Deed of Transfer in the mid nineteenth century.[13] The Jouberts sold the farm to Thomas Adams and Charles John Easton in the 1890s before the war. Adams and Easton formed a partnership under the company of Easton and Adams, which subdivided the farm into plots.[14] These landowners were British officers who participated in the war on behalf of the Crown government.[15] By then, it was usual for white landowners who suffered the economic effects of the war to sell their land to Africans.[16] During this time in the Transvaal most landowners had gone bankrupt.[17] The economy of the Transvaal was in a parlous state and Britain was hesitant to become too deeply involved with the problems of the province.[18] These circumstances forced many white landowners to sell their properties. Among the new owners were British generals who owned land in different parts of the country. Like other whites, Adams and Eaton took advantage of the post-war setbacks and sold land to Africans.

They also capitalised on the land tenure case that Tsewu won in 1905, which allowed Africans to own and register land in the Transvaal. After the subdivision of Weldebeesfontein farm, the area was named Evaton and was declared a freehold settlement. The name Evaton was derived from the combination of Eve Adams and Easton, the owners of the farm, the blending of Eve and Easton formed Evaton. In the context of South Africa, the freehold status of Evaton implied that the locale was not a location, a 'native' village or 'native' hostel under the Native Urban Areas Act of 1923. The settlement was not defined by this Act, set apart or laid out by any local authority, nor was it under the jurisdiction of any urban location. Before 1936, Evaton was not scheduled as a 'native area', and the acquisition of properties by Africans was made lawful by the Governor General under Section 1 of the Natives' Land Act of 1913. The status of Evaton was not even defined in Section 35 of the Native Administration Act No 38 of 1927.

Since the settlement was not set apart or reserved for African occupation, it was also open for occupation by white residents.[19] The freehold status provided local residents with the autonomy to build independent churches and schools without any government intervention. Residents could also trade freely without being regulated, and could own land, an economic resource that was not easy for Africans to acquire. Evaton provided a sense of belonging, a social structure where the previously disadvantaged could begin to reconstruct an African identity and dignity. It is where residents embraced strict social mores of the time, aspiring to middle class standards of conduct, dress and speech as part of uplifting the African race. The formation of Evaton could be located within the broader African struggles for land ownership and autonomy. The struggle for land-ownership was waged by different African groups, which included sharecroppers, chiefs and the educated Africans[20], who are referred to in the literature as the modern elite. These groups responded to the land dispossession that took place in the eighteenth and nineteenth centuries. Land dispossession and the entrenchment of capitalist agriculture reached a devastating conclusion in the state's relocation or forced removal and policies in the 1950s and 1960s.[21] The responses to dispossession and displacement differed from region to region. In the urban Transvaal, particularly in the Reef, this struggle was organised by clergies under the auspices of Ethiopianism.[22]

The origins of this movement can be traced to its founder, Rev Nehemiah Tile, who left the Wesleyan Missionary Society and formed the Tembu National Church in 1882. Tile and other members of the movement responded to the colour bar that persisted inside white churches by forming their own independent churches under the control of black people. For instance, Rev Tsewu, who led the Free Church Mission in Johannesburg before buying property in Evaton, was suspected of having been involved in the Ethiopian movement.[23] He was also charged with mismanagement of the congregation's affairs, including funds 'with a view to worldly gain'.[24] With an aim of investigating the matter, Mzimba was sent by the Presbytery of Kaffraria to assist in dealing with the problems.[25] For these allegations the synod of Kaffraria decided to dismiss Tsewu and replaced him with Rev C. R. Hamilton, a white priest. African congregants did not receive the replacement of Tsewu by a white pastor well. It was regarded an unfair judgement. In response to his dismissal, Tsewu established the Independent Native Presbyterian Church, although he thought that the newly formed church would reunite eventually with the white mother body.[26]

By 1903, the Johannesburg congregation was transferred to the care of the Transvaal Presbytery and Tsewu realised that the prospects of reunion were impractical.[27] As a result, Tsewu remained in Johannesburg and subsequently joined the American African Methodist Episcopal Church (AME), which was different from his protestations about being Presbyterian.[28] It is clear from Tsewu's experience that there were many factors that affected African clergies. The most important factor for the Ethiopianists who submitted themselves to the AME church was access to land. As the church was rapidly expanding, there was a demand for land where they could build churches and schools.

For many urban Africans in the Reef, particularly the educated, Ethiopianism offered an avenue for the search for personal advancement. It also offered an avenue for expressing vague feelings of nationalism by people whose traditional institutions were being undermined.[29] On the issue of land, Tsewu believed 'that the Natives ought to be allowed to buy land in their own names, and have title deeds in their own names.'[30] This struggle was of great importance among the educated pioneers of Evaton before the area was conceived, and it united them. This struggle emerged from the discrimination that existed in white churches and it broadened into more fundamental issues that included economic and social aspects, along with the land question.

This social and economic situation has been examined by many social historians[31] who studied the circumstances that might have led these professionals to seek the autonomy and respectability that Evaton embodied. More importantly, these socio-economic circumstances played an important role in altering the consciousness of religious professionals. This social class reflected powerlessness and helplessness in a socio-economic situation that was increasingly repressive. This class began to lean towards promoting unity among themselves in order to protect their limited privileges. To some extent, this radicalised some of these professionals. Rev Edward Tsewu is an example. The Native Commissioner of Johannesburg described Tsewu as someone who was troublesome and made impudent demands for explanations from His Excellency.[32]

Before dissenting from mainstream churches, African clergies seem to have played less of a direct political role pertaining to issues of land. Discrimination, however, pushed church leaders into the political arena which focused on two issues - education and land.[33] Educated Africans were anxious to seek higher education, and this issue was later taken up by Rev Jantjie Zachariah (JZ) Tantsi under the auspices of the African Methodist Episcopal Church who built the Wilberforce Institute in Evaton. They also rejected white control and continued to raise the question of land which, according to Campbell, 'stood as the ultimate emblem of European domination.'[34]

Their political desire for land was supported by sharecroppers who were increasingly being displaced from white farms. During the post-Anglo-Boer war recovery in the countryside, thousands of highly skilled sharecroppers returned to the farms to trigger a remarkable economic revival. On many farms' sharecroppers found old landlords unwilling to accept their service back on their farms. Those who were accepted were told to cull their herds or vacate the land.[35] This situation was exacerbated by the implementation of the Rights of Coloured Persons in Respect of Fixed Property Act 42 of 1908. The Act required tenants - mostly sharecroppers - to sign contracts, which brought them within the ambit of law.[36] This Act required that sharecroppers should register their wives and children as servants in white farms. These changes were not well received by many sharecroppers who left the countryside to towns where they united with the educated elite.[37] The solidarity between these African groups was derived from their mutual desire for land ownership and an end to the racial discrimination that they suffered at the hands of the white priests and landlords. This commonality drew some of the sharecroppers into the religious ranks of the AME church.[38] This explains how, why and who formed the community of Evaton.

The examination of the origins of Evaton as a residential area provides a grounded empirical study of the ways in which land-ownership was tied up in the various historical dynamics that facilitated its establishment. These dynamics included a number of factors that possibly led to the formation of Evaton as an autonomous residential area. Firstly, the origins of Evaton can be attributed to an African American influence that was perpetuated by a frequent trans-Atlantic movement of people, ideology and institutions that created multifaceted relationships between Africans in America and South Africa. Secondly, to the resistance of the Ethiopian movement.[39] Thirdly, to the development of separatist churches that sought to own land where they could build schools and churches. Finally, to the emergence of a new class of educated Africans who were committed to non-racial ideals gleaned from Christianity and supported by the theory and to some extent the practice of Cape politics.[40]

The AME Bishop, Henry McNeal Turner, who came to South Africa in 1896 to serve the interests of the AME Church, formalised its connection with Ethiopian churches. According to Campbell, Turner provided a vehicle for educated Africans to challenge the Crown government on the issue of land.[41] In fact, Ethiopianists such as Rev Tsewu, Tantsi, and many others, drew great inspiration from Bishop Turner's action of buying an AME property next to Queenstown. Before the arrival of the African American Bishop, Ethiopianists had hungered for institutions of learning of their own. In the Transvaal, they were perpetually haunted by laws that regulated African landowners. Historians such as Feinberg and Bergh have contributed to our understanding of African land ownership before 1905, the period before Evaton was founded. In their paper they note that 'Article 159 of the Volksraad Resolution of 18 June 1855 explicitly stated that all people of colour were excluded from citizenship and the right to obtain land in freehold.'[42]

In view of these serious land-ownership complications, Ethiopianists, who later incorporated their churches into the AME, were left with much less freedom with regard to land ownership than their white counterparts. Their ambition of buying land where they could build schools and churches was severely constrained by legal restrictions that inhibited them from registering their land and restricted their ability to expand their churches and school building mission. In the immediate aftermath of the war, leaders of the Ethiopian movement played a prominent role in the agitation for land. Among them was J.Z. Tansti who was by then a pastor of a large congregation in downtown Johannesburg. He 'badgered the Pretoria administration on the issues [of land], demanding freehold right'.[43] Tantsi's effort was fruitless, and together with Rev Tsewu, D. H. Hlathi, John Mtshula, Marshall Maxeke, J.Z. Tansti's son James and dozens of Ethiopianists, raised funds to legally challenge the Crown government's land tenure policy.[44] The Supreme Court's judgement set aside the existing rule on the ground that since it had been established by a mere resolution of the Volksraad and not properly enacted, it had no force of law.[45] This case was represented by Tsewu who responded to the government's denial to register his property in Klipriviersoog (the farm where Kliptown is currently standing) as a central case that represented all Africans. The judgement in Tsewu's case made it lawful for Africans to buy white farms in 1905. In Campbell's opinion, Tsewu's victory was perhaps the greatest African political victory in the entire reconstruction period after the South African War.[46] When the Adams and Eaton Company subdivided Weldebeesfontein farm, Ethiopianists began buying land from the company at Weldebeesfontein. J.Z. Tantsi walked from Phillip Street in Johannesburg to Weldebeesfontein Farm No 12 in April 1905 when he heard that the farm that was to be renamed Evaton was being subdivided into plots. He then bought a property where he built the Lillian Derrick Institute, a school that was renamed Wilberforce in 1908.[47]

At the same time, African farmers began arriving from different parts of the country to buy properties. Evaton also attracted 'detribalised' educated residents who acquired their education from mission schools. Among the mission-educated stand buyers were clergymen and teachers. Other occupations represented in this group included a few court interpreters, insurance agents, nurses, bank clerks and bookkeepers.[48] Similar to Alexandra, Evaton appears to have represented a fair-cross section of South African ethnic groups, particularly from the Sotho-Tswana and Nguni. For example, the Tsewu were of Xhosa origin while the Mokgothu were of Tswana-Sotho origin. They belonged to different church denominations with the most prominent one being the AME church. They also came from different places. For instance, the Qupes came from small towns of the Free State, while the Tanstis, Tsewus and Mqubulis came from Reef mining towns where they were attracted by economic opportunities that urban centres offered. By that time, these professionals had carved out niches for themselves in the Reef. Evaton also received rural teachers like E. D. Mashabane, Matsolo and many others.[49] Mashabane taught in the rural Free State and was transferred by the Methodist Church to Evaton after the sharecropping enterprise dwindled. Their different geographical origins as well as diverse church denominations signified a sharp contrast among these professionals. For instance, those who came from the urban centres like James Tantsi, Abram Mgqibisa, and Samson Mtintso were affiliated to the AME church and represented a large proportion of the Ethiopian movement.[50] They were detached from white missionaries but connected to African Americans. The explanation of how this association came about is examined in the literature on the AME church in South Africa and the United States.[51] This contrast was, however, overshadowed by common Christian beliefs, missionary teachings, Victorian liberalism and the increasingly racial discriminatory legislation that was influenced by the changing political, economic and social needs of the colonial economy.

Before coming to Evaton, the urban group was subjected to municipal laws that included pass raids. Their presence in municipal townships was legalised bypass documents. Like any other township residents of the time, this religious contingent experienced the trauma of pass raids. Their personal autonomy, including freedom of movement, was limited because they had to apply for permits for almost every activity and movement. [52] As the stands they occupied were leased from the municipality, they had no right over them, and they could not alter or extend them without official consent. It was no wonder that many professionals rushed to purchase land in Evaton when the stands were sold to African buyers. The autonomy that Evaton offered lured many urban dwellers to Evaton.

Unlike in the Cape, Africans in the Transvaal enjoyed less legal protection and socio-economic circumstances were uninviting. It was worse in Johannesburg where Rev Tsewu and Tantsi practised their theological profession. These professionals found themselves faced with post-Anglo-Boer war socio-economic problems that exacerbated their burdens as preachers and comforters of urban communities.

Among the educated residents and other inhabitants of the area, Tantsi was the first to occupy Evaton when he purchased property in Bodea Road in 1905. As highlighted previously, as important as the land issue was, the chief focus of the Ethiopianists remained education. Evaton seemed an ideal place where the Ethiopianists' lifelong desire to build an institution of learning of their own could be achieved. With the help of AME church donations, Tantsi bought a property where the Lillian Derick Institute was built in 1908. By that time, some of his children, Adelaide, James, and Harsan, along with a group of young African singers who went to England and America as a choir with Paul Xiniwe, the choir master. All returned from America as graduates with a bachelor's degree from Wilberforce College in Ohio. They influenced elders who were already under the AME church to rename the Lillian Derick Institute the Wilberforce College.[53] In other words, they excitedly believed that they had brought American educational institutions and modernity to Africa. Lulat points out that African graduates hoped that from its humble origins, the Wilberforce Institute would grow into a credible post-high school educational institution. However, the lack of funds and the impact of segregation and later apartheid had a negative impact on its growth.[54]

The Tantsi family was one of the most prominent families in the early days of Evaton, owning a stand in Bodea Road not far from Tsewu's home, as well as the Wilberforce Institute. Originally, the Tantsis were from Pretoria but their professional engagement at Wilberforce and their attachment to the AME church made them become part of the Evaton community,[55] and constituted the first contingent of families who bought properties. After establishing the Institute, Rev J.Z. Tantsi, who was pre-occupied by missionary work in Johannesburg, left his son, Dr. James Yapi Tantsi, an American graduate and the first principal of Wilberforce, to occupy his property in Evaton. The administrative demands of the AME which was growing rapidly forced James, who had succeeded his father at Wilberforce, to reluctantly relinquish the principal's post at the Institute for the pulpit. His educational background and sincerity, as well as ecclesiastical influence over his colleagues increased until the AME church decided to appoint him as general superintendent of the church in the Transvaal. During his term as superintendent, the younger Tantsi bought stands in different freehold areas of the Transvaal for the expansion of the AME church.[56] He collaborated with the Maxekes, and together they bought property in Kliptown where they built the church. They also acquired land in Boksburg where Marshal Maxeke died in the late 1920s. James gave his principal's post to his brother Harsan who served less than a year in 1909. He was succeeded by Henry Msikinya, also a resident of Evaton and an American graduate who took over and became the Institute's principal until 1912.⁵⁷ After a short illness, Henry died in 1912 and was buried in Number I cemetery, Evaton.

The Tsewus also shared a similar status in the area. Edward Tsewu was respected by neighbours not only as a clergyman but for his achievement in regard to the land issue. Among the early educated families who came to Evaton after 1908 were the Qupes, Makhenes, Mokgothus,⁵⁸ and the parents of David Opperman who became a teacher in Ohlange in 1915 and later the principal of Wilberforce. Opperman was a member of a remarkable families that contributed to the establishment of the AME church and Wilberforce in Evaton.⁵⁹ There were also the Masizas, Motshwaris, Maxekes, Mgqibisas, Matsolos, Mazibukos, and Magayas. The first few years of Evaton's establishment were the beginning of the great undertaking. There were very few residents, perhaps because Evaton was not known by many aspirant land buyers. Due to the lack of census documents, it is not easy to give an accurate number of residents during this period. Suffice to say that the area was sparsely populated with scattered humble buildings that served as family dwellings.⁶⁰ The residents of the time were gardeners and farmers whilst others kept livestock ranging from chickens to cows. Other activities that took place during this period were public works that were done communally which demanded the digging of pits for water, the building of roads, digging up of toilets and the building of churches that were also used as schools.⁶¹ Most of them occupied stands that were close to the school and their houses varied not just by the material used but by the square footage in layout and design. They also varied in family size and house size. Most of the local houses had a porch or 'stoep' 'where the families could cool off during the summer season. It is where neighbours would drop by, chat and exchange gossip.'⁶²

Wilberforce as a pillar foundation in Evaton

A few years after its establishment, word spread about the establishment of the African- controlled school in Evaton and the availability of land in the area. Landless Africans came in small numbers from other regions of the country to buy land. The school was dedicated to the promotion of economic growth and a professional opportunity for African children, especially in improving technical skills that would enable them to qualify for artisanal and other professional occupations. It is difficult to know the real reason that prompted the Ethiopianist clergy to establish Wilberforce. The obvious one was for their children to acquire education that addressed the African needs. At that time, mission educated Africans increasingly found that their skills opened up new employment opportunities, such as teaching occupations in different schools. Another possible explanation was the fact that there was a lack of educational opportunities for Africans in the Transvaal. This was unlike in the Eastern Cape, and the Transkeian territories where more and more missionary schools were opened in the nineteenth century. The Transvaal, particularly the urban part, had only one mission school, Kilnerton in Pretoria. This school was under the Wesleyan missionary institution. At that time, few Africans could go much further than Standard IV in the Transvaal. It was only Lovedale and Adams College in both the Eastern Cape and Natal that provided schooling up to the level of the matriculation examination. Additional education was generally limited to teacher training at Kilnerton. African students were denied admission to the white institutions offering preparation for university degrees. At the same time, the government officials had long promoted white education over African education and thus gave little funding for the latter. In the Cape, for instance, teaching certificates granted were racially divided and this generated anger among Africans.⁶³ All these difficulties implied that Africans could not advance in these schools.

Another reason for the establishment of the Wilberforce Institute was that they wanted a school that would produce students who could acquire higher education, so as to be able to enter the ministry of the independent churches. This was achieved when Rev Coan opened up RR Wright Seminary School which was part of the Wilberforce Institute. The institute offered African students' secondary education, a curriculum in liberal arts, teachers training and vocational skills. The institute was not merely a centre for imparting knowledge and skills, but it helped to develop respect, independent thinking, and self-determination. What distinguished Wilberforce from other missionary schools was its educational programme and social responsibility that took full cognisance of community needs and the life from which pupils came. Its immense influence in local social circles was always felt. From its beginning, the school represented the African reaction to the offer of Western schooling, an effort that moved beyond the capacity of the mission churches. The school became critical of several aspects of the colonial education, particularly the ways in which it defamed indigenous customs as 'savagery' and barbaric. It represented African pride and dreams that lay at the very heart of the African aspiration, pushed by the conviction that education opens the door to success. Although some Africans achieved education, they continued to suffer discrimination based on their skin colour. The Wilberforce Institute continued to inspire Africans to crave and embrace education as the ultimate solution. Its advocacy for African education was based on the African Methodist Episcopal (AME) Church's nineteenth century doctrinal statements and publications. In these documents AME church leaders and writers explicitly stated that education was a necessary component for black liberation.⁶⁴ The institute was not merely a centre for imparting knowledge and skills, but it helped its products to develop respect, independent thinking, and self-determination. Its curriculum was adopted from the Tuskegee model that emphasised self-help and freedom from direct white control. The school curriculum was thickened by the institute's staff, the American graduates that reflected on the continental problem from the broadened perspective in their teaching. These graduates also advocated political quiescence on one hand and hard work on the other.[65] They were convinced that the struggle and triumph of African Americans could inspire Africans in this country. Like its sister school, Ohlange Institute, a school that was founded by Dr. Rev. John Dube at Inanda, the Wilberforce Institute epitomised Tuskegee. It stressed industrial education and African self-help. For Africans, the institution stood out as a shining beacon of hope for African social and economic upliftment. Like its sister school, Wilberforce received wide publicity in African press. This is evident in *Umteteleli waBantu* where there was always a column and advert about the school.[66]

In its early years the Institute was small with few funds and could not accommodate its boarding students. It was under the sponsorship of the AME, which lacked funds to pay ministerial salaries. Ministers fended for themselves, subsisting on whatever the local congregation could scrape together.[67] Driven by the spirit of self-help, local residents, church and non-church members were determined to do all they could to keep the school afloat. The homes of the Mokgothus and the Maxekes, for instance served as dormitories and girls from all the denominations were accommodated.[68] Unlike other mission schools like Kilnerton that was committed to educate children of the Methodist adherents only, Wilberforce staff members believed that cultural traditions and denominational identity could not have value above human relationships. The school was committed to friendship and collaboration across barriers.[69] The Wilberforce tradition became to a large extent the tradition of Evaton. In fact, Evaton was home to people working at Wilberforce, like the Mokgothus and others associated with the Institute. For professionals who were linked to the school, Wilberforce served as a point of entry to Evaton. For example, Rev and Mrs Mokgothu, who were from the Free State, came to Evaton through AME/ Wilberforce channels.

Although the school was controlled by the AME church, it attracted people from all over the Free State and other regions of South Africa. For instance, Boy Masiza recalled that his grandfather 'came to Evaton in 1906, he was from the Orange Free State, he came when he heard that Tantsi was building a school and there were bigger stands that were available in the area.'[70] Masiza was father to Hamilton Masiza, one of the initial groups of Wilberforce students who later graduated from Fort Hare before taking up the principalship of the United Mission School in Kimberley in the 1920s. The Masizas were Catholics and not Ethiopians or members of the AME church, but their commitment to the upliftment of the local community propelled them to contribute towards the building of the school. Masiza was a builder and a brick maker. Along with Mr. Motsolo, who was also a member of the Catholic Church, they helped Rev. Tantsi and Tsewu to erect the first buildings of the Institute.

Rev. James Henry Mazibuko was one of the founders of the AME church who also settled in Evaton because of the school. He worked very closely with Father Mokone, Charlotte Maxeke's uncle, who was the founder of the AME church. He was the first minister of the AME church in Evaton.[71] When he arrived he bought property not far from Rev. Tsewu.[72] The geographical clustering of the founders of Wilberforce indicates that the part of Evaton that was next to Wilberforce used to be occupied by educated residents who were also attached to the Institute. Considering that Evaton was sparsely populated and the number of educated families was almost twenty to thirty-five per cent of the total number of the community[73], to be an educated African or a priest in the first quarter of the twentieth century was to assume a position associated with high status and respectability among African communities. By then the number of educated Africans was low in South Africa. Many local African clergymen who received ordination were excellent preachers, proudly associated with internal church mobility. Teaching on the other hand, demanded high levels of academic proficiency, ensuring that teachers were able to pass a thorough examination of the Royal curriculum. The failure of the central government to commit itself in local education meant that local teachers had to work independently without state support and resources. Their ability to work independently sustained them a respectable identity in Evaton.[74]

In this community a teacher was a mediator of a particular construction of knowledge, attitudes and dispositions in the context of the realities of a small settlement of the Vaal. The presence of an educated contingent cultivated a distinct social character and identity that distinguished Evaton from other freehold settlements. Evaton became one of the freehold settlements in the Transvaal with a large number of educated residents. Self-sufficiency, economic independence and African unity were the most valued ideologies among this group. The principles that personified local educated residents were nurtured by Christian teachings and the ideology that underpins the foundation of Ethiopianism. These principles had the weightiest influence on the later generation of Evaton residents that played an important role towards the formation of the Pan-African Congress (PAC). The presence of a large proportion of educated Africans reveals that class divisions were more pronounced in Evaton, and were associated with the occupations of ministers of religion, teachers and clerks. The local class composition consisted of former sharecroppers, educated Africans and former independent farmers. The increasing segregating practices in the post-Anglo Boer War played an important role in connecting these classes. They were tightly connected by a common urgent need for land. At the early stage of Evaton's development, land was an overriding issue which prompted these classes to redefine themselves in the new settlement with land issues bonding them despite differences in life experiences, social and political aspirations. The educated class identified with a new political initiative and its members, like Henry Ngcayiya, the Maxekes, Tantsi and many others, became unquestionably influential in the formation of the South African National Native Congress (SANNC).

Spatially, the educated residents formed what could be defined by two sets of dimensions, a common educational and religious background. Mr. M.J. Qupe, who came to Evaton after acquiring a post as a commerce teacher, was not a member of the AME church, but the influential role of the local AME church persuaded him to convert and become one of the AME adherents. It was not only the Qupes who came as adherents of European-controlled churches. There were others like Rev. Faku of the Anglican Church. Faku was from Pondoland and spent some time in Johannesburg serving as a priest in Doornfontein before buying property in Evaton. His daughter, Eleanor Faku, married Tolityi Magaya, one of the American graduates and the fifth principal of Wilberforce. He succeeded Marshal Maxeke who left the school and joined his wife Charlotte when they opened up a school at GaRamokgopa in the Batlokoa region of the Northern Transvaal.[75] Upon his return from the United States of America, where he studied at Wilberforce and Lincoln Colleges, Magaya bought property and settled in Evaton where he became a principal.[76] Magaya was one of the pioneers of Evaton who played an important role in the development of Wilberforce and the local AME church in Evaton. He died in 1924 and was buried in No. 1 cemetery in Evaton.

The influx of the first wave of educated residents in Evaton was disturbed by two factors, the promulgation of the 1913 Land Act and, more importantly, the outbreak of the First World War. The 1913 Act was preceded by the formation of the African National Native Congress.[77] This organisation advocated for land-ownership, African economic upliftment and the extension of franchise to Coloureds outside the Cape. It identified politically with the British as opposed to the Boers. As early as the turn of the twentieth century, the AME church was popular among the Cape Coloureds. The man who was behind its popularity was Francis Macdonald Gow, a prominent member of Cape Town's Coloured community and a leader of the AME Church in the Western Cape. Gow was the father of Francis Herman who later became the principal of Wilberforce after World War I and the first African Bishop of the AME church.[78]

Towards the end of the war in 1918, the school reopened and, in the same year, the Native Affairs Department concluded that Africans could continue to purchase properties.[79] As indicated, during this period, the purchase of land was conditional. The post-war period marked the beginning of a new chapter in Evaton's history with the arrival of more educated residents who bought stands in the area. This period saw the arrival of Dr. F. Herman Gow who succeeded Rev. Magaya as a principal at the Wilberforce Institute. Gow was from the Cape, the son of an African-Caribbean man who married a Cape Coloured lady. Gow was an American graduate of the Tuskegee Institute who settled in Evaton after being offered the post of principal at the Institute. Gow's administrative activities stretched from the school campus to Evaton. Along with other educated residents, he was active in administrative matters. In the 1930s, he worked very closely with Commissioner Bunting to form the Advisory Committee that aimed at replacing the headman's control in Evaton.[80]

Gow was joined by Simon Mqubuli who had spent most of his time working in Klipspruit as a teacher before coming to Evaton. Mqubuli, who was born in Graaf Reinet, Eastern Cape, received his higher education at Lovedale where he was awarded a teacher's certificate. In Evaton, he became a teacher and later the principal of the African Independent School.[81] Other families that came to Evaton during this period were the Khumalo family who were originally from Natal. Rev. Benjamin Khumalo was a Methodist pastor who, after World War I, bought property in Evaton where he settled with his wife, Johanna Khumalo, who was a matron in Wilberforce during the time of Magaya's principalship. In 1920 Khumalo's daughter Angelina got married to Dr. John Dube, the first president of the African National Congress. She was his second wife and their wedding was held in Evaton.[82]

The deeds records indicate that many other educated residents relocated after the war and it appears that most of these professionals were attracted by the expansion of the Institute and its developed educational programmes. At the same time, the school offered a Junior Certificate and a three-year teaching diploma. The school also offered trade and printing courses. Wilberforce insisted not only on academic achievements but required students to spend some time doing manual work. It emphasised the dignity of manual work, especially working with soil. Apart from academia, perhaps the best advertising medium for the Institute was music, which was recorded by gramophone companies.[83] Wilberforce became popular for its African American spiritual music and those who were far away from the Institute, whenever they needed special African American spiritual music, turned to Wilberforce. These songs include '*Sanibona*', a song composed by R.T. Caluza.[84] Wilberforce students were exposed to the violin, piano and voice lessons, activities that gave them an opportunity to be known and see other parts of the country. At this early stage in Wilberforce's history, ex-choir singers like Mrs Maxeke were active in teaching music to the learner group of Masiza and Opperman.

By this time, the school's infrastructure was also developing. For instance, new buildings like the Eliza Gregg Hall were built and the school facilities were expanding. Additionally, the student body and teaching staff increased. On his 1919 visit, the Pass Officer of Vereeniging reported:

> I find it is divided into two sections for educational purpose, consisting of primary school in which there are 12 boarders and 36 day scholars (54 boys and 44 girls) …The Primary School is held in the separate building about 150 yards from the main building, there are four teachers two men and two women who have the work divided between them in 7 classes, under personal supervision of E.T. Magaya who is also the principal, people are from all parts of the Union.[85]

This was the primary school report that was attached to the institution. This report sheds light on the expansion of the school. Another strong marketing force that contributed to the arrival of more educated residents was the school's connection with African Americans who visited the school regularly. Subsequently, the changing character of this school attracted the best highly qualified teachers who also bought properties in Evaton. One of the prominent teachers and a mother who came to Evaton after the war was Mrs Eva Morake. Morake studied at two American Universities: Wilberforce University, where she acquired a junior degree in Humanities, and Columbia University, where she graduated with a Master of Arts. After graduating from the latter, she was offered a post in Columbia University that would have required her to remain and teach there. However, because of her devotion to her people's advancement, she decided to come back and work in Evaton.[86] Morake was the first African woman to receive a Master's degree from Columbia University and she was also the first in South Africa. In her letter to Dr. Xuma, she wrote

> In spite of many attractive government offers for teaching or supervision, at various provinces and protectorates... I accepted Bishop's Sims offer...as Principal of Wilberforce... Comparatively I knew I was making sacrifice, but said that in the full belief I was not only doing patriotic duty but was also making my small contribution in the cause and advancement of African Methodism in South Africa.[87]

This letter proves that after the First World War both Evaton and the Wilberforce Institute received committed professionals who were not only interested in advancing their personal status but also that of fellow Africans. Evaton was characterised by the zeal for economic independence and the spirit of self-advancement through education. Its social character encouraged the local community to seek ways of making a living without being dependent on wage labouring. The presence of Wilberforce as an African institution that symbolised African pride had a long-term impact on the history of Evaton. It encouraged local children to search for education as the means of achieving success and racial progress. The school was seen as an institution that would meet the skills that African people needed to survive. Founders of the school improvised and devised innovative means to improve African education.

Most of the educated residents were in fact born after the 1850s, which meant that their lives were intimately affected by colonialism. They personally witnessed the discovery of gold and how it transformed the life of Africans into economic dependency. They observed how an African labour force was created on a scale that left little room for African economic prosperity. They suffered different forms of segregation. As a result, they saw education and self-employment as the only means of avoiding the ranks of common labourers. The common suffering that local residents experienced in different geographical locations at the hands of white clergy, superintendents and other white officials created a social mechanism which promoted solidarity in this community. It is possible that these experiences offered a political ideology that manifested itself later during the bus boycott of 1957 and the role that Evaton played in the formation of political movements such as the Pan African Congress.[88]

The community appeared to be a troubled community that was regarded as prone to protests. This was evident during oral interviews when interviewees expressed their views on the land dispossession and displacement from which the pioneers suffered. This was confirmed by the Native Commissioner's report which highlighted the complaints of industrialists in the area who were unwilling to employ people of Evaton because of their radical politics.[89] Evaton represented a political stance that reflected on a broader political canvas. This was evident when some residents and teachers of Evaton like the Maxekes, Tantsi, and Ngcayiya actively took part in the formation of the South African Native National Congress in 1912.

African landless farmers and the new settlement of Evaton

The African landless farmers who came to establish themselves as subsistence farmers in Evaton were sharecroppers from the Transvaal and Orange Free State. There were also groups of *Oorlams* and independent farmers from Natal. The overwhelming majority of these groups were sharecroppers. These newcomers arrived in the early stage of Evaton with clear ambitions about their role in the area. Their aim was to practice agriculture and re-establish themselves as commercial farmers. The group of sharecroppers who bought properties in Evaton was divided into different categories based on their origins and geographical locations. For example, some were BaTswana, while others were BaSotho and abeNguni. Among the BaTswana were the BaKgatla BaMakau and other small groups of the Tswana language groups. The Basotho were BaKwena, BaFokeng and others. Among the beNguni were amaZulu, amaXhosa and amaSwazi. These groups were pushed by different socio-economic and political reasons to venture into sharecropping.[90] These farmers shared the similar experience of having been pushed off white farmland which had provided them with a means of livelihood. In addition, they had moved from one farm to another with the aim of searching for opportunities of accumulation under the patronage of a white landlord. One of the most significant common aspects which bonded this group was the fact that before the establishment of Evaton in 1905, they had no property rights. Some lived as squatters or renters on private farms, and they were legally debarred from holding properties in their own names in both the Free State and Transvaal.[91]

When these groups arrived, Evaton was in its embryonic stage and there was not much happening. Pioneers were simply establishing themselves, and the construction and clearing of the fields remained the major focus. Nobody doubted that the task of establishing Evaton as a settlement was daunting. It demanded committed, industrious and energetic individuals. In its early stage of development, local residents had to lay out gardens which would be a source of nourishment for their families, erect houses, dig toilet pits and wells, open up roads, fence their properties and select suitable pastures for their herds.[92] This process included whatever could defray the cost of the establishment. The pioneers not only established themselves in the new area but also took responsibility of building Evaton from scratch. On their arrival, the area was young and unspoiled with veld grass and uninhabited. Their responsibility was to shape its physical and community development.[93] Fortunately, these groups had acquired skills from mission stations and white farms, which enabled them to understand the processes of public works and the physical development that included digging wells, clearing fields and building houses.

One of the sharecropping communities that arrived before the formation of the Union in 1910 were members of the Bakgatla Bamakau, who came from De Welt in the northwest of the Transvaal.[94] The Bakgatla were Tswana people drawn from the ranks of the increasingly beleaguered African peasantry in the nineteenth century. After the seizure of their land by Boers in the 1860s, some members of this clan depended on white land for their livelihood. They practiced what was locally known as *halfde* in Afrikaans *or* sharecropping enterprise. The experience of the Seremi family is representative to Bakgatla sharecroppers. Dwight Seremi recalls the growing tension on white-owned farms that forced his parents to buy property in Evaton:

> My father came to Evaton after Pienaar with whom he had a contract became jealous because my father had lots of cattle and money that he accumulated and that time some Boers were beginning to buy agricultural machines. When you became rich, the farmer became jealous especially when you were hardworking and at the time when you get rich, he would make you to spend unnecessarily by saying why don't you buy this plough this is not good. When you were prospering you didn't know where you put your money because other farmers will see you there in the post office depositing money and jealousy will creep in and later on came this thing of tractors and you were not allowed to buy tractor because *hulle krap die land* [they are damaging land]. They would also say this chap is competing with me and I am the owner of the land no no it's too much. Moreover, no *kaffir* was allowed to write examination when we are planting.[95]

Seremi's account embodies some of the common experiences of the larger social group as recorded in the literature on sharecropping.[96] The Seremi family ventured into sharecropping after Dwight's grandfather left their traditional land and converted to Christianity. By then, Christianity offered education and alternative economic opportunities that opened up for converts. On white farmland, the Seremis embarked upon entrepreneurial activities such as selling agricultural products after harvests. Agriculture and land were used in conjunction to produce saleable agricultural products that brought cash. For this family, Christianity provided a favourable opportunity for new economic relations that many Africans took advantage of as well as the drive to economic security.[97] The Seremis' exposure to the white economy introduced Dwight's father to different artisanal skills which enabled him to meet some economic needs in Evaton when subsistence farming ceased in the 1940s.

The Seremi family heard from other members of the Bakgatla clan that stands were available in Evaton and they 'crossed rivers and mountain ranges to begin life for themselves in the land beyond the farmlands.'[98] The Seremi's wagon was drawn by an impressive span of fourteen powerful oxen and it carried all their belongings. Daniel Seremi's family consisted of his wife and six children. As early as 1907, the group of Bakgatla sharecroppers who used the clan name Kgabu moved to Evaton. Among those who moved to the township were the Seremis, Moagis, Seshabelas and many others. Although some were scattered all over the area, the group of Bakgatlas who represented the pioneers were located in the old Evaton next to Number 1 Cemetery along Avondale Road.

On their arrival the Seremis bought property with cash in an area called Number 1. The property was bought from the proceeds that Dwight's father accumulated through his sharecropping enterprise. Some of the family cash was acquired from the sale of cattle and farm implements. At that time, the sale of stands was administered by John Malay, an agent who looked after the company's interests. Little is known about how much the company sold stands for during this period. From 1905 to 1935, there was less government involvement, and there was no inspection that oversaw the subdivision of stands. The first group of residents used cash to buy properties which implied that there were no applications for mortgages. The transaction was simple: it included two parties, the landowner and the buyer. It was only after the promulgation of the 1913 Land Act that aspirant land buyers were required by law to be granted permission by the Governor General for the transfer of land.[99] By 1918, aspirant buyers had to apply for the Governor General's consent before they could purchase any property in the area. It was only the Governor who was authorised by new laws to give local buyers permission to purchase properties in the township.[100] In the late 1930s and 1940s, when many buyers applied for bonds, the Governor General became responsible for the approval of bonds. In those years, the township was not scheduled as a Native Area and there was no official control; it was only proclaimed as a released area under the Native Land Act 18 of 1936. 'The only surviving documents that we have at our disposal present us with prices ranging from 1930s onwards.'[101] When the Seremis arrived, there were very few families. Among these families were J.Z. Tantsi's family and Sophia Maria Adams family, a coloured family unit that bought plot 3 and 4 in Block L23 in 1905.[102]

The Seremis and other members of Bakgatla residents were likely attracted by the bigger stands of one acre and the availability of common grazing land. Paul Seshabela remembers that 'my father was forced to come and buy property in Evaton because he disagreed with the Boer on products that were supposed to be shared among them.'[103] When the Seshabelas arrived, they came with their agricultural implements, furniture, agricultural skills and their cattle which they had accumulated through savings from the sale of grains. The Seremis and Seshabelas shared similar backgrounds. These families were all Christians. For instance, the Seshabelas were African Methodists. Although Paul's father did not have a formal education, he was driven by the hope that Evaton and the presence of the Wilberforce Institute would at least give his children an opportunity to study. They all settled in one geographical location in Evaton. The Seremis and Seshabelas shared a similar history. They had a long record of moving from one farm to another. Before Paul's father bought property in the area, he switched from one farm to another. Life stories told by these families reveal the experiences of the same class and draw a picture of what happened to this Bakgatla group and how they ended up in Evaton.

A second group of farmers who settled in Evaton were drawn from the class of small independent farmers in Natal who were owners of registered land. While sharecroppers were landless, they accessed land by entering into economic arrangements where they controlled labour, skills, implements and draught power. Terms of tenure with the landlord were normally negotiated verbally, depending on the productive resources and power of the contractors. Independent farmers saw land ownership as an opportunity for breaking away from traditional communal cultivation. These farmers believed that investing in small plots of land and cultivating intensively through family labour was the only way to economic prosperity.[104] What differentiated these farmers from sharecroppers was their land-ownership background. Sharecroppers were a landless group and they relied on white land for their livelihood, whereas independent farmers had land.

There would obviously have been many reasons why these Christian independent farmers left tribal land, why they later decided to engage in food production and exchange, which was relatively non-monetary, while their Christian cultural values encouraged them to be entrepreneurial. It is, therefore, important to put it clearly that Evaton was different from the tribal reserves in that there were no chiefs that demanded annually a certain amount of harvest in a form of tribute. In the western perception, this tribute might be interpreted as taxation that provided considerable security for all inhabitants, particularly for the aged and physically-disabled. In Evaton, the educated elites, sharecroppers and independent farmers were free to trade without business licencing regulations that affected trade in municipal controlled townships. This was possibly the reason why independent farmers and sharecroppers entered into communal production relationships. Even though this relationship existed, it is possible that some local farmers were more prosperous than others. Despite a number of informants describing Evaton families as homogeneous, some families lived a precarious life that depended on others. This is evident when one drives around viewing architectural structures of different families. There were those that lived in mud shabby houses while others lived in architecturally- attractive houses. In other words, there was class distinction. It is also possible that some residents worked for others, but this was not mentioned during interviews.

The Dlaminis and Mbheles, who were originally from Natal, were representative of the independent farmers in Evaton. Absolom Dlamini's grandfather was an *inyanga*, a traditional healer. He left his traditional land where he was born because of a family dispute that forced him to migrate in the mid-1890s. In those years, it was common for Africans in Natal who disagreed with their traditional families to move to mission stations and become Christian converts.[105] One of the factors that attracted Natal Africans to mission stations was the availability of land. Dlamini, however, avoided settling on a mission station. As an *inyanga* who relied more on ancestral healing power, his avoidance was based on the fact that Christianity threatened the ritual powers African patriarchs derived as intermediaries between the living and the ancestors.[106] Another factor that kept Dlamini within traditional circles was the implementation of 'Msunduzi rules' drawn up by American missionaries in 1879. These rules prohibited church members from participating in polygamy, bride-wealth exchange, or levirate marriage, or from drinking alcohol or smoking marijuana.[107] He therefore left Weenen and moved to Driefontein where he bought property and got married.[108]

According to Absolom, 'It is where he left some of his children and wives to occupy his properties when he moved to the Free State.'[109] His advantage was that his traditional healing profession was lucrative;[110] people who consulted him for different illnesses and problems paid with cattle. Unlike the Bakgatla families, who were landless before coming to Evaton, the Dlaminis enjoyed property rights long before Evaton was established. They had property in Ladysmith and as independent farmers. As we shall see below, the difference between sharecroppers in Evaton could be measured materially.

Dlamini was not a Christian convert and his traditional profession gained him economic prosperity. His healing vocation enabled him to travel all over the country and to some parts of Lesotho curing the sick. While working in the Orange Free State, he was consulted by a certain white landlord who had heard of Dlamini's healing powers. This farmer's wealth was limited by his unproductive land, so Dlamini apparently used his spiritual power to solve the farmer's problem. Dlamini became relatively wealthy and was a polygamist with three wives and more than ten children. He moved to Evaton in 1908.[111] He bought four stands that suited the size of his family with some of his stands shared among his children. What is striking about these pioneers is that they demonstrate that the Evaton community was made up of socio-economically differentiated individuals. The Dlaminis were not Christian but traditionalists who believed in ancestors. Since Dlamini was an *inyanga*, he was distinct from the Bakgatla Christian families who emphasised the significance of education. Dlamini's children were not focused on educated but followed his footsteps of maintaining economic independence. Even today Absolom Dlamini's grandson owns a butchery that was operated by his father who used his father's cattle to start the business.

Another independent farmer that arrived at the same time as the Dlaminis was J.J. Mbhele who came from Natal in 1907. Mbhele bought a small farm that comprised of six stands. He was an independent farmer in Kokspruit, Newcastle.[112] Unlike in the Boer Republics, as early as the second half of the nineteenth century, Nguni peasants had access to a range of land parcels that sustained them as independent producers in Natal. In Natal, Africans were divided into different categories. There were independent food producers who intermittently worked as wage labourers and their submission to employment depended on their desire for cash income. This group sold its labour to supplement earnings from the sale of agricultural produce. Some were traditional subsistence farmers, who were independent of colonial economy.[113] There were independent farmers like Mbhele who never submitted themselves to wage earnings. Apart from farming, he operated a transport business that hauled goods that came with the midnight train from Johannesburg to local shops.[114] According to Daniel, 'he would come back and leave the wagon there and take the cattle to the farm because it was not far from the station; it was right in town where ISCOR is currently located. He would take his cattle there for grazing and in the evening he would go back to the station.'[115] Mbhele became a prosperous commercial farmer. He left Natal and moved to Boksburg where he also bought property in 1906. For reasons unknown to his grandson Daniel, he left Boksburg and came to Evaton where he bought properties in the Bodea

Road next to the Wilberforce Institute, the area that was occupied by educated residents who worked at the school. Though plots of land were small in Evaton, he started farming and he kept livestock.

Oral testimonies reveal that these newcomers were not from the Cape, nor were they descendants of the Cape aborigines but were descendants of African communities. Jacob Sibeko recalled, 'my father told me that these people were captives of the Boers during raids, they were captured as children and grew up as Boers, they speak Afrikaans, they behave like Afrikaners and they like Afrikaans.'[116] Delius and Trapido[117] pioneered the literature on the formation of *Oorlams,* and Bonner added more to the nascent literature on the *Oorlam*. Bonner documented how in the late 1840s, the Swazis, 'by far and away the most important dealers in captives in the eastern Trans – Vaal,' raided children from their weaker neighbours such as the Kopa and the Tonga and sold them to Afrikaners in the eastern Transvaal.[118] Like sharecroppers, the Evaton *Oorlams* were a multi-skilled group from white farms in the Orange Free State and Transvaal. They accumulated farming and artisanal skills from the white farms and mission schools. It is apparent from the accounts presented below that the *Oorlams* were not just distinct from other Africans in their range of economic skills and practices. As servants on Boer farms, they were trained in a variety of skills such as stonecutting and building, brick making, cookery, veterinary and folk medicine, literacy in Dutch, wagon repair, hunting, gun maintenance, making cheese and plough farming.

Among the members of the *Oorlams* community were Mr. Van Der Merwe, who was a stonemason, John Malay, who looked after the Easton, Adams and Company's interest, Sophia Maria Adams who bought Plot 3 and 4 on Block 123 in 1905, and F. W. Francis who owned Plot 8 and 9 in the Block 139 which he bought in 1910. In the late 1960s and early 1970s, these residents became victims of the Group Areas Act which forced them out of Evaton. It is currently difficult to trace their families. Abel Tshawe's testimony informs us that 'they were just like us and some were black like me most of them were captives during the annexation wars; they were not Cape coloureds: we used to call them makatoos in the farms.'[119] In Evaton, self-sufficient *Oorlams* came along with families of sharecroppers from the Transvaal and Orange Free State and independent farmers from the Cape and Natal colonies.

In the period after the First World War, a second wave of sharecroppers arrived in Evaton. This group belonged to the Bakwena and other groups of sharecroppers, and they came from the surrounding Mid-Vaal farms, mostly from the Vereeniging Estate. When this group came to Evaton, South Africa was experiencing socio-political changes that left a mark on the administration and acquisition of properties in Evaton. This period saw the acceleration of restrictions on African land ownership.[120] The government's desire was to see Africans in segregated areas that secured a labour supply for urban industries. As a result, the 1913 Land Act was imposed to satisfy the government's wish. The most important provision of the Act stated that Africans could no longer buy, lease, or in any other manner acquire land outside a scheduled area, except by acquiring that land from another African. Europeans were prohibited from buying or leasing land from an African. Only Africans could buy land within the scheduled areas.[121] It will be demonstrated how these changes impacted on the land purchase process, how the pre-war land acquisition differed from the post–war purchase, and how aspiring buyers were affected by this transformation.

The Bakwena groups were originally from the Magaliesburg area and belonged to sedentary polities that practised agriculture and pastoralism. Their peaceful settlement in the area was disturbed by colonial interventions, most importantly wars, that included the *Difaqane* and Ndebele raids in the mid-nineteenth century. These disruptions affected this group in different ways. Some fled to Lesotho; some subjected themselves to the Boers and other neighbouring African polities; and some sought refuge on mission stations.[122] When sharecropping opportunities began to emerge for Africans, some members of the Bakwena joined this economic venture.

Similar reasons that pushed the group of pioneering sharecroppers off white farms affected the Bakwena sharecroppers. These factors include the introduction of mechanisation. When white landlords began to use steam machines, the prospects of African farmers continuing sharecropping dwindled.[123] The position of Bakwena commercial farmers on white-owned land was becoming increasingly precarious and many Africans in rural areas began to seek land not under white ownership. As a result, many African farmers who were desperate to settle on their own properties gathered to consider the difficult circumstances that they were experiencing.[124] In a meeting that was held by the Bakwena sharecroppers in 1913, Abram Mogale remembered that

> ...in that meeting it is where problems that face our parents were discussed intensively, it is where we heard that stands were available in Evaton., some of the Bakwenas regrouped themselves under Chief Mamogale and bought properties somewhere in the Northwest of Transvaal, but my father did not join that group...[125]

For the Bakwena sharecroppers, this was one of the most traumatic and tormenting periods – it is described by Tim Keegan as the first 'forced removal' on a large-scale from white farms.[126] The Mogales, Mokwenas and other families who came from the surrounding farms decided to explore opportunities for buying land in Evaton. These tenant farmers saw Evaton as a place where there was more space for them to re-establish themselves and where they could also exercise their economic autonomy and continue to practice agriculture. Part of this was the presence of the Wilberforce Institute, an African-owned school that was developing into one of the most respected schools in the country and where their children could study and further their education.

The 1913 Land Act

The 1913 Land Act effectively prevented further purchase of land in Evaton. It also undermined all other African options to labour tenancy. Furthermore, it had a severe impact on sharecroppers. Jackson Mokwena remembers that his father and other members of the Bakwena families would wake up early in the morning and ride their bicycles from the surrounding mid-Vaal farms to Evaton where they would wait for the company officials responsible for selling properties. Mokwena recollected:

> ...it became difficult to buy properties during this time because our fathers had to apply to the Governor General for his approval...this was a long process they had to wait for ages... [127]

In the period between 1913 and 1918, the purchase of stands in Evaton was suspended, a result of the outbreak of World War I and the implementation of the 1913 Land Act. At the end of 1918, the land transfer process began to get complicated due to the implementation of the 1913 Land Act. The latter confused Native Affairs Department officials who did not possess any legal expertise for assessing the status of Evaton in relation to the Act. Hence, after the implementation of the 1913 Land Act and during the war, land purchases in Evaton were suspended. The demand for land purchases by Africans continued to increase, however, so the government sought to identify a different approach to the sale of land to Africans in Evaton.

Prime Minister Louis Botha's solution was to introduce the Native Affairs Administration Bill in 1917, which sought to impose a uniform system of control on African-owned land.[128] This Bill granted aspirant buyers of Evaton a way forward by including the Governor General in the process of transferring land. The Governor General was given the status of the sole trustee of Evaton, which implied that aspirant buyers were required by law to apply for consent from the Governor who was given the power to approve and disapprove their applications. The purchase of land became highly bureaucratised. The purchaser had to commission lawyers who would draft legal documents that applied to the Governor General on his or her behalf and then the letter would go through the office of the Secretary of Native Affairs to the Governor's office.[129]

When the Governor General had approved the application, the letter would also go via the office of the Secretary to the lawyers who would then hand it to the applicant. In some instances, the application was turned down, especially when an applicant was unable to furnish required details.[130] The surviving documents do not indicate how many applications were rejected. The purchase of land was also delayed by the war, and it took more than two years before prospective buyers were given a way forward. Mofokeng recalls that 'during the First World War everything came into standstill,'[131] and his father had to wait for several years before he could buy property in 1918. In view of the unsettled state of the country owing to the war, it appeared as if the purchase of land in Evaton was kept at abeyance. Aspirant buyers had to be temporarily accommodated by local property holders, while some such as the Mogales rented in Top Location, a township next to Vereeniging. Some families like James Mokwena's were accommodated by the Nhlapo family for two years while they waited for the approval of their application from the Governor General. Some members of this group did not, however, persevere; they gave up and moved on to other areas. James recalls that some of them went to the Zeerust area, while others sold their livestock and farm implements and joined the labour market in Johannesburg.[132]

After lengthy inter-departmental discussions and deliberations, the Department of Native Affairs agreed to the principle of 'natives' acquiring property in the township, subject to certain conditions. One of the conditions drew the Governor General as the sole trustee who would approve transactions during purchase. In 1918 land purchases commenced again, and stands were sold for 26 pounds between 1918 to 1930. Apart from African buyers, coloured buyers such as James Derbyshire, who later became a local bus operator, bought properties under the new conditions that regulated land purchases.[133] It is this period that saw the second wave of residents that comprised the Mofokengs, the Bakwenas and many others flocking into Evaton. What emerges from historical recollections is that the group of African farmers who made up Evaton was diverse, but they all shared a background of economic independence and business experience, which laid a foundation for the emergence of local enterprises in the following decades. They represented a group of Africans who shifted from the slumbering traditional rural sector economy to commercial agriculture. They only enjoyed this type of agricultural practice in the rural Highveld before coming to Evaton. This class developed a new nationalist-oriented consciousness that owes its roots to the presence of the educated neighbours. This consciousness appeared to underpin the local community in which cultural origins and division played a role in dividing them. Though they lacked tribal attributes, they were distinctly African in nature, with an inherent African mentality of communalism.

For these reasons, they saw chiefs as agents that were manipulated for the colonial indirect rule. They were deemed as instrumental in shaping reserves to be labour pools. This degraded Africans into serfdom. There are two different explanations that could possibly explain the Christian farmers' attitude. Some of these Christian farmers were adherents of churches that broke away from the mainstream churches and shared anti-colonial sentiments with these churches. It should be noted that by the 1890s, the idea of Africans asserting themselves anew in religious and political arena was catching on.[134] These Christians represented the new breed of nationalism that rose to prominence later. Another explanation could be associated with the Christian stereotypical teaching that looked down upon African countryside as backward. For these farmers, modernisation was the key although they viewed it from different angles. For them modernism was viewed as a key to economic progress and independence and an avenue for economic development. The emergence of different forms of enterprises which will be examined in detail in the following chapter provides us with empirical evidence and an explanation for the persistence of their economic independence. The consciousness behind economic independence was derived from sharecropping and independent farming enterprises. Apart from common social forces that pushed them to purchase properties in Evaton, these residents were differentiated, and their history of dispossession and movement varied from one family to another. Diversification among them can be attributed to their geographical origins, socio-economic status, education, history of land ownership, and religious beliefs. For instance, the Bakgatla and Bakwena group were different from the Dlaminis and the Mbhele who were Zulu independent farmers that enjoyed the privilege of land ownership long before Evaton was established. These Zulu farmers were largely distinguished by their religious beliefs, conventional practices and household composition. Mbhele was a Christian with one wife, while the Dlaminis were traditionalists and polygamists with three wives.[135] Unlike the Bakgatla and Bakwena who had a tenuous history of tenancy on white farms, the Mbheles and Dlaminis had a long history of independence and land possession. For example, the Native Affairs Commissioner of Maphumulo district complained that 'The Kafirs are now much more insubordinate and impatient of control; they are rapidly becoming rich and independent.'[136] This implied that the group of independent farmers from Natal had a very strong background of economic independence that also impacted on their relative political independence.

This speaks to the distinctiveness of Natal in particular as a regional economy as well as the area where entry into some kind of relationship with a white farmer was somewhat less attractive. On the contrary, the Highveld was attractive despite the fact that African farmers controlled their labour, plough and seed. They were not independent because of landlessness. Considering the independence of these farmers and the uniqueness of the area where they came, there seems to be few, if any, examples in Evaton of this rank. The sharecroppers from the Highveld of Transvaal and Free State outnumbered independent farmers from Natal in Evaton. In fact, sharecroppers formed a substantial proportion of the new settler community and their needs for plentiful land. For the sharecroppers, access to Evaton was determined by a number of factors that impacted on the lives of the early residents. One of the most significant was the fact that before the establishment of Evaton in 1905, early inhabitants of the area had no property rights. Some lived as squatters or renters in private farms while others rented in the old municipality townships. They were legally debarred from holding properties in their own names. Moreover, for many decades, early settlers of Evaton lived under a colonial system whose administration was bound up in the cruelties of land dispossession and absurdities. Before buying properties in Evaton, land ownership in the Transvaal, particularly in the Rand which was rich in mineral deposits, was not easily accessible to Africans or poor whites. The right to land ownership in the Rand was tied to subsurface rights that mining magnates enjoyed. It was worse in the Orange Free State where Africans were not allowed to purchase land.[137] From the outset, Evaton attracted diverse landless settlers who were cut off from places that they were deeply attached to; some of them, like the sharecroppers,[138] had been moving from one farm to another. This raises the question of attitudes and how independent farmers defined themselves as an exclusive group in the community of sharecroppers.

The settlement of Evaton displayed considerably diverse characters in its early population, as well as some of the common traits which drew individuals to Evaton, and this made the area distinct. Seemingly, there was a sharp contrast between sharecroppers and independent farmers. These differences give us greater insight into how and who formed the community of Evaton and how a number of economic, social and political factors shaped the manner in which these residents perceived their surroundings. All these factors contributed to the peculiarity of the Evaton community. This also sheds light on entrepreneurship perhaps as a form of resistance to the labour market, though the resistance is slippery because of its openness to a wide range of interpretations.

When we examine the divisions of these farmers we begin to see different experiences within the Evaton community as the group of former landless farmers like the Seremis, Mogale and many other groups coming together with the group of former landowners to form a community. The Natal contingent was made up of residents who enjoyed the right to land ownership long before the Bakgatlas and Bakwenas. They were more affluent than the landless sharecroppers who quickly felt the effects of being dislocated from the farms. The Natal group, like the Mbheles and the Dlaminis, continued to enjoy the proceeds of what they had accumulated over many years. Absolom

Dlamini's testimony shed light on how his grandfather's wealth lasted: 'even here in Evaton he was still spending the money that he saved'.[139] This is demonstrated by the fact that in the subsequent years of Evaton's development when the subsistence economy was increasingly troubled by demographics that led to local socio-economic change, Mbhele's economic muscle allowed him to buy two expensive cars that he used as taxis to ferry residents to Johannesburg. Furthermore, the Dlaminis opened up a butchery that still operates today.[140] On the other hand, Dwight Seremi's father struggled to maintain his economic independence, and he intermittently joined the labour market and became the builder of mining compounds in the Reef. Dwight recalls that 'he built many compounds in the mines and he also built a school in Sharpeville.'[141] This tells us that after some years of establishing themselves in Evaton, some residents clung to their economic independence while others were forced by circumstance to give up and join the labour market. It was the same with Nicholas Motloung who submitted himself to the labour market without any attempt to maintain his economic autonomy.

An analysis of the resident's building styles reveals a lot about the status of the local residents. The interim report to the Minister of Public Health in 1939 reported that in some houses there were ceilings and the usual dung smeared on the floors and that the majority of the structures were two or three rooms with insufficient ventilation which made Evaton mainly rural.[142] However, at that time the Mbhele's house was modernised with a pitched roof and a decorated column, wooden floors and door frames. Such buildings were rare in the area. This sheds light on the different economic status' of the residents because the same report stated that the majority of residents in subsequent years appeared to be impoverished.[143]

Local Administration

Although this study focuses on the African section of Evaton, for the better understanding of how the township was administered it is important to also take account of how the white section of Evaton was governed. Our familiarity with the manner in which the white area was administered, will later assist in this discussion to draw a picture on how local white administration shaped by-laws that controlled local entrepreneurship. Evaton was divided into two sections. There was the white and the African section. These two racially divided segments of Evaton were divided by a street called Union Road. The majority of white residents were mainly Afrikaners who were displaced by a number of factors on the farms. These factors included natural disasters, the capitalisation of agriculture, rapid industrialisation and lack of available land which offered adequate subsistence. The white section was under the control of the Evaton Health Committee (EHC).

After a petition that was signed by 68 white residents, who styled themselves as Evaton residents, the EHC was formed in 1936. The petition lobbied against deplorable health conditions that were caused by the encroachment of African livestock in white open spaces of Evaton. Whites complained to the District Surgeon that the native herds caused fly nuisance and unhygienic conditions. After several meetings with the government officials, the Evaton Health Committee (EHC) was formed in 1936. In one of the letters that was addressed to the Native Commissioner, Baillie wrote,

> the Native is as arrogant and defiant as ever, even more so now that the 'pound' has been closed at Evaton, he continues to invade the white man's area with impunity knowing full well that neither the white or the police as he is a Supreme Lord. The young Native has grown up in the atmosphere created by his fathers, viz

trampling upon whites and openly defying them, and are also just as arrogant as their elders.[144]

Perhaps, Ballie's tone, along with the establishment of EHC could be better understood within the context of Hertzog's reshaping of Afrikaner political attitude that responded to the *volks* suffering and defeat. The local racial friction reached a point where Baillie and his people felt that the position in Evaton was such that they would welcome a decision of the government to take over all from whites and compensate them and let them clear out, and hand over the lots to the natives so that the white man can find a place to live in peace which was not possible in a reserve containing thousands of natives along them.[145]

In terms of any law Evaton was not scheduled or declared a 'native village' and neither was the place in terms of any law a private location or farm. It was not a location or a hostel under the Native Urban Areas Act of 1923. It was not defined or set apart by any urban local authority.[146] The acquisition of land was made lawful by the Governor General under Section 1 of the Native Land Act of 1913. The area was not even under the Native Administration Act of 1927. This qualified the African section to be independently governed by *Izibonda,* the headman.[147] The *Izibonda* styled themselves as the village administration board. They used the chieftainship model of controlling Evaton. They tried cases with power of appeal vested on them, but they had little or no formal education. The position of *izibonda* granted some residents, such as the Seremis and other residents, with different roles and responsibilities within the community. For instance, records reveal that Daniel Seremi became an assistant headman. At that time, the area was experiencing the growth of local common law that gave its inhabitants a greater access to local self-control. In turn, Africans who had been for decades denied the privilege of decision-making began to have a place in decision-making on how local affairs should be administered. In a letter, Commissioner S.J. Bunting indicated that in the early days of Evaton, these administrative bodies were endorsed by the Native Affairs Department.[148] It is possible that this form of administration served as a strategy of excluding white Native Commissioners from local affairs. Perhaps, most importantly, this type of administration illustrates the complexities of unpopular resistance that was expressed in freehold areas. It captures a distinct form of a less institutionalised strategy of resistance. Paul Seshabela informs us that the governing committee under *izibonda* was responsible for local law and order especially during local family or neighbourhood disputes. In the 1930s, the township was under the headmanship of Mr. P. Ngoqo, who was assisted by Petrus Mahlangu and Daniel Seremi.[149] Both local authorities were allowed by the community to try cases. This implies that residents of Evaton governed themselves and enjoyed considerable freedom from government interference. This local governance was, however, opposed by a small section of the community, particularly the educated residents. This educated group organised themselves under the Village Board of Management, which had an office in the Wilberforce Institute. The group dissatisfaction was reflected in a letter written to the Commissioner of Native Affairs by Herman Gow and James Tantsi, the representatives of the educated residents from Evaton. In this letter Gow and Tantsi wrote:

> We have been instructed by the Village Board of Management to lay before you the continuous and malicious propaganda of Mr. P. Ngoqo to whom you issued certain specific direction some time ago. He carries on as follows:
> 1.   Advertised and presided at a public meeting on 15 of March, styling himself headman of Evaton

2. He authorized Petrus Mahlangu and Daniel Seremi to try cases, with powers of appeal vested in himself

3. In various other ways he has studiously endeavoured to make the Board an of non-effect among the people

4. A serious issue has arisen between Mathew Mphse and Isaac Paulengl; we want to bring about peaceful settlement by asking Rapuleng to meet us with Mpshe. Rapuleng answered, being duly influenced, that he will not submit to any other but Ngoqo's investigation

The situation is, to put it mildly, SERIOUS, and we therefore ask direction from you as will put a stop to this dangerous reputation of the proper function of the Board.[150]

This letter reveals how complex, indeterminate and contentious the local administration was, particularly with the majority of residents favouring a headman style of administration. The 'headman party' was in control and the 'educated party' was opposing. Perhaps these internal differences emanated from the fact that the formation of the Evaton community occurred in cohorts. When it comes to the understanding of the local community, during its formation, residents with similar cultural backgrounds tended to consolidate around social and cultural nodes that define its belonging. Numerically, the educated party was smaller than the headman party. For instance, the Native Commissioner wrote,

I have just received a petition signed by 136 members of the opposition party opposing the present order of things and stating that they are altogether excluded in matters pertaining township.[151]

The reason why the local administration style became effective was because the people of Evaton did not like to include white magistrates in their affairs. However, internal struggles between these two cohorts might have been triggered by the internal pattern or practice that the headmen's party followed, which was not aligned to the educated party's expectations. It is possible that it was not administrative autonomy that the educated cohort opposed, but the approach of the headman's committee.

The struggle for the local independent administration reflects on local dissatisfaction with the central government. It also demonstrates how the Evaton community challenged the political order of the time. Furthermore, it expresses another mode of protest that was less popularised. This type of resistance is clearly reflected in a letter that was written by Paul Motaung who clearly stated that:

> The object is mostly for the purpose of disciplinary measures among themselves, as they fear that, by not having any body they can entrust with their Domestic Affairs, and avoid police being called unnecessarily at times. Which thing might force the government to put police right in their township. In brief Sir it is the wish of the residents that all discrepancies and any affair affecting the residents …should be dealt with by the Board of Control first and if they have to be gone into by any authority or police the Board of Control should recommend.[152]

This community notion made it possible for the headman's committee to play an important role. This was a symptom of protest against the white administrative institution that was intensifying in African urban areas.

With the rise of territorial segregation under the 1936 Native Trust and Land Act, and the systematic enforcement of influx control that began in 1938, the freehold status of Evaton and its lack of official control began to trouble the government. The government appointed a Social and Economic Planning Council to devise a blueprint for the post war reform. An interdepartmental committee under Smit's chair was also tasked to investigate the health, educational and social condition of urban Africans. This urged the Native Affairs Department to propose the amendment of the 1927 Native Administration Act that Evaton was protected from. The aim of this amendment was to establish local authority in Evaton. After lengthy correspondences, debates and meetings that resisted the establishment of any kind of control, particularly from the headman party in the 1930s, the enlightened group favoured the proposal. As a result, they passed the resolution that the local authority should be established. This resolution was adopted in the meeting that was held at Wilberforce on 25 March 1944. This diverse way of thinking on administrative matters reflects on social relations, class consciousness and local politics. It demonstrates how each class perceived the conception of local governance differently. This shall be addressed below. In support of the resolution, the Additional Native Commissioner wrote:

> The reason I am in favour of the establishment of a Body of Control, is that the population of the township as a whole consists of an enlightened and orderly…the Magistrate and the police on the absence of crime…the fact in favour of the scheme outweigh those against.[153]

In opposition, the headman party felt that they should be allowed to continue to govern themselves. For many years, they had been enjoying a considerable freedom from government control or interference and they felt that they never abused that freedom. They felt that they were capable of framing their own regulations. This was expressed in a letter written by S.P. Bunting, a Johannesburg lawyer who represented the proportion of local residents that favoured the headman. Bunting wrote, 'village life was on the whole peaceful and undisturbed until the recent arrival of the new police official who they say had embarked on a new regime of prosecution and interference in village life.[154] This action foreshadowed the character of the new forms of local control. As the discussion unfolds, we shall see how this new form of control impacted on local entrepreneurship.

Conclusion

The aim of this chapter was to explain how different people who made up the Evaton community from its inception cultivated the distinctiveness of the settlement, and how a diverse population coalesced into a community that emphasised social and economic autonomy. This community saw planned municipal townships as controlled settlements that disrupt relative autonomy. This was achieved by shedding light on who these pioneers were, where they came from, what attracted them to the area and what pushed them out of their previous areas. Additionally, it explored what kind of socio-economic dynamics emerged in this community as well as attitudes towards land-ownership and economic independence. The following chapters demonstrate how an understanding of these dynamics provides us with the rationale on why the pioneering residents preferred to maintain their economic independence that was later expressed through enterprises, which is the core issue of this book, and how Evaton became a space that was favourable for the continuation of money-making enterprises. Evaton provided local resident's space as a defence mechanism against demands made on them by the Industrial Revolution. Furthermore, their struggle against increased dependency in wage labour affected the shape of the Evaton community over time. These chapters also help us map out the changing economic profile of early residents, particularly those who moved from commercial agricultural enterprises to retail and service-related entrepreneurship. It is fair to conclude that in the following decades most of the families were unable to escape wage labour but the families who are represented in this chapter demonstrated their ability to escape the labour market during a time when surrounding industries that mushroomed in the 1940s demanded local labour.

The chapter illustrated that the local community and its socio-economic traditions were shaped by the majority landless farmers from the Highveld and former land-owners from Natal as well as land-thirsty urbanites. The most important force that motivated this group to settle in Evaton was to own land. This group, however, demonstrated different ways in how they would use their land. Educated residents, for example, wanted land for building schools and churches while the former farmers wanted to re-establish their agricultural enterprises for commercial benefit. Their aspirations sadly did not materialise due to the size of the stands which only allowed farming for household food supplies. This prompted these farmers to revert to the old ways of the African peasantry. One of the most common aspirations among the former sharecroppers and independent famers was to maintain their economic independence at a time when many Africans were drawn into the expanding labour market. The notion of economic independence that was achieved through land ownership proves, therefore, to be central to this chapter and the following chapters.

Perhaps this is one of the most important aspects that made Evaton distinctive from other freehold areas that were rapidly urbanised because of smaller stands and their proximity to the city. There are three features that could be attributed to the maintenance of economic autonomy which Evaton provided to its pioneers. These aspects were land ownership, the size of stands, and grazing land. The area also provided former landless farmers an opportunity of owning land, which satisfied their lifelong desire. This opportunity was coupled with local level decision-making in the administrative affairs of the area. Local residents enjoyed the power of deciding where community service amenities that were designed to improve the lives of the local community members should be built. For them, Evaton provided a space where they could express themselves freely and move without restraint from authorities. In other words, Evaton marked an achievement especially with land issues not only for farmers but also for educated urban residents. It was a place where autonomy was expressed through access to land use rights. This enabled educated residents to build the Wilberforce Institute.

Notes

[1] J. Guy, *The destruction of the Zulu Kingdom: The Civil War in Zululand, 1879-1884*, London Longman Publishers, 1979

[2] P. Delius, *The Land Belong to Us: The Pedi Polity, the Boers and the British in the Nineteenth Century* Transvaal, Berkeley, University of California Press, 1984, p.1

[3] L. Thompson, *A History of South Africa*, Yale, Yale University Press, 1990

[4] M. D Ramoroka, 'The History of the Barolong in the District of Mafikeng: A study of the Intra Batswana Ethnicity and Political Culture from 1852-1950,' Unpublished PhD Thesis, University of Zululand.

[5] A. Manson, 'Christopher Bethel and the Securing of the Bechuanaland Frontier, 1878-1884" *in Journal of Southern African Studies*, Volume 24, Number 3, 1998.

[6] M.D. Ramoroka, The History of the Barolong.

[7] D. P. Curtin, *The Image of Africa: British Ideas and Action, 1780 -1850*, London, 1965.

[8] A. Odendaal, *The Founders: The Origins of the ANC and the Struggle for Democracy in South Africa*, Pretoria, Jacana Media, 2012 P. Rich, 'Black Peasant and Ethiopianism in South Africa 1896-1915,' A Conference paper that was

delivered in the Conference on the History of Opposition in Johannesburg, July 1978 N. Etherington, Religion and Resistance in Natal in A Lissoni et al (ed), *One Hundred Years of the ANC: Debating Liberation Histories Today*,2012. J. Campbell. *The Songs of Zion: The African Methodist Episcopal Church in United States and South Africa, Chapel Hill,* University of North Carolina, 1998, G. Shepperson, ' Ethiopianism and African Nationalism,' *Phylon,*Vol.14 1940-1956 Q.N. 'Parson, Independency and Ethiopianism among the Tswana in the late 19th and early twentieth century,' Collected Seminar Papers, Institute of Common Wealth Studies G Shepperson 'Ethiopianism and African Nationalism,' *Phylon.*

[9] E. Letsoalo, Land Reform in South Africa, Green Paper on South African Land Policy, 1987.

[10] W. Du Plessis, 'Historical Overview: Evolution of Land Tenure and Administration System in South Africa' International Conference Paper, Orlando, Florida, 1996.

[11] Ibid

[12] J. Bergh and H Feinberg, 'Trusteeship and Black Land Ownership During the Nineteenth and the Twentieth Century,' *Kleio, 36: 1, 170-193, 2004.*

[13] Surveyor General Office, Akter van Transport, NMS Staatsprokureur, Micro Filmed 3401/73/D3/b

[14] National Archive of South Africa, Transfer of stands, file NTS, 1447/56, 3 September1949

[15] Interview with Dwight Seremi, conducted by Vusi Kumalo, 21 May 2011, Evaton

[16] A. Classen, For whites only: Land ownership in South Africa in M. De Klerk (ed) *A Harvest of Discontent*, Cape Town, IDASA, 1992

[17] R. H. Davenport. Native Land Act, 1913, *Black Sash,* 1983

[18] Ibid

[19] Ibid

[20] The substantial literature on the educated refers to this class of certified Africans as an 'educated elite'. The author will avoid using the concept 'elite' which is controversial and is maybe an inaccurate characterisation of this class. My argument is based on the fact that class

composition of this group changed over time depending on the circumstances. The term 'elite' obscures the extent to which they were drawn from an oppressed and economically deprived grouping. For instance, the income of some members of this group was increasingly inadequate to sustain their family's survival. Although this group was educated, their qualifications were of little help to them in a period in which concerted efforts were being made to suppress the development of the African middle class. The case of Evaton explains this better where some uneducated residents like the Dlaminis, who were traditionalist, were more affluent than many members of this class. Therefore, the author will avoid using the term elite and will refer to this group as educated residents, professionals or certified residents.

[21] W. Beinart, P. Delius and S. Trapido, *Putting the Plough on the Ground: Accumulation and Dispossession in Rural South Africa 1850-1930*, Johannesburg, Ravan Press, 1986

[22] The term ought to be applied to some aspect of the independent churches in South African church movement whose origins may be traced back to the 1870s. Ethiopianism was started by African Christians who abandoned mission churches. They were later drawn to the AME Church by the promise of education. Many left European churches precisely because of the limitations they encountered in mission schools. For them the AME offered an ideal solution to the problem. Given their exaggerated notion about African American educational attainments, it was easy for the early Ethiopians to believe that they had at last found the key that would unlock the future of the race. For further details see J. Campbell. The Songs of Zion: The African Methodist Episcopal Church in United States and South Africa, Chapel Hill, University of North Carolina, 1998, G. Shepperson, 'Ethiopianism and African Nationalism,' *Phylon,* Vol.14 1940-1956

[23] Ethiopianism was resented by white government officials and missionaries. Missionaries were so hurt and enraged by Ethiopianism that they rarely stopped to ask who specifically had defected to the movement or why. This movement was characterised as menacing, and it was denounced in Natal by government officials as calculated to destroy European rule. The authorities in Natal and some parts of the Cape Colony prohibited it.

²⁴ G.A. Duncan, 'Pull up a Good Tree and Push it Outside, The Rev Edward Tsewu Dispute with the Free Church of Scotland Mission' *http: ngtt. Journal. ac.za*

²⁵ G. A. Duncan Pull up a Good Tree and Push it outside: The Rev Tsewu dispute with the Free Church of Scotland Mission, http://ngtt. Journals. ac.za

²⁶ Ibid

²⁷ Ibid

²⁸ Ibid

²⁹ Ibid, p. 9

³⁰Ibid

³¹ P. Bonner, The Transvaal Native Congress 1917-190: Radicalisation of the Black Petty Bourgeoisie on the Rand in S, Marks and R. Rathbone, (ed) *Industrialisation and Social Change in South Africa: African Class Formation, Culture and Consciousness 1870-1930*. New York, Longman Group 1982. G Balandier *Sociology of Black Africa* London, 1970 P. Rich, 'Ministering to the White Man's Needs: The Development of Urban Segregation in South Africa, 1913-1923', History Workshop Conference Paper, University of the Witwatersrand, 1978

³²National Archives of South Africa, A report from the Secretary of Native Affairs, File, SNA 287, NA 2870, 1905

³³ J. Campbell, The Songs of Zion

³⁴ ibid

³⁵ Ibid

³⁶ Ibid

³⁷ Ibid

³⁸ On sharecropping and the AME church see T. Keegan 'Crisis and Catharis in the Development of Capitalism in South African Agriculture, *African Affairs*, No. 4. 84. 1984, pp? J. Campbell. *The Songs of Zion*, p, 152

³⁹ G. Shepperson, 'Ethiopianism and African Nationalism', *Phylon*, Vol. 14. No.1 1940-1956, pp, 9-18

⁴⁰ P. Walshe, 'The Origins of African Political Consciousness in South Africa,' *Journal of Modern African Studies*, Vol. 7 No. 4, 1969, pp. 583-610

⁴¹ J. Campbell, *The Songs of Zion*, p. 137

⁴² J. Bergh and H. Feinberg, 'Trusteeship and Black Landownership, p. 175.

⁴³ J. Campbell, *The Songs of Zion*, p. 153.

⁴⁴ Ibid, p. 153.

⁴⁵ *The Black Sash Magazine,* 1983, p. 25.

⁴⁶ J. Campbell, *The Songs of Zion*, p. 153.

⁴⁷ J. M. Nhlapo, *Wilberforce Institution*, Boikhutso Institute, 1947.

⁴⁸ Interview with D Qupe, conducted by Vusi Kumalo, 12 May 2011, Evaton.

⁴⁹ Today there is a high school in Evaton named after Mashabane who taught people like Barney Ngakane in rural Free State.

⁵⁰ The roots of Ethiopianism may be traced to the early years of the nineteenth century with the struggle of the anti-colonialist Nxele and the development of an African indigenous theology by Ntsikana. Both developed a religious synthesis of African traditional religion and Christianity which 'demonstrate the turbulence in the symbolic world occasioned by the coming of the Europeans. It is clear that Ethiopians saw a convergence of the political and the religious motives and methods. However, in conceiving the reason for the founding of the Black Church as being primarily missiological even to the extent of visualising the principle of the ecumenical dimension of Christian mission, they were the formulators of the concept of Pan-Africanism. They preached that the church in colonial South Africa and the entire African population should be so developed, freed and equipped that it can go out and serve other people.' For details see G. A. Duncan Pull up Good Tree and Push it outside: J.R. Cochrane, *Servants of Power: the role of the English speaking churches in South Africa 1903-1930* Johannesburg: Ravan Press, 1987, G. Cuthbertson, 'Missionary Imperialism and Colonial Warfare: London Missionary Society attitudes to the South African War, 1899-1902.' *South African Historical Journal,* 19:93-114, 1987 G. Cuthbertson, 'Cave of Adullam: Missionary Reaction to Ethiopianism at Lovedale, 1898-1902.' *Missionalia* 19 No.1, April, 1991 pp, 57-64.

⁵¹ J. Campbell, The Songs of Zion

[52] H. Bradford, 'Mass Movement and the Petty Bourgeoisie: The Social Origins of the ICU leadership, 1924-19,' *The Journal of African History*, Vol 25, No 3, 1984 pp 295-310

[53] Ibid

[54] Y. G-m Lulat. *United States Relations with South Africa: A Critical Overview*, New York, Peter Lang Publishers, 2008, p. 441

[55] Interview with David Qupe, conducted by Vusi Kumalo, 21 July 2011. Evaton

[56] T. D. Mweli Skota *The African Yearly Register*, Johannesburg R.L. Esson and Co The Orange Press.

[57] J. Nhlapo, *Wilberforce Institute*.

[58] Interview with Ben Tsotetsi, conducted by Vusi Kumalo, 12 May 2011, Evaton.

[59] Interview with Ben Tsotetsi, conducted by Vusi Kumalo, 12 May 2011, Evaton.

[60] Ibid

[61] Ibid

[62] Interview with Enoch Madonsela, conducted by Vusi Kumalo, 13 August 2012, Evaton.

[63] S.D, Gish A.B Xuma, *African, American, South Africa*, New York, New York University Press, 2000

[64] D J Childs, The Black Church and the American Education: The African Methodist Episcopal Church Educating for Liberation, unpublished PhD Thesis, University of Miami, 2009

[65] Y. G-m Lulat. United State Relations with South Africa: A Critical overview, New York, Peter Lang Publishers, 2008, p. 441

[66] **Umteteli wa Bantu** (Mouthpiece of the People) was a newspaper, established by the Chamber of Mines and the Native Recruiting Corporation (NRC) after the 1920 mineworkers strike.

[67] J. Campbell, The Social Origins of African Methodism in the Free State, Seminar Paper delivered at African Studies Institute at the University of the Witwatersrand 1993

[68] J. M. Nhlapo, *Wilberforce Institution*, p.7

[69] Interview conducted with Motlalepule Chabaku by Vusi Kumalo, 5 May 2010, Evaton

[70] Interview with Boy Masiza, conducted by Vusi Kumalo, 12 October 2011, Evaton.

[71] J.M. Nhlapo *Wilberforce Institute*.

[72] Ibid

[73] National Archive of South Africa, Native Commissioner's Report, NTS 361/364, 1938.

[74] Ibid

[75] T.D. Mweli Skota, *The African Yearly Register*, Johannesburg, R.L. Esson and Co. Ltd, 1932; T.D. Mweli Skota, *The African Who's Who*, Johannesburg, Central News Agency, 1965.

[76] J.M. Nhlapo, *Wilberforce Institute*.

[77] Ibid

[78] J. Campbell, The Social Origins of African Methodism in the Free State, Seminar Paper that was delivered at African Studies Institute at the University of the Witwatersrand 1993.

[79] National Archive of South Africa, A letter from the Native Commissioner to the Secretary of Native Affairs on Evaton Administration matters, File, NTS 361/364 27 July 1930.

[80] Ibid

[81] T. D. Mweli Skota *The African Yearly Register*.

[82] H. Hughes *First President: A life of John L Dube, founding president of the ANC*, Johannesburg, Jacana Media, 2011.

[83] J. M. Nhlapo *Wilberforce Institution*, 1947 Unpublished Manuscript, J.M. Nhlapo Papers, A1006 Historical Papers.

[84] *Sanibona,* ILAM CR3735, Wilberforce Institute Singers, 1940, Digital Innovation South Africa, University of KwaZulu Natal.

[85] Pass Officer report on his visit to Wilberforce Primary Section, 5 December 1919 NTS 373/56 National Archives of South Africa.

[86] Historical Papers, University of the Witwatersrand, A letter written by Eva Morake to Dr A.B. Xuma, Xuma Papers, 10 March 1937.

[87] Ibid

[88] In 1957, the Public Utility Transport Corporation (PUTCO) in South Africa raised the bus fare from 4d to 5d for commuters in Johannesburg. This was equivalent to 2 pennies or 1 shilling (15c) more that the South Africans would need to pay a week. As a result, these Africans in Evaton and Alexandra launched a bus boycott exclaiming, "Azikhwelwa!"

[89] National Archive of South Africa, A letter from the Native Commissioner to the Director of Native Labour File 361/363, undated.

[90] T. Keegan 'Crisis and Catharis'.

[91] Ibid

[92] Interview with James Moore, conducted by Vusi Kumalo, Evaton, 21 June 2012.

[93] Interview with Paul Seshabela, conducted by Vusi Kumalo, Evaton, 28 April 2012.

[94] Interview with Dwight Seremi, conducted with Vusi Kumalo, Evaton, 12 May 2011.

[95] Interview with Mjikisi Maseko, conducted by Vusi Kumalo, 11 June 2011, Evaton.

[96] T. Keegan, *Facing the Storm: Portrait of Black Lives in Rural South Africa*, London, Zed Books, 1988.

[97] Ibid.

[98] Interview with Dwight Seremi

[99] Untitled document from the Secretary of Native Affairs, NTS 361/364 National Archives of South Africa.

[100] A letter from J. De Roos to the Secretary of Native Affairs 1 December 1916, JUS 240 3/881/16 National Archives of South Africa.

[101] Native Affairs Department on Evaton Location: Native Township on 9th September 1938 This report was gathered by the author from Tladi Kekane's private collection, and it is difficult for the author to locate where it comes from in the National Archives. For reference purposes this report will be stored in the History Workshop Archives located at the Origins Centre at the University of the Witwatersrand.

[102] National Archives of South Africa, A letter written by Easton Adams Company to the Secretary Health Committee, File NTS 361-364, 21 March 1936.

[103] Interview with Paul Seshabela, conducted by Vusi Khumalo, 17 June 2009, Evaton.

[104] J. Lambert, 'African reasons for purchasing land in Natal in the late 19th, early 20th centuries,' *African Historical Review*, Vol. 31.1 1999.

[105] See, for example, the examination of the prominent Wesleyan station Edendale in S. Meintjes, 'Edendale, 1850-1906: a Case Study of Rural Transformation and Class Formation in an African Mission in Natal', PhD dissertation University of London, 1988, N. Etherington, *Preachers, Peasants, and Politics in Southeast Africa*, 1835-1880 London, 1978.

[106] Interview with Absolom Dlamini, conducted by Vusi Khumalo, 12 May 2011, Evaton.

[107] M. Mahoney, 'The Millennium comes to Mapumulo: Popular Christianity in Rural Natal' 1866-1906, *Journal of Southern Africa Studies*, Vol. 25 No 3, 1999, pp. 375-391.

[108] Interview with Lucy Dlamini, conducted by Vusi Kumalo, 12 March 2010, Evaton.

[109] Interview with Absolom Dlamini.

[110] Ibid

[111] Interview with Absolom Dlamini conducted by Vusi Kumalo, 12 March 2010, Evaton.

[112] Interview with Daniel Motuba, conducted by Vusi Kumalo, 25 May 2011, Evaton.

[113] S Meintjes, 'Edendale, 1850-1906: A Case Study of Rural Transformation and Class Formation in an African Mission in Natal', PhD dissertation, University of London, 1988.

[114] Ibid

[115] Interview with Daniel Motuba.

[116] Interview with Jacob Sibeko, conducted by Vusi Kumalo, 23 May 2011, Evaton.

[117] P. Delius and S. Trapido, 'Inboekseling and Oorlams: The Creation and Transformation of Servile Class, in B. Bozzoli (ed), *In Town and Countryside in the Transvaal: Capitalist Penetration and Popular Response*, Johannesburg, Ravan Press, 1983.

[118] P. Bonner, *Kings, Commoners and Concessionaires: The Evolution and Dissolution of the Nineteenth-Century Swazi State*, Cambridge, Cambridge Press 1983, p, 81-84.

[119] Interview with Abel Tshawe, conducted by Vusi Kumalo, 13 May 2013, Evaton.

[120] ibid

[121] H. Feinberg. 'The 1913 Land Act in South Africa: Politics, Race and Segregation in the early 20th Century,' *International Journal of African Historical Studies*, Vol 26 No.1 pp 65-109.

[122] S. Trapido, Putting the Plough on the Ground, in S. Trapido, et al (ed) *Putting the Plough on the Ground*, Johannesburg, Ravan Press, 1986.

[123] Ibid

[124] Interview with Jackson Mokwena, conducted by Vusi Kumalo, 12 June 2012, Evaton.

[125] Interview with Abram Mogale, conducted by Vusi Kumalo, 30 June 2012, Evaton.

[126] T. Keegan, *Facing the Storm: Portraits of Black Lives in Rural South Africa*. London, Zed Books 1988.

[127] Interview with Jackson Mokwena, conducted by Vusi Kumalo 12 June 2012, Evaton.

[128] T. R. H Davenport, *South Africa: A Modern History*, London McMillan Press, 1991.

[129] National Archives of South Africa, A letter from the Secretary for Native Affairs to the Secretary for Justice, File, JUS 240 3/881/6, 20 November 1916.

[130] Ibid.

[131] Interview with Jacob Mofokeng, conducted by Vusi Kumalo, 9 June 2011, Evaton

[132] Interview with James Mogale, conducted by Vusi Kumalo, 18 July 2011, Evaton

[133] National Archive of South Africa, A Letter from Macrobert and De Villiers Attorneys to the Secretary for Native Affairs, File NTS 376 252/26, 16 January 1930

[134] S. D Gish, *A.B. Xuma, African, American, South African*.

[135] Interview with Daniel Motuba, conducted by Vusi Kumalo, 12 May 2011, Evaton.

[136] Quoted in H Slater, The Changing Pattern of Economic Relations in Rural Natal, http:// sas – space. Ac.uk/3657/1

[137] M. Chanock *The Making of South African Legal Culture: Fear, Favour, and Prejudice*, Cambridge, Cambridge University Press.

[138] In the central Highveld and bushveld regions Africans continued to live on farms acquired by Afrikaners through the conquest of the Ndebele under Mzilikazi and local polities, or by purchase. African labour was needed by the white farmers, so half of the crop was kept by the white landlord and half was kept by African workers. In many regions African sharecroppers flourished and were able to rebuild their herds as well as acquire wagons and agricultural implements. However, once white farmers obtained more political power, they caused the sharecropping system to be modified into one of labour tenancy in which tenants had to provide wage labour and could retain a third of the total crop.

[139][139] Interview with Absolom Dlamini.

[140] Interview with Oupa Motuba.

[141] Interview with Dwight Seremi.

[142] National Archive of South Africa, Interim Report No. 7 in respect of Evaton, District Vereeniging in the Province of the Transvaal, File NTS 361/364, 11 March 1939.

[143] Ibid

[144] National Archives of South Africa A letter from H.H Baillie to the Native Commissioner, NTS 361/364, 15, October 1934

[145] Ibid

[146] National Archive of South Africa National Archives of South Africa A letter from S P Bunting to the Native Commissioner, NTS 361/364, 15, November 1934

[147] Ibid

[148] National Archive of South Africa, A letter from S. J Bunting to the Secretary of the Native Commissioner, NTS 361/364, 23 November 1942.

[149] National Archives of South Africa, A letter from H. Gow and J Tantsi to the Commissioner of Native Affairs, NTS 361-364, 27 March 1931.

[150] Ibid

[151] National Archive of South Africa, A letter written by the Native Commissioner to the Secretary for Native Affairs, NTS 361/364, 31 July 1930.

[152] National Archive of South Africa, A letter written by Paul Motaung to unknown Lawyer, NTS 361/364 dated 11 November 1944.

[153] National Archive of South Africa, A letter written by the Additional Native Commissioner to the Director of Native Labour NTS 361/364, 23 March 1944.

[154] National Archive of South Africa, A letter written by S.P Bunting to the Secretary for Native Affairs, NTS 361/364, 11 December 1931.

Chapter 2

Subsistence farming and economic independence

Introduction

In the previous chapter it was demonstrated how the presence of educated residents associated to the Wilberforce Institute and local churches, as well as the Institute itself, expressed the distinctiveness of Evaton. This social expression did not only represent the uniqueness of the settlement, but it characterises and confirms Evaton's relative autonomy. At the point at which this analysis begins, Africans were already deeply affected by successive waves of land dispossession. Their independent economic status was undermined. These fundamental changes in the rural economy pushed many Africans to urban areas. This implies that the level of dependence on wage labour was increasing among Africans. These changes differed, however, from one settlement to another. In Evaton, the process of proletarianisation appeared to be more complex. For instance, local families practised subsistence farming, which contributed to their economic independence. Similar to the presence of Wilberforce and the educated residents, the local economy provided one of the major economic expressions of autonomy and uniqueness of Evaton. Equally important, it provided the settlement with dignity, economic security and self-respect.

More interestingly, the existence of a subsistence economy delayed local incorporation into wage labour beyond what other freehold townships experienced on the Reef. For local residents, this type of farming presented an alternative livelihood that prevented locals from giving up entering into the labour market. It satisfied the consumption needs for many families. Pressure on arable soil began to show, however, when migrants from rural areas began to find space in which to settle. Dependence on wage labour rose sharply, arable land was severely constrained by rooms that were built on arable land to accommodate newcomers. Population growth also hampered grazing land, and locals were forced to reduce their livestock. In the face of these fundamental changes, the process of proletarianisation was inescapable. Nonetheless, there were residents who were able to escape the general experience of entering into the labour market. These residents opened up different types of entrepreneurial activities that catered for the increasing number in population. The emerging local enterprises had deep implications in the local struggle against economic dependence and social differentiation.

The aim of this chapter is to examine how subsistence farming sustained the local economic independence and distinctiveness of Evaton. This explains why and how the deterioration of subsistence farming led to the development of African entrepreneurship. The chapter also reveals how some residents, particularly sharecroppers who had entrepreneurial taste, ventured into entrepreneurial activities with an aim of sustaining a life-long goal of becoming economically independent. This explanation provides us with an economic trajectory from farming to entrepreneurship - this was what made the settlement so special. The first part of the chapter focuses on subsistence farming and its development. The second part explores the population pressure and how it constrained local farming. The final section of the chapter discusses the emergence of entrepreneurship and the types of entrepreneurial activities that materialised.

Subsistence Farming

During the early period of Evaton, the availability of big stands provided enough agricultural space for subsistence farming. During interviews one of the informants, Sonto Kekane, recalls: 'we had maize and different kinds of vegetables, we also had fruit trees like grape, apple, apricots and pears, and it was green all over with trees and plants.'[1] In the first decade of the twentieth century, the low level of industrialisation in the surrounding areas opened up space that could be used for ploughing and grazing. Other land parcels of Weldebeesfontein farm were unoccupied and unutilised, and large areas of land was used for grazing. When properties were sold by the Easton and Adams Company in the form of blocks, they consisted of a number of individually owned erven. Each of these plots had its own arable land, title deeds, and the right to common grazing land.[2] Stands were divided into two, the larger stands were 40, 800 square feet and the smaller ones were 291 square roods (a measure of land area equal to a quarter of an acre) and 96 square feet.[3] Subsistence farming became one or the other feature of the pioneering stage in Evaton. Although land was small compared to the land that the former sharecroppers worked on white farms, it was enough for subsistence purposes. This is supported by Mjikisi Maseko's recollection:

> ...we never starved in Evaton families were productive units....we as children worked with our parents ploughing fields, my father was strict he wanted us to work and we worked, we also looked after cattle... 'hey man there was nothing people of Evaton were practising agriculture, they were just planting in their stands for example I would plant this place there was no poverty there was maize in these stands we were not starving there was sorghum as well you see there were buses there was also a grinding stone

where people will grind their corn and we were not starving and suffering here in Evaton.[4]

Tsepo Khanyi pointed out a grinding stone that her mother used and observed:

> we looked down upon people from urban areas because they bought everything while we were planting everything, here at home we grinded (sic) *mabele (sorghum)* and made *ting* sour porridge that is made out of sorghum. We never bought *mabele* or maize we planted, and we exchanged with other families.[5]

In Evaton's early years, local residents reverted to the old ways of the African peasantry. They grew their own food and lived as an inter-dependent community that was bonded by reciprocity. Each family was responsible for producing its own food that would take care of its subsistence needs. Local families were not dependent on food that was purchased from grocery stores. Indeed, there were very few household items that were bought from the grocery store and they were secondary to daily food consumption. Perhaps the local families were also enmeshed in monetary relations, but this assumption is not clear from the interviews. What is clear from the interviews is the relationship between land and agricultural practice. This claim paints a picture that the local agricultural practice minimised dependence on local money relations. Money was, however, used for external purchases of some household commodities, schoolbooks, for travelling cost and other needs. It was further used for school fees that were paid in local schools, such as the Wilberforce. Most interviews emphasised the significance of land over money. Seshabela recalled that 'our fathers believed that land ownership especially the size of stands that they owned helped them not to depend on wage employment.'[6] Land was a major resource for economic stability, and it was where food was sourced through agriculture and cattle relied on it for grazing. The local economy was characterised by a complex interrelationship between cattle-holding and cultivation and a family labour's participation in the subsistence economy. Local economic strength involved processes of economic calculation which originated from and were directed towards the material interests and well-being of the individual family.

The local agricultural practices were blended with pre-colonial indigenous economic systems and social links that bonded Evaton families together. For instance, during harvest time, different families would exchange crops in the form of bartering. This was observed by Paul Seshabela who recalled 'one man will plant potatoes another one will plant mealies and they would barter after harvest.'[7] Early residents formed work parties that were based on traditional African economic welfare. These parties worked as *letsema* in SeTswana or *ilima* in the Zulu language. Sonto recounted,

> ... every year when we were about to plant, we had *letsema* a certain old-man would come with his donkeys and turn the soil of all the houses on our street, his name was Mankune. We worked as a community, everyone would go help out from the first house till the last one.[8]

Work parties are widely reported in pre-industrial ethnography. As far as south-eastern Africa is concerned, the first detailed description by a social scientist seems to be of the Lovedu.[9] Kuckertz noted that classical ethnographies stress two elements, the first being some kind of reciprocally rendered assistance or service, the other one being an enactment of a social value rather than an economic affair.[10] During this period many public works activities like building, pit digging, and clearing of fields appealed to local residents not necessarily because of financial rewards but because of mutual assistance.

This is evident in the letter that J. B. Malindisa, the Induna of the National Royal Club of the Evaton branch, wrote to the Native Commissioner which reads as follows:

> People are poor and make their living on ploughing and getting twelve bags of mealies a year. What we do out here in Evaton as we see that we are poor we help each other as; one dies we make collection of foodstuff and grave is dug by men free of charge and also taking of the body is taken by wagon free of charge.[11]

This letter is an intriguing document that supports the claim of informants. For the great majority of Evatonians, in the early part of the settlement's development the community offered security. There were no private undertakers that would be paid when an individual died, no funeral insurance for individuals. In terms of crisis, the community had to play an important role in burying the dead. Apart from funerals, the local community was bonded together by different activities that were done communally. The notion of individualism was not known, the social group or the community was more important than an individual's right and privileges. Sharing was central to the community of Evaton. This affirms social connectedness, human value, trust and dignity. Seshabela remarks, 'it was not like today when people just come to bury the dead without contributing something'[12] There existed an emphasis on social bonds and mutual interdependence, such that the good of the individual was closely intertwined with the good of the group.

This helps to account for why before the 1930s, local development was done communally and why Wilberforce, the first school, was built by a group of local artisans who never wanted any payment.[13] Apart from Wilberforce, many churches and local community centres were built by local artisans. Among these artisans were Makhene, a brick-maker, Motuba, a teacher and wagon maker, Mareletsi, a bricklayer, Pooe, a baker, Tswagong and Rapodile, bricklayers and makers, Mamasile, a scotch roof maker, Marago, a wagon maker and a crafter of wagon wheels, and many others like Sonto's grandfather, a shoemaker.[14] There were also stonemasons like Meku's grandfather, leatherworkers, wood carvers, carpenters, wagon builders, teachers, clergy, iron smelters, herbalists and so forth. Mission schools and exposure to the white economy provided these residents with the basis for independent commodity production that served as the foundation of local entrepreneurship.

An Evaton family that required the service of the *letsema* would invite *letsema* members and prepare food and traditional beer. Co-operation between homesteads occurred particularly in the form of borrowing draught animals for ploughing and harvesting and in organising work-parties for hoeing and weeding. This implied that the individual household required help from other homesteads for many of its domestic as well as economic activities. In Western terms, it could be argued that work operated in a contractual form where an individual participant was indebted to provide equal service to the previously serviced party.

In addition to agricultural work, these parties were also responsible for public works such as building roads. During the physical development of Evaton, these co-operatives became a very important unit for public works and local administration. They became functional during road works, digging pits, clearing fields for cultivation, school building and other local development projects. This is reflected in William Mokwena's testimony on the establishment of the school,

> ....They talk about this they were in the coal yard, somebody said no man each household should contribute pound and we will go and challenge commissioners. Then they started collecting this

money pound per stand. After they collected they went to commissioner wearing coats, they said hey man here is our money we want the school. The amount of money that the elders collected shocked the commissioner... [said the commissioner] I will take it to the bank, the elders said no talk to the government then you will come back to us.[15]

Evaton residents adhered to communal work for the security that it offered. This form of communalism was socially instrumental for maintaining social order and reducing jealousy among lazy families. Every family was obliged to participate so as to avoid greed. Mjikisi Maseko pointed out that these parties also provided people an opportunity to debate social problems.[16] It is where gossip was exchanged, the news providing an informal forum wherein actions of community members were discussed and evaluated and if necessary censured.[17] Within this discourse, an African philosopher John Mbiti summed up this socio-cultural practice in the following statement: 'I am because we are, and since we are therefore I am'.[18] This is what the people of Evaton believed.

Like in any other African rural settlement, livestock, particularly cattle, was a major form of capital in Evaton. Sheep and goats were secondary although sheep were more commercial for their skins. However, in Evaton, the sheepskin trade was not practised.[19] Though animals were occasionally killed for meat, cattle produced many useful domestic products such as milk which was fermented to make *amasi* (sour milk), one of the principal items of the local community. Milk, whether sour or fresh, was a staple food with varieties of grain. Cattle also provided meat for feasting and cow dung for floor decoration, fuel and manure as well as skins that were used for shoes, robes, sandals and other leather commodities. Oxen were used for drawing ploughs and wagons.

In cases of family economic crises, cattle were exchanged for cash. For instance, Aubrey Mofokeng remembered that in order for his parents to pay his fees at Adams College, they had to sell cattle to some Afrikaners.[20] It was common in those years for the residents of Evaton to sell their cattle in order to pay school fees for their children. At that time, residents defined wealth in terms of cattle. Thus, a household with many head of cattle was regarded as rich. For each and every local family, cattle acquisition was the main ambition and it was a source of worries and joys.[21] Another major use of livestock was for acquiring wives which was a common cultural practice in Southern Africa. By then, livestock farming was favoured, and the fact that the area was sparsely populated while its topographical formation was flat meant that the area was immune to soil erosion.

However, from the late 1920s and early 1930s, the number of cattle gradually decreased because of population growth that impacted on grazing land. In 1938 the Secretary for Native Affairs reported that 'natives residing in the Township and that between them they owned about 3,750 head of large stock (including horses) and 600 small stock'.[22] During this period the area had 200 acres of grazing land which was inadequate for local needs.[23] Initially Evaton had an adequate amount of open space that was left for grazing and other purpose. This was noted in a letter from Mr. Easton, one of the owners of Weldebeesfontein, who wrote to the Secretary for Native Affairs where he stated that 'it is not intended to deprive this Native community of all open spaces...it is not intended to sell the whole of the lands'. [24] The decrease of livestock could therefore be attributed to the shortage of common grazing land, as well as to various factors, such as the 1930s drought that was locally known as *'leruli'*. This deficiency may have contributed to the decrease in cattle due to the resulting difficulties in grazing. In the early 1930s, when depression and drought threatened to overwhelm the farming sector, the government supplied white farmers with cattle feed and financial aid, but similar assistance was not extended to African farmers whose ability to market their grain crops was severely impaired by the high mortality amongst draught oxen and donkeys.[25] Sources indicate that by 1937, Evaton, which was 1,300 morgen in extent, already had 1,700 plots which were sold to residents. The local Special Justice for Peace estimated that the residents' population was between 14000 and 20000.[26]

Although these families produced enough for subsistence, they were living under capitalism and had to cope with capitalist demands. For instance, they had to pay colonial taxes, sponsor their children's education and sustain other household needs. Furthermore, they had to deal with changes in consumption tastes as Evaton families were beginning to experience new needs and desires that were similar to those of white people. Moreover, families of the early residents valued education driven by the strong belief that education would provide the means to advance them in civilization. Hence the acquisition of artisanal skills was desirable. Lily Nondala pointed out that when she arrived with her parents from Sophiatown in 1933, it was during the drought period and people were starving.[27] Nondala's testimony that touches on the natural impact on agriculture may be linked to a letter from Hope Baillie to D. Gunn, the acting entomologist in which Baillie complained about the ladybirds that were destroying pumpkins. In response, Mr. Gunn wrote 'with reference to your inquiry regarding the destruction of ladybird I have honour to state that the best remedy to be employed against them is undoubtedly arsenate of load...should be sprayed upon plants'.[28]

Population growth and the demise of subsistence farming

Evaton saw the arrival of some educated families that came during this period. One of the most well-known families was the Nhlapo family that came from Reitz, Orange Free State. This family came after Jacob Nhlapo received an invitation from Bishop R.R. Wright, a presiding bishop of the AME church, to come and work at Wilberforce Institute as principal. Nhlapo served as principal from 1940 to 1947.[29] At Wilberforce, he contributed by purchasing an additional seven morgen of land where he erected more buildings that extended the Institute.[30] At the same time, the area saw the arrival of Moses Kekane's family. Kekane came from Sophiatown where he was a teacher and later became the principal. In Sophiatown, Kekane had been banned from teaching because of the role that he played in the formation of the Transvaal United African Teachers Association (TUATA).[31] According to his son, Tladi Kekane,

> ….after my father was banned from teaching my aunt who was also a teacher and a shop owner in Evaton called him to come and manage her shop. The aim was to keep him busy because he could not practice as a teacher and he had no income. He then worked at Nkabani General Dealer and managed to buy property in the area'.[32]

It is possible that Evaton served as a refuge for politically rebellious individuals and persons who were frustrated by stringent government control. One of the most important factors that attracted a large proportion of educated people was the expansion of Wilberforce, which by 1936 had more than 35 students. This number increased over the next few years to accommodate more than 200 students.[33] By this time, Evaton's appeal, however, lay not only in the autonomy it offered but in the availability of education. The Wilberforce Institute made Evaton special and distinct – it attracted students from all over Southern Africa. This is exemplified by learners who came from as far as Northern Rhodesia (Zambia). Ethel Chunga, for instance, came from Nkana, Northern Rhodesia. In her letter of application, she stated:

> ...the immigration Authorities here advised me to consult you and the Commissioner of Immigration... Any arrangement which will be arrived at will be greatly appreciated the concession to read fare from Ndola to Evaton. I will send an advance of school fees amounting to £4 at the beginning of the next month.[34]

By 1940 there were educated people who came to Evaton, even from as far away as the United States of America. One of the African-Americans who became the eighth principal of Wilberforce was Dr. J.M. White who came with his wife J. White, who became the secretary of the Institute in the late 1930s.[35] When Bishop Wright of the AME went to America in 1938, he talked a great deal about the Institute and this inspired Dr. Jeophus Roosevelt Coan, a professor of Old Testament Theology at Morris Brown Institute, Atlanta, to come to South Africa with him. Coan helped to establish the R.R. Wright School of Religion on the campus of the Wilberforce Institute in Evaton. In 1940, he was selected to become the first Black superintendent of the Wilberforce Institute.[36] Coan served as a missionary in South Africa for nine years. This was one of the social aspects that made Evaton distinctive from other freehold settlements. The presence of these African-Americans in Evaton could be accounted to the ideas of racial upliftment and African advancement that were grounded in the Pan Africanist framework that inspired the foundation of the Wilberforce Institute. The presence of the African-American professionals was motivated by a desire to uplift and redeem Africa. Their participation at the Wilberforce Institute dovetailed what the first group of African-American missionaries had cultivated in the last decade of the nineteenth century in South Africa. The path that Coan and White followed was the trail that was paved by the earlier African-Americans. They came to Evaton to develop new professional skills that were going to be useful to Africans in South Africa. At that time many theological schools did not accept aspirant priests from independent spiritual churches, but the R.R. Wright Theological School at the Wilberforce Institute welcomed these applicants. Like the Wilberforce Institute, R.R. Wright did not cater for the children of the adherents of the AME church only but kept it open for learners from different denominations, as well as for those who were not attached to any denomination. The educational output of this college, in line with others at the time, was well captured by Sunkler[37] who stated that:

> Besides the president himself (now deceased), there were forty-eight ministers' in the Church. Of the forty-eight ministers one was a graduate from a Negro Teachers' College in the United States; six had South African Teachers' Certificates; one had passed Standard VII; five Standard VI; three Standard V; fourteen Standard IV; eight Standard III; and eight Standard II. As for additional theological training, nine of these men had studied at three different Mission Bible Institutes, while thirteen others had been working in Mission Churches and presumably taken some Bible study there, and twenty-three had had "private studies" in theology. The Holy Communion Church of South Africa: one of the ministers has attained a Standard IV in school; the bishop himself and the three ministers claim knowledge of Zulu or Xhosa, but none of them has had any theological training whatsoever.[38]

The coming of Dr. Coan in Evaton encouraged African religious priests from independent churches to develop a sense of pride. Coan transported African-American religious and educational achievement to South Africa. The arrival of Dr. White and Coan in Evaton sustained and continually reshaped the close trans-Atlantic ties between Africans in the United States and South Africa. As a distinct freehold settlement, Evaton represented the space where the effort to forge connections between African Americans and Africans was expressed. This connection became a primary focus of the Wilberforce Institute. From its inception the Institute maintained close ties with the United States. Apart from the connection that was cultivated by the dozens of American graduates in the early stage of Wilberforce's development, the American ties were further maintained by Eva Mahuma Morake, who graduated with a Master's Degree from Columbia University. In the 1930s, she became the first female principal of the Institute. In Wilberforce, Morake worked very close with Dr. Xuma who was the treasurer of the Institute in the 1930s. Xuma himself had strong ties with America to an extent that he got married to Madie Hall, the African-American graduate from Columbia University. [39]

During this period, the settlement and its population was expanding. According to the report of the Health Inspector, 151 plots were sold, and a clause inserted into the deed of sale that these plots could not be subdivided. By 1941, 71 houses were built on the plots and the value of dwellings and improvement was estimated by the Native Commissioner of Vereeniging at £12 010.[40] The arrival of these property buyers and the further subdivision of Weldebeesfontein Farm, however, meant that grazing land became too small to provide pastures for livestock, and residents were compelled to sell their livestock even though they provided milk for subsistence.

As mentioned, the freehold status and location of Evaton, which was geographically located in the heart of a large industrial area, attracted many newcomers from different parts of the country. During this period, the urban Transvaal was being industrialised and many freehold areas in the Reef experienced population growth which changed their character. The examination of Alexandra and Sophiatown presents us with a typical example of freehold settlements that experienced population growth earlier than Evaton. Population growth in these townships was shaped by institutional forces and the relative autonomy that these settlements presented. These socio-political forces enable one to explain why these settlements became overpopulated. There was a combination of factors that led to the overpopulation of these freehold areas. These reasons range from the changing residential arrangements in the Rand to pass laws. Pass laws became one of the most important factors that accelerated population growth in the freehold townships of Johannesburg. What is clear from many studies is that urban life for male immigrants remained conditional.[41] Apart from institutional factors, the owners of freehold plots in these settlements, especially those who were burdened with bonds which were used for building solid structures, saw sub-letting shacks and rooms to new arrivals as a means of income.[42]

As a freehold area that was far from Johannesburg it experienced changes in a different way from other freehold settlements. The changing conditions in the settlement came along with increasing constraints on land use that affected the local subsistence economy and the economic independence of local inhabitants. These circumstances forced local residents to change their economic activities, impacting their socio-economic occupations. Before the arrival of the newcomers in the mid-1930s, the land available for agriculture and grazing was abundant, and the human movement into the urban areas from the surrounding countryside was small compared to what was later to come. It was, however, not the same when Dr. Clark, a Deputy Chief Health Inspector, visited the area in 1940. During these years, wage labour migrants were finding it increasingly difficult to find suitably priced residential accommodation as no new houses were being built.[43] In consequence, many labour migrants looked to Evaton as a place in the region where they could settle freely without being required to obtain permits that authorised them to be in the settlement. The increasing population and the room letting enterprise were reported by the

Additional Native Commissioner to the Director of Native Labour.

> This released area has increased exceedingly rapidly in population owing to its proximity to Johannesburg, and to the absolute lack of control over community. Most of standholders owning large houses keep lodgers, others have permitted the building of one and two roomed huts on their stands...sanitary convenience available on any one stand are quite inadequate for all residents. [44]

Similar conditions were observed by Dr. Clark who was alarmed during his inspection by the changing conditions in the settlement. He reported, 'Natives in Peri-Urban Areas outside Released Area, were likely to be irksome and that these natives would tend to move away from control into released area and so aggravated the position in Evaton.[45] Many stand-holders in Evaton took advantage of the situation and sublet rooms to migrants. In response, Clark reported that the area had become congested and that slum conditions were beginning to appear in Small Farms. He further concluded that these conditions posed a danger of contamination and infection.[46] By 1939, it was estimated that the population increased from 12 000 to approximately 40 000 residents.[47] This suggests that Evaton's population doubled in just a few years. This congestion did not only pose a danger to health conditions but also contributed to the end of subsistence farming.

Physically, the new development changed the pattern of land use. Agricultural fields were transformed into residential space where rooms were built for tenants, and these dwellings were built on arable land. Depending on the landlord's choice, many yards had five to ten rooms, but the largest number of rooms that were built during this period had 30 rooms and all were rented out to newcomers.[48] From an administrative point of view, this transition introduced threats to the *izibonda's* administrative power and to the local autonomy and freehold status of Evaton. This was recognised by Edward Thornton, the chairman of the Peri-Urban Health Board, who was troubled by the influx of newcomers. He called for the establishment of a local authority that would be equipped to provide essential services to control the influx of 'undesirable elements and to prevent the further development of slums condition'.[49]

There were external forces that pushed many newcomers to the freehold township of Evaton. These forces included the state influx control measures and tight control over the daily lives of urban Africans; the regulation of African entrepreneurship; and the adverse conditions that forced African labour tenants from white farmlands. Population growth and the decline of subsistence farming cannot solely be attributed to the arrival of rural wage labour migrants who rented rooms. One of the most pressing factors on subsistence was the removal of Top Location that led to the establishment of Sharpeville.[50] Top Location had many tenants who rented rooms and a large proportion of these tenants did not qualify for housing schemes in the newly-established Sharpeville. Still more reprehensible was the failure of the location administration to make use of its resources to control the illegal brewing of beer and the massive inflow of its principal manufacturers – predominantly Basotho women.[51] When Top Location was relocated to Sharpeville, these groups of women and other immigrants, particularly those who did not qualify for the new housing allocation, streamed into Evaton. Joshua Vilakazi recalls:

> Many Basotho came here when Top was demolished and the new space and rules in the new location were not the same. The municipality became strict and beer brewing was closely monitored.[52]

Oral evidence indicates that if beer brewers had gone to Sharpeville rather than Evaton, it would have certainly spelled the end of their beer brewing enterprises.[53] The freehold status of Evaton made the area more attractive than the new Sharpeville, where occupation was regulated. According to Mamokiti Seloane, a former beer brewer who now lives in Evaton, 'We would not go to Sharpeville because the 'blackjacks' [as municipality police were called] were very strict and some of us never had pass books'.[54] This removal of Top Location was not well received by beer brewer tenants, mostly Basotho from Lesotho. Mohlalepule Moloi recalls 'it was meant to impoverish us when they removed us from Top, where we had been close to town and never needed transport money because we just walked to wherever we wanted to go'.[55] Women who rented rooms in Evaton Small Farms were independent single women. They were beer brewers or self-employed dressmakers and tailors.[56] They often came independently to the towns, sometimes because of broken families, and were likely to settle more permanently than men.[57] The presence of the women turned Evaton into a centre of attraction for male migrants who spent lonely months without their loved ones. Maseko recollects, '...over weekends migrants from all over the Reef would come for weekend drinking spree'.[58] Tladi recalls 'There were many parties that were held over weekends by Basotho people. They turned Small Farms into little Lesotho, and they were also organised as regional factions'.[59]

During the 1940s, many urbanised Africans from the Johannesburg peri-urban area, slum yards, municipal locations and white-owned yards chose to relocate to Evaton. These urbanites bought properties and set up homes in Evaton. Geographically, the settlement was expanding, and its growth was accelerated by the arrival of these newcomers. It was less than five years before the Edward Nathan and Friedland Attorneys made application on behalf of the Adams and Easton family to sell the grazing land. An extract from the application that was investigated by the Native Affairs Commissioner reads as follows:

> That a clause be inserted in the deed of sale to the effect that the holding may not be subdivided and that no person other than the owner or the member of his family or may reside on such holding. The condition of sale contain a clause to effect that, in the event of the purchaser making default in the payment of any instalment and the sale being cancelled by reason of such default, the sellers shall be bound to refund to the purchaser all monies paid by him less a reasonable sum as commission, etc., not exceeding 10%.[60]

Some of these newcomers brought their wives and children, while single men like Mogoerane organised marriages with women from Evaton or from other areas. Most urban workers who relocated to Evaton were employed in the Reef towns that surrounded Johannesburg. They were relatively poor and most of them relied on bonds for the purchase as well as construction of their properties. Some were single women who could not qualify for a mortgage bond. This is illustrated by the letter of mortgage bond application of N.E. Sechaba. In this letter I. P. O'Driscoll wrote:

> The relative documents were forwarded by this office to the Assistant Native Commissioner, Evaton who was instructed to ascertain from a woman, Sechaba, the reason for the bond…her sources of income, and whether she understood the obligations imposed by the bond and the result to meet failure such obligation…I do not recommend official approval of this transaction, as I feel that the woman will be incurring an obligation which may prove to be beyond her means to meet and

which may possibly result in the loss of property in the event of such failure on her part.[61]

During this period Evaton saw more women buying properties. Francis Yina's letter of bond application confirms the number of women who bought properties. In this letter, F.H. Behrmann wrote '...the loan to erect a brick building under an iron roof to be used as a fresh vegetable and fruit shop'.[62] The urban newcomers could be divided into three categories. In the 1930s, there were tenants from the freehold locations of the Reef which were already overpopulated by working people in the 1930s,[63] backyard dwellers from white yards, and those who held leasehold properties in municipal areas. For example, there were the Nondalas, Moagis and other families that came from the freehold area of Sophiatown. There were also the Khumalos who were domestic servants in white premises and were forced out by municipal policies that attempted to restrict the increase of African families living on white premises.[64] Those who came from the eastern and western municipality townships were the Nxumalos, Mokgoju and other families. Lily Nondala recollects that her father decided to buy property in Evaton because the area was quiet and peaceful with big yards. Her testimony sheds light on how the peaceful social atmosphere in Evaton attracted urbanites especially from other overcrowded African settlements. John Dandala, who came with his family in the same period from Sophiatown, recalled,

> ….many people in Sophiatown did not know the names of their neighbours. It was the opposite in Evaton where residents were ready to help whenever their neighbours were in need. The relationship among residents was so close that we usually attended ceremonies whether traditional or other of each and every family. Elders would help and contribute presents and food.[65]

In those years, Sophiatown and city centre slums such as Malay Camp and Doornfontein were affected by subletting since landlords were attempting to generate more profit. As a result, they would crowd their plots with many tenants for the sake of gaining profit. Parnell recorded that landlords 'could honestly claim to have rented 35 families, 145 were found on his property.'[66] This implied that urban landlords were unscrupulous and that they did not adhere to health and safety measures that were in place to avoid overcrowding in these settlements. The average stand in places like Sophiatown had seven to eight families living in a single room. The Nondalas were joined by the Khumalo family. In his own words, the late Alf Kumalo, a former *Rand Daily Mail, Bantu World* and *Drum* reporter and photographer, recalled,

> We lived in Lyndhurst, we lived in Alexandra, we also lived in Bedfordview, when it was still bushy, as you see. Now there are many buildings. There was nothing, by then there were only white small farms. We occupied one of the houses that was left by some white people. Then from there we went to Alexandra. When we left, I was thirteen, in 1943. But before that my father took me and showed me a place that he bought, because other members of the family had gone to Natal for Christmas as it was during school holidays. So, I lived in Evaton until the sixties. We still have our family stand there on 8th Street Evaton. There are tenants living there.[67]

A number of points that emerge from these individual histories inform us that Evaton was peaceful, clean and well ordered - it was not overpopulated, and the area enjoyed the elements of reciprocity and non-monetary ties that bonded community members. 'Evaton is one of the most orderly places I know of in the Transvaal,' said Sol Plaatjie, testifying to the Native Economic Commission.[68] At this stage, residents of

Evaton appeared to be cordial to each other, and the environment was greener than in Sophiatown where there was no space for greenery. This seems to be of importance in many testimonies. Lily Nondala remembered,

> it was very nice very nice ... people who lived here had love and they were strong and united and the house you could count then the houses here I remember it was the house of Boshego and Lejoge, the house of Matsego and Mogojo there and there in the corner.[69]

Considering a number of informants who claim that Evaton was peaceful, it appears that Evaton was a tranquil place possibly with residents who espoused the principle of reciprocity. In view of the fact that many freehold townships in the Reef were troubled by urban social ills, such as delinquency, faction fighting, domestic violence, beer brewing, internal class struggles, and sexual experiences of African urban women who were blamed by white officials for urban disorder. At the same time, the increasing numbers of Basotho migrants on the mines were beginning to take jobs in the heavy engineering sector in the towns, and a large proportion settled in Evaton. In Evaton, the Basotho migrants were grouped into two factions, the group of Ralekeke and Palama.[70] The violent behaviour and the social impact of the Basotho manifested itself during the clash that erupted during the Evaton bus boycott of 1956. Perhaps informants' memories of the state of local tranquillity are coloured by romanticism. It could be argued that its tranquillity, combined with the cooperation among local residents, attracted urban dwellers that saw Evaton as the island of security against urban institutional harassment and frustration. In urban spaces where they came from they were deprived of this kind of environment. However, it is likely that the somewhat idyllic account of reciprocity and corporation obscure less equal relationships that drew an element of exploitation and monetary ties.

Another pressure on subsistence farming resulted from the natural growth of families. In order to accommodate this growth, paternal inheritance prevailed in the settlement. All the male off-spring split the land at each generation and dwellings had to be built within the property. At the same time, the geographical mobility of young males was constrained not only by the availability of land but also by the existing laws that restricted mobility and the freedom of choosing where one should settle. For example, William Ndlovu recounts:

> When we became young men, our father subdivided this property for us, you see there it's my brother's house and it is where we used to plough mealies. We did not have a choice we had to stay because it was not easy to find places in urban Johannesburg because of laws.[71]

There were a substantial number of entrepreneurs who bought properties in Evaton, and most were from the Reef. There were various reasons that drew these families to Evaton. One of the common pulling forces was the autonomy that the area enjoyed. This was coupled with the abundance of land available at an affordable price. These urbanites had means to set up homes there, particularly the entrepreneurs who were relatively prosperous. Due to the restrictive measures implemented in the urban areas in the 1940s, entrepreneurs such as J.C.P. Mavimbela and Paul Mosaka struggled to thrive in the municipal locations of Johannesburg.[72] They saw Evaton as an alternative area where they could prosper. In Johannesburg, these entrepreneurs rendered a valuable service to their communities as they had the potential to make a profit from their respective enterprises. The trade regulations and policies of local authorities, however, limited their growth. For example, trading sites were allocated on the basis of a quota determined by the number of houses to be served, and a number of trading sites owned by the council were leased to traders. Also, municipal laws did not allow traders to have more than one business in the area and this stifled economic progress.[73] In Campbell's view the lives of these African businesspeople,

> suggests the inability of… [these] elite[s] to give… [themselves] any secure material reality. Buffeted by hostile government legislation, confined to impoverished, segregated locations, forever starved of capital, the elite was constantly compressed back into the classes beneath it.[74]

For the growth of their enterprises, entrepreneurs found the freehold status of Evaton welcoming. For instance, the ground which they occupied and built their business premises on belonged to them and could be theirs in perpetuity. They could build, demolish, rent or sell without any restrictions. Their presence had an impact on the economic and social dynamics in Evaton. Some, like Mavimbela, commuted to their businesses in the Johannesburg area from Evaton. He could do this most likely because he could afford to buy a car.[75] Among urban entrepreneurs, relocating to Evaton was seen as politically and economically proactive, and a way of circumventing the oppressive restrictions of municipal townships.[76]

The relocation of urban entrepreneurs included freehold businessmen such as Mkhwanazi, who came from Sophiatown, and the Nkabindes, who were tenants in Alexandra. Elizabeth Nkabinde's family originally came from Natal and had moved to Alexandra. In Alexandra the Nkabindes opened up a small shop where Dudu worked for her husband in 1937. When they came to Alexandra, Dudu's husband taught her how to run a shop. She recalls:

when we arrived here in the township he taught me how to run the shop. I worked in the shop and he would go, and order and he also taught me how to stock the shop. We would go together to the wholesale. We would also go to Lever Brothers. [77]

It could be argued that small businesses initially required family labour to survive. For the Nkabindes, marriage provided the couple an opportunity to become self-employed. He started an under-capitalised business in the form of an unstated partnership between himself and his wife. Many small businesses were unable to bear the costs of formally employed labour and started out this way. So, while the role of women in the domestic sphere was emphasised by communities, their contribution to the family economy often went unrecognised.

In order to buy property in Evaton, Dudu's husband was encouraged by his landlord who related the benefit of owning property in a freehold area. Dudu recalls:

> Because he liked my husband and they were in good terms, he said; You know what my son, I enjoy staying with you, but I would also like you to have your own place... So that if you are old you should enjoy in your own place. I don't mean that I am chasing you away if you still want to stay and run your business please carry on.[78]

Entrepreneurs bought property in Evaton in preference to other areas. The weight of evidence indicates that these entrepreneurs were attracted by business opportunities and the relative autonomy that Evaton offered. What emerges from Dudu's testimony is the fact that her stand was located next to Golden Highway, a main road that linked Johannesburg and the Orange Free State.

Perhaps population growth was not the sole cause of the decline of subsistence farming. There were other possible causes such as the natural environment, the state policy and attitude towards freehold areas, as well as poor agricultural development. It is possible that Evaton like any other settlement became vulnerable to climate change that was coupled with socio-economic, demographic, and policy trends limiting their capacity to adapt to change. Unlike the white commercial farming sector that received state support, the local small-scale farming received no support from the state. There were no support services catering for local agriculture. This included technical and scientific support that was directed to white farmers. Efforts in support of the African agriculture was restricted to African reserves where state-sponsored programmes like the Betterment Scheme that was designed to arrest and reverse the destruction of natural resources and improve agricultural production were officially implemented.[79] Long-term sustainability of a subsistence economy depends on the state relief programmes. Dwight Seremi recalls that 'agriculture was destroyed by drought that was known as *leruli*, just before the Second World War, that time access to water became a serious problem and crops died in the field'.[80] Abel Nkosi recalled that 'during the Second World War there was drought that was felt by individual household and the entire community of Evaton; cattle and crops died.'[81]

It is likely that local agriculture was deliberately neglected by the state because Evaton's local economy was not in line with the state labour system. Perhaps this was the strategy to discourage local farmers from supporting themselves with agriculture and make them dependent on neighbouring industries for survival. It is possible that the state was operating within the broader national framework that was noted in Natal when the Native Affairs Commissioner complained "The Kafirs are now much more insubordinate and impatient of control they are rapidly becoming rich and independent".[82] Clearly, this state of affairs in Evaton transformed the settlement from being an independent enclave into a labour reservoir that secured the supply of cheap labour to Vereeniging and Johannesburg. This implied that Evaton experienced a decline of the number of economically independent residents and the rise of local wage labourers.

It is, therefore, likely that population growth and the aforementioned factors had a negative impact towards agricultural development, especially subsistence farming. While subsistence production has been shown to be important for household food security, the productivity of smallholder agricultural production declined and was quite low, in some cases was given as the reason for the abandonment of agricultural production. Mjikisi Maseko recalls 'after the building of rooms we were left with very small gardens and we could not survive on them as before. This pushed many people of Evaton to work for ISCOR and other factories'.[83] The testimonies of many of those who lived in Evaton in the 1940s confirmed that a large numbers of local residents were employed by ISCOR. Johannes Mokoena's recalls 'I remember in 1944 I was 12 years old and there were very few buses here. In the morning you will see many bicycles and donkey drawn carts that transported elderly male to ISCOR'.[84] Joseph Lubisi remarked 'As young as I was I did not have an opportunity of going to school and I was forced to work at ISCOR. I started working there in 1947, I was 17 years old, by then there was no Sebokeng the only township that was there was Sharpeville which was still new and small, and many people whom I worked with were from Evaton'.[85] Much of these employment opportunities were perhaps moulded by the fact that Evaton was the largest African township in the Vereeniging/Vanderbijlpark region. With its large population, the township had the potential of providing labour to ISCOR. The only township that served a similar purpose was Sharpeville, but it was small with stable families and fewer migrants. Another possible factor that led Evaton to supply large numbers of labour to ISCOR could be attributed to the relocation of Top

Location. Before the relocation, the town of Vereeniging had its own township that accommodated the African workforce. In addition, many companies accommodated their staff which meant that local companies could afford the expense of building compounds for their workforce.[86] But many compounds were taken down when inhabitants of Top Location were removed in the 1940s. When Sharpeville was established, restrictive influx control measures made it difficult for newcomers who wanted to make entry into the township. The municipal control of Sharpeville homogenised its residents who shared almost similar life conditions. Unregistered migrants who were attracted by the surrounding industries were consequently obliged to secure accommodation in the peri-urban settlement of Evaton. It was these factors, which almost certainly explain why Evaton supplied much of the ISCOR labour force.

Transformation of local residents from the agricultural sector to other non-agricultural sectors, was unavoidable and employment in large-scale industries was the sector which absorbed the growing labour force. The question arises as to what happened to the group of residents who wanted to maintain their economic independence; how the local absorption into wage labour created social differentiation; and how the levels of economic independence differed from one resident to another. The process of economic independence will be explored largely by means of different life histories. All these changes meant that Evaton grew rapidly, commodity markets expanded, and the new market emerged. The settlement deviated considerably from the ideal type of subsistence farming into an urban community that depended on the wage labour market. Agriculture had always been very important for Evaton's economy and livelihood. The decline of subsistence economy implied that local families had to change their means of livelihood and perhaps what they consumed and the way they consumed it. The historical significance of this period represents a shift in family economy from subsistence farming to a money-based economy. The decline of the subsistence economy left only one alternative open to the local dwellers - the opening of the labour market. For the local inhabitants who wanted to maintain economic independence venturing into local entrepreneurship was the only alternative. Local entrepreneurship that emerged during this period was closely tied to the inner dynamic which local households and families generated within a context that was increasingly determined by market and monetary relationships.

The emergence of entrepreneurship

The late 1930s and early 1940s can be perceived as a watershed in the history of Evaton's local economy. This period was marked by fundamental changes that occurred in food distribution patterns, transport operation and local artisanal specialisations. This work argues that after the decline of subsistence farming in the late 1930s, new forms of entrepreneurship in Evaton began to take shape. The rapid growth of neighbouring industries and the government intervention in local affairs introduced a complex administrative problem and challenges for local enterprises. These challenges were visible in the local meat industry, shops and in some artisanal activities, such as shoe making. For local enterprises, all these developments impacted on capital, facilities and other resources. Before the decline of subsistence farming, local entrepreneurship existed in a less recognisable and essentially formal form which bore little relation to the post-1930s entrepreneurial environment. The rise of entrepreneurship resulted from the aforementioned prevailing socio-economic dynamics that emerged during this period. These social and economic aspects included population growth and the decline of subsistence farming. They facilitated the emergence of new local entrepreneurs and the growth of new entrepreneurial activities.

The term entrepreneurship is common to the vocabularies of most people today. However, for this study the term occupies a prominent position. In the context of Evaton, entrepreneurship has a special meaning. It could be explained and interpreted within the context of local, social and economic change. It is by and large explained through the decline of subsistence economic activity that resulted from the dramatic impact of industrialisation, and urban growth that demanded the emergence of the new local businesses. For this research agenda, entrepreneurship pertains to any type of local commercial activity creatively innovated for commercial gain. This commercial activity introduced new good and services that appealed to the community of Evaton.

The local economic transformation created new forms of economic relations that were based on monetary ties. The rapid population growth suggests that from the late 1930s to about 1947 there was a fairly dramatic rise in levels of consumption. This period represented quite a different socio-economic character from the subsistence farming era. It presented a significant change in food consumption and production in the settlement. Dwight Seremi explains the nature of this economy:

> Our agricultural space was reduced by the development of rooms and population growth and the expansion of the settlement impacted on grazing land. We then stopped producing crops that we use to get from our garden; it was the beginning of dependence. Many shops emerged. We started buying things that we used to grow.[87]

The decline in a subsistence economy introduced change in the local consumer demands for goods and services as well as in local food supplies which depended on the frequency of purchase and the type of shops that emerged. It created an adjustment in consumption and retailing that reshaped economic activities and occupations, and also introduced new structures of markets in Evaton. Given the emergence of the new economic institutions and infrastructure, new values and development goals altered the lives of the Evatonians.

This transformation influenced the path to new economic development that was determined by the emergence of small-scale enterprises, mostly grocery stores. These shops included Barong, Motuba, Moagi, Makgaleme and many others that were owned by former sharecroppers, educated residents and former labour tenants. It is possible that venturing into shop-keeping enterprises was an effort to fit within the changing local environment, or some means to obtain freedom and improve economic status. In order to achieve this status, residents like Zebulon Vilakazi applied for a loan with the intention to operate a cartage business from which he expected to receive approximately £10.0.0 per month.[88] For others, it was simply a strategy for survival. The commercial means they used created and sustained a sense of economic progress, purpose, and community while they sought integration into South Africa commercial society. Their stores were smaller, more labour intensive, and located in neighbourhoods that demanded their services. They were not only small-scale in terms of volume, but also in size of workforce. For the community of Evaton, these stores occupied a position of enormous structural and social importance - they were the large single retail sector that fed the whole community. They determined how local families would get food. All the inhabitants of Evaton came into contact with these stores; they undeniably mattered in local people's lives. Sergeant Pretorius noted that these shops were not registered, 'there were no shop ordinances in force, except the Sunday law.[89] For the first few years of their existence, their management was not shaped by government policy but independently. The minimal government intervention enabled local shopkeepers to operate freely.

Attention needs to be given to the changes in food consumption and the levels of consumer demands, frequencies of purchase and the types of shops used. During the subsistence period, patterns of food demand were characterised by fewer purchases of food. Reciprocity and non-monetary ties of various kinds, such as kinship, prevailed. These social relations of production maintained household reproduction in the settlement. Small-scale intensive labour by family members with simple technology was sufficient for subsistence. The oral evidence and primary sources do not indicate where and how food was purchased during the subsistence farming period, but emphasise the continuance of subsistence farming as the main supplier of food in the settlement. Little is known about the kind of stores that existed. In his publication, Dr. Nhlapo indicated that Rev. C. Mokgothu was 'the first African shopkeeper and butcher at Evaton'.[90] As one of the first residents to buy a stand, his shop and butchery was established long before 1930. It is not known what kind of foodstuffs and other commodities were sold in these old shops, and how frequently customers purchased goods from them. As an enclave in the early part of the twentieth century, Evaton appeared to be economically diverse with artisans that provided a basis for petty commodity production. The accessibility of different skills made the settlement self-sufficient, and the availability of small-scale local service centres that provided only the most basic needs made Evaton self-sufficient. The geographical location and the high costs of transport also contributed to the settlement's isolation.

In an attempt to describe how Evaton's subsistence economy was practised before its decline, a number of informants tend to emphasise the notion of reciprocity and self-sufficiency. Lily Nondala remarks 'local residents produced not only food but also clothing and furniture. All these were exchanged through barter.'[91] Agreeing with Lily, Paul Seshabela reached a similar conclusion: 'food that was purchased was in fairly small quantity, 'we never relied on stores because we had everything we just bartered. We had basic foodstuffs like *mabele* and vegetables, from shops we would buy things like sugar but we never used sugar that much'.[92] Clothing was locally manufactured and one would buy through agricultural products', said Donald Dube.[93] A large number of these families were Christians, former productive commercial farmers under share-cropping arrangement with cultural values and a strong background of an entrepreneurial attitude. As early as the 1890s, some of these families accumulated capital through agricultural markets. At the same time, these families were different from subsistence cultivators of the earlier period, some were educated families and were exposed to money economy long before Evaton was established.

Before coming to Evaton some of the share-cropping families disposed their surplus to local storekeepers, merchants and millers.[94] Everything these families produced were valuable resources from which they could earn profit. In the context of the rural Highveld, poorer labour tenants would work for richer sharecroppers in return for bags of mealies and communal work was sourced from the kinfolks. This is evident in Tim Keegan's work who studied sharecroppers in their rural arrangement before relocating to Evaton. Keegan noted that 'when the harvest on Zaaiplaas failed in 1895, Emelia Molefe [who bought property in Evaton][95] and her mother paid an extended visit to her aunt in Rustenburg…assisting in the harvest and threshing wheat. At the end of the season, her aunt gave them ten bags of sorghum'.[96] Taking into account the socio-economic values of the local residents who formed the Evaton community, it appears as if these idyllic accounts downplay unequal social relationships that existed during the subsistence period. The Evaton community was not homogeneous, there were wealthy and poor residents, and those who were unfortunate possibly worked for or provided services to the richer families. This questions the notion of *letsema*. It is possible that *letsema* existed but to a certain extent it accommodated class differentiation. The informants' narrative reflects much less on unequal relationships that flourished in Evaton. It is possible that the community consciousness that emerged in Evaton created a situation in which members of the community did not recognise themselves as socially differentiated in terms of class. From the interviews it is evident that the gap between the educated and economic class was big, but the nostalgia and community bonds that bound this community together overshadowed this distinction. This social phenomenon urges us to rethink the concept 'class' and its meaning in the minds of community members. From the outsider's point of view, class distinction in this community may be attributed to materialism and accumulation. This raises the question as to whether or not material possession really mattered in the minds of the community. It is possible that material possession did not matter that much as the community account reflects on it as homogeneous. Class distinction, however, is clearly exemplified by the different opinions between the educated and non-educated residents around local governance. As mentioned, the township did not have formal control. In the 1940s, the question that troubled the central government was the type of control that was to be implemented in the township. After lengthy meetings and correspondence, there was disagreement between different groups of residents. In a meeting at the Wilberforce Institute held for the purpose of considering the provisions of the amendment of the Local Authority Act 38 of 1927, about six prominent male residents under the leadership of Dr. Nhlapo and Mqubuli expressed the opinion that 'it would be desirable for a local authority to manage the affairs of the community'.[97] Due to their better understanding of the western form of administration, the group of educated residents under the leadership of Dr. Nhlapo accepted the proposal. The less educated residents in the community, particularly ex-sharecroppers, opposed the proposal.[98] These divergences clearly illustrate class distinction and local community struggle. Furthermore, class was clearly demonstrated in the architectural design of houses in Evaton. In terms of aesthetics, these houses clearly demonstrate class differentiation. Furthermore, products from these homesteads were bartered - bartering was possibly practised among kinsmen and women or among close family friends. A letter of Zebulon Vilakazi's bond application supports this argument: '£5.10.0 being board and lodging paid by his sons. This excludes the income that he obtains from the cultivation of his land'.[99] From this evidence, it is clear that some residents sold their agricultural products to local consumers. This implies that Christian values that some local residents adopted inculcated the idea of accumulation, improvement and material achievement.

Grocery shops

With the decline of subsistence farming, local residents began to purchase more foodstuffs like meat, sorghum and other household goods. This period marked the shift from a subsistence economy to a money-based local economy. This change facilitated the emergence of new shops and butcheries that became important as suppliers of food. The appearance of new shops was also facilitated by the increased levels of population that created greater levels of demands, with the number of residents doubling as compared to the subsistence period when the population was estimated to be about 12 000.[100] Inevitably, the system of supply prompted business-minded local residents like the Motubas to open up new shops that would keep up the pace with the growth of consumer demand. Many shops were unspecialised general stores. They were a major source of groceries because they had to meet the recurring daily or at most weekly demands. In his description, Oupa Motuba recalls that these shops were located in the neighbourhood and so shopping trips were for a short distance and local.

As the number of shops increased, they developed a distinct architectural format, with fascia boards, hanging signs, projecting or bow windows, and painted boundaries which delineated the boundaries of the premises and marked them out as retail shops.[101] The shop front advertised the business to the passing public by proclaiming its fashionable standing and drawing attention to extensive window displays.[102] In terms of labour these stores used family labour. This was the case with the Motuba family store - family contribution to their store was immense. Daniel recalls that it circumvented conflict between the role of Mrs Motuba as an entrepreneur and a housewife. As a mother she was not depressed by the multiple roles, she had to help my father.'[103] The contributions of family as a working unit played an important role in the smooth operation of these family enterprises. This could be attributed to the reason why the Motuba's shop still exists today. In the case of Mary Maseko, a female shopkeeper, she was assisted by her daughter and her brother.[104]

The local shops were in direct competition with each other for the attention of consumers. Many of them commonly sold groceries, but others like the Barolong one, a general dealer, sold a diverse range of goods.[105] One of the commodities that these shops sold very fast was paraffin and candles. During this period Evaton was not electrified, it only relied on candles and paraffin that served as the local fuel.[106] Wood and coal were also used but paraffin was largely used for cooking using a primus stove and for lights. A primus stove was easier and faster than firewood. The reason why migrants and other local workers preferred paraffin was because they did not have time for coal and wood. Apart from shops, there were also bakeries that supplied local consumers with bread, cakes and biscuits. One of the most popular bakers was Mr. Pooe who used an underground oven for baking and who was later joined by Mrs Nkabinde who also made bread, cakes and biscuits.

Due to the lack of archival sources, it is difficult to measure the average number of customers per shop. The greatest increase in shops was, however, definitely associated with food retailing. Retail enterprises expanded quickly and the larger section of Evaton's population in the second half of the twentieth century was able to spend more on food. As indicated earlier, local autonomy attracted entrepreneurs from municipal townships and the freehold areas of the Reef. Among these entrepreneurs were Paul Mosaka, J.C.P. Mavimbela, Jabula Mkhwanazi and many others.[107] In Evaton, local shop owners were free to design and develop enough shelving space for their stock. They could build for themselves without conforming to the standardised plans which superintendents required in a municipal controlled township.[108] There was no need for the approval of building plans or a waiting period for plan approval as typically happened in townships. Interestingly, there was also no stipulated period to complete the construction of a trading building. Evaton also offered women an opportunity to own shops. One woman who may be representative was Mary Maseko, the daughter of Jabula Mkhwanazi, the owner of Vukaphansi Bus Services. Mary took over her father's store and expanded it by opening up a restaurant. She also smuggled alcohol. In those days, many migrants preferred to eat out. For them, it was convenient because it saved them cooking time. Most of the local wage labour migrants did not have their families with them and lived and ate their meals in local restaurants and in their boarding houses. Most of them would not have had cooking facilities and skills.[109] Mary's restaurant sold take-away food, and she had space for those who wanted to eat inside. One of her old customers recalls:

Mary's fast food was tasty, and was reasonably of good value, and it was extremely convenient to eat there because we never had time to cook. I mean we would arrive at home from work at about seven and there was not time for cooking.[110]

Local economic change appeared to coincide with change in local food consumption. The overriding question is: are these changes related to changes in population composition shifts that occurred or with the rapid urbanisation that took place in Evaton? Due to the lack of health records, we do not know how change in food consumption marked a shift in health problems and diseases that emerged. This opens up a new gap for research that needs to be done on local food change. Changes in food consumption did not only see the emergence of grocery shops, but also meat, fruit and vegetable supplies. The supply of green groceries is difficult to reconstruct due to the lack of archival sources. The only surviving records indicate that there were middlemen dealing with fresh products. One of the documented private dealers was R. J. Phooko, who served as a middleman between the rural producers and urban market product buyers. His exemption application letter stated that he was a partner in the Native General Agency which was operated by five 'natives' who received stock and farm produce from 'natives' in the countryside and sold it in the urban market.[111] Phooko's son, James, recalls that 'my father and his partners never succeeded because greenstuffs were perishable and they never had refrigerated storage'.[112] Other oral evidence indicates that 'some fruits and vegetable were bought from the surrounding farms; they were bought in wholesale quantities and sold in the settlement'.[113]

Butcheries

One of the most important entrepreneurial activities was butcheries. Local butcheries were not controlled, and local butchers slaughtered livestock in their backyards without any official inspection. The slaughter poles were grossly Unsanitary. Seremi describes them as ramshackle wood-and-iron structures. Cattle, sheep and pigs were slaughtered by neighbouring boys who were rewarded in a form of offal.[114] Like the new shops, many butchers appeared during this period and they seem to be the first specialised shops in Evaton. The supply of meat in Evaton was dominated by producer-retailers and small-scale butchers, such as Dlamini whose family still operates a butchery even today. Many of these butchers, like Mokgoju, were cattle dealers who had a long history of dealing with cattle.[115] These butchers supplied a growing number of working-class people who were forced to buy meat nearly every day because of the lack of household refrigeration. The analysis of population growth and the decline of subsistence farming portray that by the 1940s the meat supply was under growing demand from the local consumers.

The expanding demand for meat meant that a settlement as large as Evaton was more and more dependent on local butchers. There was a considerable amount of meat trading within Evaton to supply the growing number of meat eaters. This was confirmed by Nhlapo who recalls 'we never bought meat from outside. Livestock was easily available in Evaton'.[116] The accounts of several local butchers reveal that for the first five years of the 1940s many retail butchers were making their own arrangements for slaughtering animals.[117] Rodseth, a health inspector, reported that 'each butchery had its own slaughter place, and nobody saw to it. In other words, they were not regulated'.[118] Agreeing with the health inspector, Isaac Nhlapo indicated that butcher operations were not regulated. Butchers did as they pleased; their shops were badly ventilated and there were no fridges.[119] This implies that there were no means of keeping meat fresh. As a result, butchers tried to find room on their own shop premises to do their early morning slaughtering for selling the same day.

These unhygienic practices continued to take place in the homes and shops of the butchers until the Director of Native Agriculture took note of them in the mid-1940s. In his struggle for control of this enterprise, the Director wrote:

> absences of control the police find it impossible to check stock theft, black market in meat and general lawlessness. At the raid conducted under the auspices of the Meat Control Board last November six 5-ton lorry loads of beef illegally slaughtered in Evaton area were removed.[120]

This letter forced the Peri-Urban Health Board to take control over the market. We shall see in the following chapter how these regulations impacted the local meat industry.

Transport enterprise

As Evaton was going through a process of urbanisation owing to the high rate of population growth with an increasing labour force, the demand for more transport was unavoidable. The availability of well-paying large industries in Johannesburg attracted the majority of the local workforce who preferred to work in the city. This was observed by Dr. Fourie, a local health inspector in his 1938 report: 'The majority of breadwinners whose family resides in the Township are employed either on the Reef [or in Vereeniging]'.[121] By the 1940s, very few households owned vehicles in Evaton. Instead, in many households, there were bicycles, donkeys and horses. Seremi recalls 'it was the Mbheles, the Ntshalintshalis, the Dlaminis and very few other families that had cars'.[122] Due to the distance from Evaton to Johannesburg and other industrial centres like Vereeniging, local residents had no choice but to use some form of transport to get to work on time. The only available means of transport was the train. Seremi recollects:

> By then Johannesburg was very far because trains were slow and local residents did not go to Johannesburg regularly; there were no taxis some elders would cycle to Johannesburg, going there it was a really long trip, by then almost every household had the bicycle, we also used them when we go to Evaton station.[123]

In the absence of local support from the central government, the development of a transport business in Evaton was primarily due to the initiative of the residents themselves. This does not ignore that the government introduced railway services that could transport locals to respective destinations. The availability of the train was not sufficient as the only means of transport that ferried the growing number of workforce to industrial centres. Train services had to be supplemented by bus and taxi services which were only introduced in the late 1930s. This gap became an opportunity for some vehicle owners who opened up new commercial activities of transporting residents from their homes to their workplaces, and backwards and forwards to nearby towns and cities.

Two aspects of this are of particular interest. Firstly, the pioneers of transport enterprises tended to be former sharecroppers and independent farmers. And secondly, they had a long history of enterprising. Mbhele, for example, was a transport rider in Newcastle[124] and Mkhwanazi was a hotelier in Sophiatown.[125] The autonomy that Evaton offered for this operation and the financial rewards attracted other operators such as Derbyshire,[126] a coloured man from Kliptown who bought property from James Kunene for 100 pounds in 1928.[127]

These entrepreneurs operated in a *laissez-faire* environment. Mjikisi recalls 'they would overload their cars and buses'.[128] They also used family labour, as it was the case with Mkhwanazi, the owner of Vukaphansi Bus Service, who used her daughter, Mary, to sell tickets. Most of these bus operators experienced difficulty in maintaining their vehicles. According to Mary,

> ...the reason why my father company's fell was the fact that he bought old buses, and there were a number of breakdowns, we would wake early in the morning and push the bus. This led to irregularity of service sometimes the bus will work and sometimes not[129]

As the bus operation were not enough to cater for the growing population of Evaton, there was a need for a taxi operation that would supplement bus services. The introduction of taxis[130]in Evaton represented a change in the history of local transport. This industry was well received by local commuters and was strengthened by the perception that it was community-based. Mbhele, the innovator of this enterprise, was well known among the commuters. Daniel Motuba recounts:

> ...my grandfather J. J. Mbhele was in what is called ISCOR now in Newcastle that was his farm. It was Kokspruit.... he did farming there, and he was running transport on a wagon which was pulled by fourteen... He used to park at the Newcastle station at twelve o'clock, between twelve and one, and the train used to come in from Joburg and he would collect goods from there.[131]

Apart from ferrying the local population to work, the demands of population growth also required transport for health-related services. The freehold status of Evaton meant that it was deprived of similar services such as ambulances that were provided by the municipality in other African townships. In an emergency, there were no ambulances that could transport residents to a hospital. Taking an advantage of this gap, 'Liphoko exploited this opportunity by converting his taxi into an ambulance that catered for the larger Evaton population'.[132] At the time, Evaton had no hospital. In cases of serious illness, Dr. White, the former principal of Wilberforce, wrote in his memoirs 'we called doctors from Vereereniging. Their fee was three pounds...whenever possible we would take the sick student to his or her home. Sometimes, students were taken to Johannesburg city hospital'.[133] The only health facility that was available was Crogman Clinic which catered for primary health care. The Clinic was built by Bishop Wright in the late 1930s. It is where Dr. Xuma occasionally served as the medical officer. The clinic was under the administration of the AME Church and was attached to the Wilberforce Institute.[134]

The nearest hospital was in Vereeniging, but it catered for whites and had only a very small section for Africans. Before Baragwanath opened up in 1947, Evaton's residents preferred to use the Johannesburg Native Hospital. This might be the reason why Liphoko began an ambulance service.[135] His ambulance service operated until the mid-1950s when the government reorganisation of local entrepreneurship structure reached its peak. During this period, private ambulance services were inhibited by government intervention which monopolised it.

Skills-related enterprises

From its formation in 1905, Evaton, like other freehold areas on the Reef, was exceptionally diverse, not only in terms of the origins of its people, but also in its different classes and categories. As discussed, the largest category in the early years was former sharecroppers who came from different parts of the country. There were other educated residents and all these residents, including the sharecroppers, were skilled in different vocational specialities. The majority of these residents were Christians and they were taught skills and values appropriate to the nuclear family structure and a division of labour characteristic of pre-industrial England. Women were taught to sew and cook, and men received instruction in artisanal specialisations.[136] With a larger population, the demand for skilled services in their own workshops increased. These artisans sold their goods in their little stores and workshops. For instance, Nxumalo repaired and sold bicycles from his small workshop.[137] This local economic transformation fills a gap in our historical understanding on how the inter-dependent processes of specialisation unfolded on the ground. During this process, local artisans, retailers and consumers; all played important roles in shaping the new emerging local economy of the area, and artisans took advantage of their specialisations.

By then, specialisation and artisanal work was more complementary to investments embodying new technology rather than unskilled labour, and so capital accumulation and technological change favoured skilled over unskilled labour. Locally, skills captured what local residents needed for the development of their homes. For instance, Maseko noted that, 'by this time many residents extended their dwellings because families were expanding and others rented rooms out to migrant workers, so the service of bricklayers became important'.[138] Due to the lack of archival sources we do not know how many artisans operated in Evaton. We do not know whether they did well or not. But oral accounts indicate that with the growth of population, some artisans prospered though their prosperity was inhibited by the impact of technology, the increase in mechanisation and the industrialisation of different specialisations.[139]

This situation was worsened by the tightening of pass laws that restricted African movement in South Africa in the late 1940s. These laws increasingly limited artisanal service to the immediate vicinity of Evaton as artisans had to adjust their methods of production and produce suitable goods that met the needs of local residents. They could not move to other centres where they could serve other communities. Dan Mofokeng recalls 'my uncle who was a bricklayer was sometimes given contracts in Johannesburg where he worked independently but after pass laws he could not'.[140] Among those who prospered was Makhene, a brick maker. During the time when new rooms were built in Small Farms, many stand holders bought bricks from him.[141]

The impact of industrialisation was felt by Makhene and other brick makers when Vereeniging Brick and Tile Company was established. According to Paul Seshabela, 'Brick and Tile wanted to employ Mr. Makhene and he refused'.[142] The impact of industrialisation was also felt by many shoemakers who saw their livelihoods being destroyed, but several crafts, especially the construction trades, were largely unaffected by changes during this period. Plumbers, plasters, and imperial furniture makers thrived. Plastering remained almost the same from the pre-1940 period until the introduction of prefabricated laths in the 1950s. Many members of the builders' guild, like Seremi, prospered from this enterprise. Among the builders who were doing well were Bloke Maseko, Rapodile and Tswagong and Dwight Seremi's father, who built the school in Sharpeville location. Mamasile, on the other hand, specialised in roofing. He was an expert in scotch roofing. In the 1940s, the guild of builders and many other artisans benefited from the Native Trust Fund and its building legislation.[143] It was these African-run enterprises that built the new segregated townships like Sharpeville. Shoemakers, however, struggled. Abel Meku, for example, specialised in shoe-making but his career was affected by the decline of local cattle slaughtering and cattle keeping. For his shoe manufacturing, he relied on local hide suppliers, mostly butchers. Moreover, capital requirements for the daily running of his enterprise became expensive. He had to pay for transport and travel to remote areas where he could get hides.[144] For Meku and other local artisans, local industrialisation adversely affected the advancement of their enterprises. Abel Nhlapo recalls,

'During industrialisation the great majority of artisans found work in large factories like ISCOR Steel Works, either as foremen or in skilled manual positions'.[145]

Women hawkers

Another group of Evaton entrepreneurs, particularly women, operated their entrepreneurial activities outside of Evaton. These women, who could be regarded as itinerant traders or hawkers, were involved in trade in areas familiar to them such as nearby farms and cities. These women sold a variety of products such as vegetables, eggs and chickens as well as other non-farm products in Johannesburg. It appears that the local women entrepreneurs emerged to occupy a niche that was opened up by the inadequacies of the then existing food supply in Johannesburg. In the recorded history of food supply in Johannesburg, the market is well covered, but other distributors like hawkers seem to have largely gone unnoticed or perhaps records were not kept.[146] Opportunities for the kind of extensive small-scale entrepreneurship in which Evaton women began to specialise thrived in Johannesburg. It was long before municipal control extended pressure on African traders, particularly coffee cart street traders in Johannesburg.[147] From oral sources it is difficult to establish why local women ventured into entrepreneurship. It is, therefore, interesting to speculate on the reasons that gave rise to this degree of entrepreneurial activity. Perhaps because employment opportunities for women were largely non-existent in the early urban economy, it is possible that they ventured into entrepreneurship because they wanted to be economically independent.

In the late 1930s, there were relatively few women who sold farm products in Johannesburg. In this rough and gritty urban space, men greatly outnumbered women until rural poverty forced greater numbers of women into the city.[148] There were few women in the city and the majority of African women were involved in beer brewing. In those years their business thrived because the population of consumers was high in Johannesburg. These women generated relatively high profits out of this enterprise. Dwight recalls that 'through this enterprise our mothers made more money than our fathers, I mean they had money. On Fridays they will bring us fish and chips, clothes and other nice things'.[149] Dwight's account is supported by Christina who recollects: 'Fridays we would eat meat and enjoy when they came back from Johannesburg'.[150] Christina Meku's grandmother and her friends, including Dwight Seremi's and Paul Seshabela's mothers, were hawkers. They sold their farm products in the rich white suburbs of Johannesburg. Christina recalls:

> I was still at school and my grandmother would go and fetch chickens from a farm in the west that belonged to Mr. Van Vuuren, which would be done on Fridays. We would then slaughter the chickens and clean them, she didn't work alone, there were other ladies working with her; this one lady who has passed on too, her kids sold their place, her name was Gogo Mngomezulu, and another lady Gogo Mokgeli, she too passed, also her kids sold the place, I think it is the grand child who was left there.[151]

Christina further recounted how her grandmother and other hawkers reached Johannesburg.

> There was a garage behind the BMSC, the taxi would park there, and the ladies would then go on in different directions to sell, my grandmother sold mostly in Lower Houghton, she had pre-placed orders and would just deliver them, I was schooling at St. Peters at the time then.[152]

In Johannesburg the only place where farm products were sold was the market where prices were higher than what Evaton hawkers charged. The early morning market was for bulk-buying for dealers, hotels and restaurants, and the mines. There are later indications that the market was open to the public after 9 am.[153] Evaton female hawkers delivered products to the doorstep. This was a convenient time as well as a saving for local residents who wanted to avoid paying for transport from Market Square to the suburbs. These women had information about market and prices, and they knew who the buyers were and how to contact them.

The involvement of these hawkers in Johannesburg's economy draws our attention to the neglected issue of how Johannesburg was fed. Where and by whom was food produced, and how was it transported and distributed? Cripps has noted that there are no records that tell us where the people who fed the residents of the city came from. She further states that there is considerable information in contemporary newspapers and in accounts by visitors and pioneer recollections, although those dealt with only a section of the population (whites only).[154]

Apart from foodstuffs, some hawkers like Sonto's grandmother, sold other items. Sonto recalls:

> The family also sold brooms and clothing that my grandmother made. We would walk around Evaton selling these goods, some we called dress and n' coat. During the December holidays we would sell clothes which included beanies, brooms and straw mats...every day we were selling, at times on our way to school she would be out with five or ten brooms to go sell...There were many other dress-makers and a lot of other people who were selling too. There was a lot of trading going on, one would sell an item to one person and buy another item from someone else...[155]

Hawking was not exclusively a women's domain. There were also male hawkers like Gilman Nkutha, a former sharecropper from the Transvaal, who enjoyed a long history of economic independence. Before venturing into door to door sales, Nkutha operated a small poultry business. He reared chickens and sold eggs, chicken and chicken feathers for pillow making. Nkutha's daughter, Thembi, remembers:

> My father would go to Johannesburg market in Newtown to sell chickens to the market. My mother who also sold other products would join local women who traded in Johannesburg.[156]

Nkutha's family was business-minded; Mrs Nkutha was a basket maker and one of a group who hawked their wares in Johannesburg. In Johannesburg she sold baskets and other craft works and made traditional dresses that she sold for local weddings.[157] The poultry business moved slowly locally, and transport from Evaton to Johannesburg became expensive. On the other hand, it was not easy to sell chicken and eggs in Evaton because many households kept chickens. After realising that the poultry business was slow-moving, he switched to the livestock trade, which became problematic when grazing land dwindled due to increased population density. When Nkutha ventured into livestock, the area was already experiencing a shortage of grazing space forcing residents to hire space in the surrounding white farms.[158] Mr Engelbrecht, who owned one of the farms, was prepared to lease his grazing land for £100 per annum.[159]

These impediments led Nkutha to venture into the clothing business. 'my father did not know how to sew clothes, so he was taught by my cousin. This business became lucrative and my father made lot of money,' said Thembi.[160] Starting in 1941, with a little cash he was able to expand his enterprise: 'when he started, he used a bicycle. He later used the profit that he generated to buy a Chevrolet van'.[161] Perhaps what made

Nkutha's clothing enterprise thrive was the remoteness of the areas that he targeted. He sold in the rural Free State and Transvaal. In those years, the parts of the Orange Free State and Transvaal where Nkutha conducted his business could be described as the 'wilderness' with very small hamlets that did not adequately cater for local African communities. In these towns, transport was scarce, and it was expensive for the farming community to reach urban centres. These areas offered an opportunity for Nkutha's commercial establishment because he was not competing with other sellers and his goods were on high demand.

'People asked him to buy them things such as radios, torches, batteries, household appliance and many other goods that were not available on the farms', recalled Thembi.[162] He would give them by credit and collected the money at the end of the month; in some instances, he would collect money seasonally because some farmers paid their labourers that way. He gave credit on the basis of trust, with no legally-binding documents. Failure to repay debts - which was unusual - meant exclusion from the credit network. Nkutha operated this enterprise for more than ten years. He stopped because of his advanced age and opened up a butchery instead. In the following chapter we shall see how the implementation of regulatory measures that governed local enterprise stifled Nkutha's entrepreneurial progress.

Conclusion

The arrival of newcomers played an important role in the recovery of the old entrepreneurial habits which were overshadowed by the acquisition of stands and the local subsistence farming. Population growth also helped the former sharecroppers to venture into new entrepreneurial activities and prolong their economic independence. It could be inferred that when entrepreneurial opportunity presented itself, many entrepreneurs were on the verge of losing their economic independence. Industries were mushrooming, grazing land and agricultural space was dwindling, and there were no other means of livelihood that local entrepreneurs could rely on except for selling their labour to the surrounding factories. The arrival of newcomers could be seen as a form of relief which indirectly comforted former independent farmers and sharecroppers by preventing them from losing their life-long livelihoods.

It can, therefore, be argued that the distinctiveness of Evaton lies in the fact that the area offered a space where former sharecroppers could at least maintain or rather prolong their economic independence. It offered a space for resisting the labour market which affected many African people as early as the 1920s. Most importantly, the area provided women the freedom of creativity that expressed itself through accumulation. Local women were never confined to the kitchen. They were independent and in many cases, they generated more income than their husbands. This chapter reveals that women in Evaton viewed the world through independent lenses. However, the growth of local industries and the intervention of the central government in local affairs introduced complex administrative problems that the unrecognised pre-1930 businesses did not experience. The changing development in administration, as has been shown with butcheries, presented a serious problem that inhibited the growth of local entrepreneurship. Changes in organisational structure of butcheries were intimately related to the ways in which enterprise had to expand. Apart from government intervention, the National Party's political role, which strengthened pass laws that restrained the movement of Africans, impacted negatively on the local enterprise. As an example, the group of women who sold their products in Johannesburg were forced to abandon their enterprises.

Notes

[1] Interview with Sonto Kekane, conducted by Vusi Kumalo, 4 July 2010, Evaton.

[2] Ibid

[3] National Archive of South Africa, The Report of the Secretary for Native Affairs, File URU Vol, 524. Ref 3/881/16, 15 September 1935.

[4] Interview with Mjikisi Maseko, conducted by Vusi Kumalo, 14 May 2010, Evaton.

[5] Interview with Tsepo Khanyi, conducted by Vusi Kumalo, 3 July 2009, Evaton.

[6] Interview with Paul Seshabela, conducted by Vusi Kumalo, 12 July 2010, Evaton.

[7] Ibid

[8] Interview with Sonto Kekane.

[9] E. Krige, and J. D. Krige, The *Realm of a Rain-Queen: A Study of the Pattern of Lovedu Society.* London: Oxford University Press, 1943.

[10] H. Kuckertz,'Organizing Labour Force on Mpondoland: A New Perspective on Work Parties,' *Journal of African International Institute,* Vol 55, 1985 pp115-132.

[11] National Archive of South Africa, A letter from J. B. Malindisa to the Native Commissioner, File NTS 361/364, 28 August 1939.

[12] Interview with Paul Seshabela, April 2009,

[13] J Nhlapo, *Wilberforce.*

[14] Interview with William Mokoena, conducted by Vusi Kumalo, 21 July 2009, Evaton.

[15] Interview with William Mokoena, conducted by Vusi Kumalo, 21 July 2009, Evaton.

[16] Interview with Mjikisi Maseko.

[17] Interview with Paul Seshabela.

[18] J. Mbiti, *African Religions and Philosophies*, New York, Doubleday and Company. 1970. p. 141.

[19] Interview with Amos Moagi, conducted by Vusi Kumalo, 23 July 2010, Sebokeng

[20] Interview with Aubrey Mofokeng, conducted by Vusi Kumalo, 15 May 2011, Evaton.

[21] Interview with Thembi Nkutha, conducted by Vusi Kumalo, 23 September 2011, Evaton.

[22] National Archive of South Africa, Report of Inspection at Evaton Native Township, File NTS 361/364, 9 September 1938.

[23] Ibid

[24] National Archive of South Africa, A letter from Mr Easton to the Secretary of Native Affairs dated, File NTS 361/364, 19 November 1936.

[25] Zoutpansberg *Review*, 28 January 1936.

[26] National Archive of South Africa, Report of the Native Affairs Department, NTS 361/364, 1937.

[27] Interview with Lily Nondala, conducted by Vusi Kumalo, Evaton, 16 May 2010.

[28] National Archive of South Africa, A letter from Hope Baillie to the Acting Entomologist Mr Gunn File BNS 1/8/ 116/ 4197 National Archive of South Africa, 25 July 1909.

[29] J. Campbell *The Songs of Zion The African Methodist Church in the United States and South Africa*, Chapel Hill, University of North Caroline Press,1998.

[30] Historical Papers University of the Witwatersrand, A short biography of J M Nhlapo, Jacob Nhlapo Papers, A1007.

[31] Interview with Tladi Kekane, conducted by Vusi Kumalo, 16 July 2009, Evaton.

[32] Ibid

[33] Historical Papers, University of the Witwatersrand. A letter from Opperman to Dr Xuma on the increase of the student roll dated AB Xuma Papers, AD 834, 17 July 1938.

[34] Historical Papers, University of the Witwatersrand, A letter from Mr E. H Chunga to the Principal of Wilberforce Institute, Xuma Papers, AD 834, 7 March 1936.

[35] J. Nhlapo, *Wilberforce Institute*, Boikhutso Institute, 1949.

[36] Ibid

[37] V. Molobi, The AICS and the Theological Training with Special Reference to the St John Apostolic Church of Ma Nku, Research Institute for Theology and Religion, undated.

[38] B. G. Sunkler. *Bantu prophets in South Africa*. London: Oxford University Press, 1964, quoted by V Molobi The AICS and the Theology.

[39] I. Berger, An African American 'Mother of the Nation': Madie Hall Xuma in South Africa, 1940-1963, *Journal of African Studies, Vol 27, 2001*.

[40] Native Commissioner Report, NTS 361/364, 26 March 1946.

[41] M. Wilson and A. Mafeje, *Langa* Cape Town, Oxford University 1963, Mayer, P. 1961 Xhosa *in Town: Studies of the Bantu-speaking population of East London*, Cape Town, Oxford University Press, 1961, D. Welsh 'The Growth of Towns' in M. Wilson and L. Thompson (eds), The Oxford History of South Africa, Vol. II 1971. J. Cherry, 'The Making of an African Working Class, Port Elizabeth, 1925-1963', M. A. dissertation, University of Cape Town 1992.

[42] P. Bonner. P. N Nieftagodien, *Alexandra*, p. 6.

[43] P. Bonner, African Urbanisation on the Rand between the 1930 and 1960: Its Social Character and Political Consequences, *Journal of Southern African Studies*, Vol.21 No.1 pp, 115-129.

[44] National Archive of South Africa, A letter from the Additional Native Commissioner to the Director of Native Labour, NTS 361/364, 26 March 1946.

[45] National Archive of South Africa, A Report of the Deputy Chief Health Inspector on Local Health Condition, NTS 361-364, 17 May 1946.

[46] National Archive of South Africa, A Report of the Deputy Chief Health Inspector on Local Health Condition, NTS 361-364, 27 May 1940.

[47] National Archive of South Africa, Report of the Native Affair Commission, NTS 361/364, 1939.

[48] Personal observation that was supported by oral testimonies on the structure of the rooms that were used as early as the 1940s.

[49] National Archive of South Africa, A Report of the Deputy Chief Health Inspector on Local Health Condition, NTS 361-364, 17 May 1946.

[50] P. Frankel, *An Atrocity: Sharpeville and its Massacre*.

⁵¹ P. Bonner, 'Desirable or Undesirable Sotho women? Liquor, Prostitution and the Migration of Sotho Women to the Rand 1920-1945,' A seminar paper that was delivered in African Studies Institute, University of the Witwatersrand 1988.

⁵² Interview with Joshua Vilakazi, conducted by Vusi Kumalo, 20 May 2012, Vereeniging.

⁵³ Interview with Mamokiti Seloane, conducted by Vusi Kumalo, 21 May 2012, Sebokeng.

⁵⁴ Ibid

⁵⁵ Interview with Mohlalepule Moloi, conducted by Vusi Kumalo, 23 July 2012, Phiri.

⁵⁶ Interview with William Mokwena, conducted by Vusi Kumalo, 27 April 2010, Evaton.

⁵⁷ P Bonner, 'African Urbanisation on the Rand Between the 1930 and 1960: its Social Character and Political Consequences', *Journal of Southern African Studies*, Vol 21 No 1.

⁵⁸ Interview with Mjikisi Maseko, conducted by Vusi Kumalo, 29 December 2011, Evaton.

⁵⁹ Interview with Tladi Kekane, conducted by Vusi Kumalo, 7 July 2010, De Deur.

⁶⁰ National Archive of South Africa, The Report to the Minister of Native Affairs, NTS 361-364, 27 May 1947.

⁶¹ National Archive of South Africa, Application for Mortage Bond: N.E. Sechaba, NTS 376 252/56, 6 June 1950.

⁶² National Archive of South Africa, Application for Mortage Bond: F. Yina, NTS 376 252/56, 12 February 1944.

⁶³ Interview with Lily Nondala and Moagi, conducted by Vusi Kumalo, 12 May 2011, Evaton.

⁶⁴ S.M Parnell, Johannesburg Backyard: the slum of Doornfontein, Bertram and Prospect Township. History Workshop, University of the Witwatersrand, 1987.

⁶⁵ Interview with John Dandala, conducted by Vusi Kumalo, 20 October 2011, De Duer.

⁶⁶ Ibid, p. 9.

[67] [67] Interview with Alf Kumalo, conducted by Vusi Kumalo, 15 January 2011, Evaton.

[68] Report of Native Economic Commission 1930-1932 S. Plaatjie testimony in the UG, 22, Pretoria Government Printers.

[69] Interview with Lily Nondala, conducted by Vusi Kumalo, 19 September 2010, Evaton.

[70] Interview with Tladi Kekane, conducted by Vusi Kumalo, 20 May 2011.

[71] Interview with William Ndlovu, conducted by Vusi Kumalo, 23 November 2011, Evaton.

[72] T.D. Mweli Skota, *The African Yearly Register*, Johannesburg: R.L. Esson and Co. Ltd, 1932; T.D. Mweli Skota, *The African Who's Who*, Johannesburg: Central News Agency, 1965.

[73] L. Kuper, *An African Bourgeoisie: race, class and politics in South Africa* New Haven, Yale University Press, 1965.

[74] J. T. Campbell, T D Mweli Skota and the making and unmaking of a Black elite, A seminar paper that was delivered at History Workshop, University of the Witwatersrand, 1987.

[75] T.D. Mweli Skota, *The African Yearly Register*, Johannesburg: R.L. Esson and Co. Ltd, 1932; T.D. Mweli Skota, *The African Who's Who*, Johannesburg: Central News Agency, 1965.

[76] L Reyburn, African Traders and Problems in Johannesburg South Western Townships, Johannesburg, South African Institute of Race Relations, 1960.

[77] Interview with Dudu Nkabinde, conducted by Vusi Kumalo, 27 September 2010, Evaton.

[78] Ibid

[79] S.M. Ngcaba, The Decline of Rural Agriculture in the Rural Transkei: The Case of Mission Location in Butterworth, Unpublished Master's Thesis, Rhodes University, 2002

[80] Interview with Dwight Seremi, conducted by Vusi Kumalo, 20 March 2011, Evaton

[81] Interview with Abel Nkosi, conducted by Vusi Kumalo, 25 November 2010, Evaton

[82] Quoted in H. Slater, 'The Changing Pattern of Economic Relations in Rural Natal', http:// sas – space. ac.uk/3657/1

[83] Interview with Mjikisi Maseko, conducted by Vusi Kumalo, 20 March 2011, Evaton.

[84] Interview with Johannes Mokoena, conducted by Vusi Kumalo, 16 April, 2011, Evaton.

[85] Interview with Joseph Lubisi, conducted by Vusi Kumalo, 14 July 2012.

[86] M Chakalson, The Road to Sharpeville, A Seminar Paper presented in the Institute for African Studies at the University of the Witwatersrand, 1986.

[87] Interview with Dwight Seremi, conducted by Vusi Kumalo, 21 June 2011, Evaton.

[88] National Archive of South Africa, A letter for Zebulon Vilakazi application for bond, NTS 376 252/56, 23 June 1948.

[89] Ibid

[90] J. M. Nhlapo, *Wilberforce Institute*.

[91] Interview with Lily Nodala, conducted by Vusi Kumalo, 13 June 2011, Evaton.

[92] Interview with Paul Seshabela conducted by Vusi Kumalo, 21 May 2010, Evaton.

[93] Interview with Donald Dube, conducted by Vusi Kumalo, 22 February 2011, Evaton.

[94] T. Keegan, *Rural Transformation in industrializing South Africa, Johannesburg*, Ravan Press, 1986.

[95] After going through the collection of the Wits African Studies Institute records the author came across the testimony of Emelia Molefe on the covering page it is indicated that she bought a property in Evaton. This is even recorded during interviews.

[96] T. Keegan, *Rural Transformation in industrializing South Africa, Johannesburg*, Ravan Press, 1986, p. 78.

[97] National Archive of South Africa, A letter from the Additional Native Affairs Commissioner to the Director, 15 October 1943.

[98] Ibid

[99] National Archive of South Africa, A letter of Bond Application for Zebulon Vilakazi, 23 June 1948.

[100] National Archive of South Africa, Report of the Native Affair Commission, NTS 361/364, 1939.

[101] Interview with Oupa Motuba, conducted by Vusi Kumalo, 12 May 2010, Evaton.

[102] Interview with Elias Nhlapo, interviewed by Vusi Kumalo, 21 July 2011, Evaton. Interview with Oupa Motuba conducted by Vusi Khumalo, 23 July 2011, Evaton.

[103] Interview with Daniel Motuba, conducted by Vusi Kumalo, 23 July 2011.

[104] Interview with Mary Maseko, conducted by Vusi Kumalo, 2 July 2011, Evaton.

[105] Interview with William Mokwena, conducted by Vusi Kumalo, 21 May 2010, Evaton

[106] At that time electricity was confined largely to white areas. All African townships lacked electricity while white suburbs enjoyed the benefits of electricity. This was not right in a country where coal resources were almost unlimited. An effort was to be made to bring coal in the form of electric light and power to African townships to brighten homes and for cooking, heating, washing and refrigeration.

[107] T.D. Mweli Skota, *The African Yearly Register*, Johannesburg: R.L. Esson and Co. Ltd, 1932; T.D. Mweli Skota, *The African Who's Who*, Johannesburg: Central News Agency, 1965

[108] Urban Trade Regulations, Leo Kuper's Papers, FI 5854 Roll 1 Microfilm, UNISA

[109] Interview with Mary Maseko, conducted by Vusi Kumalo, 20 July 2011.

[110] Interview with James Dakile, conducted by Vusi Kumalo, 1 April 2011.

[111] National Archives of South Africa, A letter from R. T. Luther to the Secretary for Native Affairs, GNLB 273 National Archives of South Africa, 3 April 1917.

112 Interview with James Phooko, conducted by Vusi Kumalo, 3 July 2010, Katlehong.

113 Interview with Oupa Motuba, conducted by Vusi Kumalo, 27 July 2011.

114 Interview with Dwight Seremi, conducted by Vusi Kumalo, 13 June 2010.

115 Interview with Absolom Dlamini, conducted by Vusi Kumalo, 12 May 2011, Evaton.

116 Interview with Isaac Nhlapo, conducted by Vusi Kumalo, 20 November 2010, Sebokeng.

117 Interview with Absolom Dlamini, conducted by Vusi Kumalo, 12 May 2011, Evaton, Interview with Abel Mokgoju, conducted by Vusi Kumalo, 13 May 2012, Evaton.

118 National Archive of South Africa Peri Urban Health Inspector Report, NTS 361/ 364, 3 May 1943.

119 Interview with Isaac Nhlapo, conducted by Vusi Kumalo, 20 November 2010, Sebokeng.

120 National Archive of South Africa, Director of Native Agriculture's report on slaughter facilities NTS 361/364, 1947.

121 National Archive of South Africa, Report of the Inspection at Evaton Native Township, NTS 361-364, 9 September 1938.

122 Interview with Dwight Seremi, conducted by Vusi Kumalo, 2 July 2012, Evaton.

123 Ibid

124 Interview with Oupa Motiba, conducted by Vusi Kumalo 23 July 2011, Evaton.

125 Interview with Mary Maseko, conducted by Vusi Kumalo, 12 June 2011, Evaton.

126 Little is known about Derbyshire's venture because coloureds were dislocated by the Group Areas Act during the establishment of segregated townships such as Eldorado Park, Roshnee and other areas. Moreover, there are no archival sources that present his story. The existing evidence of Derbyshire's entrepreneurial activity could only be sourced from residents who knew his operations. The only evidence about him was presented by

John Maseko who recalled that, 'His buses ferried people from Evaton to Johannesburg and they stopped in Kliptown where they filled up gasoline and then drove people to the city. He was rich because he had other properties in Kliptown. He was also a member of Catholic Church he attended the church next to Mekus house'.

[127] National Archive of South Africa, A letter from McCrobet and De Villiers Attorneys to the Secretary for Native Affairs dated NTS 376 252/56, 16 February 1930

[128] Interview with Mjikisi Maseko, conducted by Vusi Kumalo, 20 April 2010, Evaton.

[129] Ibid

[130] Ibid

[131] Interview with Oupa Motuba, conducted by Vusi Kumalo, 28 July 2011, Evaton.

[132] Ibid

[133] A. J. White and L. White, *Dawn in Bantuland: An African Experiment or An Account of Missionary Experiences and Observation in South Africa*, Boston, Christopher Publishing House, 1953.

[134] Historical Papers, University of the Witwatersrand, Crogman Clinic Committee minutes, Xuma Papers, AD 843, 1945.

[135] Interview with Daniel Motuba, conducted by Vusi Kumalo, 26 May 2011, Evaton.

[136] S. Mentjes, Edendale 1850-1906: a case study of rural transformation and class formation in an African mission in Natal, PhD thesis, University of London,1988.

[137] Ibid

[138] Interview with Mjikisi Maseko, conducted by Vusi Kumalo, 27 July 2011, Evaton.

[139] Interview with Dwight Seremi, conducted by Vusi Kumalo, 21 May 2010, Evaton.

[140] Interview with Dan Mofokeng, conducted by Vusi Kumalo, 30 June 2010, Soweto.

[141] Ibid

[142] Interview with Paul Seshabela, conducted by Vusi Kumalo, 23 July 2010, Evaton.

[143] Interview with Paul Seshabela, conducted by Vusi Kumalo, 21 May 2010, Evaton.

[144] Ibid

[145] Interview with Abel Nhlapo, conducted by Vusi Kumalo, 21 May 2012, Evaton.

[146] Ibid

[147] C. Rogerson, *The Casual Poor of Johannesburg, South Africa: The Rise and Fall of Coffee-Cart Trading*. Ph.D. Thesis, Queen's University, Ontario, Canada, 1983.

[148] C, Burns, 'Controlling Birth 1920-1960' *Southern African Historical Journal*, Vol 50, 2004, pp, 170-198.

[149] Interview with Dwight Seremi, conducted by Vusi Kumalo, 13 October 2011, Evaton.

[150] Interview with Christina Meku, conducted by Vusi Kumalo, 4 May 2011, Evaton.

[151] Ibid

[152] Ibid

[153] E. A. Cripps, Provisioning Johannesburg, Unpublished MA thesis, University of South Africa, 2012.

[154] E. A. Cripps, 'Provisioning Johannesburg'

[155] Interview with Sonto Kekane, conducted by Vusi Kumalo, 1 April 2011.

[156] Interview with Thembi Nkutha, conducted by Vusi Kumalo, 12 May 2010.

[157] Interview with Thembi Tshabangu, conducted by Vusi Kumalo, 12 May 2011.

[158] A letter from Secretary/Treasurer to the Provincial Secretary dated 12 August 1946. The author received a copy of this letter from Tladi Kekane's private collection. For reference purpose it will be stored at the archives of the Wits History Workshop at the Origins Centre, University of the Witwatersrand.

[159] A letter from Mr Schwarzer to the Director of Native Labour 18 January 1938.

[160] Interview with Thembi Nkutha, conducted by Vusi Kumalo, 12 May 2010.

[161] Ibid

[162] Ibid

Chapter 3

Transition from unregulated to regulated trade

Introduction

The process of industrialisation in both Vereeniging and the Reef presented an important turning point in the history of the local economy in Evaton. The development of new industries attracted many rural Africans to urban industrial centres where there were greater opportunities of employment. This process correlated with the intensification of legislative frameworks and administrative procedures that regulated African life, including African entrepreneurial activities in urban areas. Since the early 1920s, African entrepreneurial activities in urban areas were regulated by the 1923 Urban Areas Act, but regulations were not rigidly enforced.[1] In those years, urban African entrepreneurship was not in the spotlight. African entrepreneurs could trade freely in segregated white central business districts that later became predominately white. After the outbreak of the Second World War, there was a rapid influx of the population into urban areas. This urged the state to amend the 1923 Urban Areas Act in the 1940s and grant local authorities more powers. As a result, local authorities strictly enforced influx control and tightened African access to entrepreneurship in urban areas.

Between 1943 and 1944 construction of new African housing declined in municipal controlled locations.[2] The rapid growing population, mostly sub-tenants, crowded into freehold settlements which fell outside of municipal control. The overcrowding of freehold areas was intensified by pass laws. In 1943, for instance, the state ordered the police to conduct passes in which 13 000 Africans were arrested.[3] In addition, the state changed its attitude towards freehold settlements. Equally significant, white pressure groups pressurised the state to remove freehold areas that surrounded white suburbs.[4] This was evident when health authorities and interested departments of the central government held joint discussions with white pressure groups where the future of freehold areas was discussed. The aim of these deliberations was to institute a system of control or to remove many freehold settlements, such as Sophiatown. Out of these considerations health and local entrepreneurship became one of the central issues. This led to the establishment of License Boards that controlled entrepreneurial activities in different freehold settlements. In this context, it is difficult to separate micro-economic development of respective freehold settlements from the broad socio-economic and political processes of the post Second World War period.

In Evaton, the genesis of regulations that controlled local entrepreneurial activities could be linked to the rapid increase of migrant sub-tenants. The presence of migrants was twofold. Firstly, it provided a market for aspiring entrepreneurs who saw the presence of a large population of newcomers as an opportunity to open up new, different forms of enterprises. Secondly, it placed Evaton in the spotlight, which prompted the state to extend its control and regulate local enterprises. In this chapter, the nexus between population growth and the evolution of local entrepreneurship, as well as the extension of urban legislative framework into Evaton, will be examined. A better understanding of the different stages of local entrepreneurial evolution will contribute to our understanding of the local administrative changes that took place in the 1940s. These changes impacted on the historical shift from unregulated to regulated commercial enterprises. More than anything else, it is the analysis of these complex historical processes that makes it essential for this chapter to reconstruct the history of local entrepreneurship.

The discussion proceeds in three parts. The first part broadly deals with the policy that controlled African entrepreneurship in urban South Africa from the 1920 to 1950s. The second section of the chapter concentrates on the evolution of local trade from 1905 to the 1940s. This part traces the trajectory of local enterprises from the time when Evaton was sparsely populated to the period of mass population relocation and rapid economic differentiation. The final section of the chapter focuses on the control of the local entrepreneurial activities. It examines the implementation of the new entrepreneurial regulations in Evaton and reveals how this initiative was associated with public safety, health, morals, and welfare.

Policy towards African enterprise

There was an underlying legislation that governed African entrepreneurship in South Africa. In order to have a better understanding of Evaton entrepreneurship, it is important to draw attention to an institutional framework as an important focus of analysis. The examination of the state institution and laws that governed African entrepreneurship provides us with a framework within which entrepreneurial activities operated. In South Africa, as in other countries, the state determined how entrepreneurship should operate. It struggled to control entrepreneurial activities which characterised the market, products to be sold and accumulation interest: this was all embedded in state policy. Generally speaking, the aim of the state entrepreneurial policy is to regulate business activities, and provide support to new and small firms. This was to be achieved in a form of information, advice, training, or finance to new enterprises.[5] Entrepreneurship is a major source of job creation, innovation and competitiveness. It is, therefore, the government's task to promote these characteristics in order to enhance the welfare of its citizens.

Before 1923, there was virtually no law that regulated African entrepreneurship; Africans traded independently without any government intervention. In a broad sense, African entrepreneurship was much freer before the 1920s than it became in the later years. While introduction of the new trade legislation was shaping up, important changes were taking place in South African urban areas. These changes included the shortage of housing, the overcrowding of urban spaces, and town-wards movement of poor whites and Africans. At the same time, the state committed itself to the curtailment of the potential development of African agriculture and sharecropping enterprises that gave Africans economic independency - this pushed many Africans to towns. In towns, infrastructural development, such as road and railway construction, demanded labour. This was in tandem with the expansion of mining, as well as the emergence of secondary industries. As a result, the high demand of labour pressed the state to tackle the manifold problems which stemmed from these socio-economic dynamics. With an attempt to solve this predicament, authorities sought to create urban areas as the white area while alienating Africans to the environment.[6] In this context, the legislation that regulated African enterprise was created within this broader institutional framework. This policy became part of the Urban Areas Act of 1923; it never stood on its own. The clause of the legislation reads as follows:

> Any urban authority which has under administration and control any location or native village may
> (a) Let sites within the location or native village for trading or business purpose
> (b) Prohibit hawking within the location or native village and

(c) Prohibit the carrying on any business within the location or native village in any other place than a site rented for trading or business purpose. Provided that-

(i) No site shall be let under paragraph (a) to a person who is not a native; and no person who is not a native shall be employed on a site so let; but

(ii) If the Minister is satisfied that the reasonable needs of the native residents are not met by business establishment on such sites, the urban local authority may carry on within the location or native village the business of a general dealer, butcher, baker or eating housekeeper and open such shops and do all such things as may be necessary for that purpose.[7]

The clauses quoted above appeared to be reluctant to assume equal business opportunities for all South African racial groups. This Act influenced the new direction of African entrepreneurship that reorganised and formalised African enterprise into retail. It limited African businesses to general dealer, butcher, baker or eating housekeeper and to the certain range of commodities sold. Africans could only sell consumer goods needed for daily use. This made African entrepreneurs realise they were in locations only temporarily. Furthermore, it guaranteed white entrepreneurs a monopoly of trading with manufactured goods, as well as running financial industries like insurance and banks in urban markets. This monopoly was enforced by law: it denied Africans an opportunity to exploit commercial opportunities. Africans who wanted to venture into the financial or manufacturing industry were denied that opportunity. This was clearly demonstrated by the letter that was written by Broomberg Graaf and Karb, the firm of lawyers that represented one of the unknown African applicants. The letter reads as follows: 'Undertakers and insurance business is not one of the services which need necessarily be provided in the white area by a Bantu entrepreneur'.[8] It was not easy for Africans to venture into the manufacturing industry. Those who ventured into the furniture industry experienced difficulties in acquiring permits for buying timber from timber-yards. The purchase of timber was under the control of the Ministry of Labour, which directed the Controller of Timbers office. This is revealed by the letter that was written by the Director of Native Labour to Dr. Xuma who represented Aaron Mokete and J. Mtimkulu who were both applying for the permit to purchase. The letter reads as follows:

> With reference to your letter of the 21st March last, and subsequent telephonic communication regarding the application of Aaron Mokete and J. Mtimkulu for permits to purchase timber for the manufacture of furniture, I have now been requested by the Controller of Timber to obtain fresh application forms from each of the two applicants concerned.
>
> As I am not in possession of the addresses of these two men, I shall appreciate it if you will kindly contact them, and advise them each to complete fresh application forms and forward these to me for transmission to the Controller.[9]

There were many regulations that prevented Africans from entering into manufacturing. These regulations emphasised the importance of context and of the understanding on how Africans were pushed into the labour market. Perhaps, most importantly, they illustrate the complexities of the combination of entrepreneurial laws and urban control. In this framework, the control of African entrepreneurship was enforced by means of open as well as veiled regulations, along with by-laws and trade licenses which formed the web of authority. The central government gave the local authorities power and the right to control, supervise trade and impose licenses on specific activities such as general dealing within the areas of jurisdiction. In the case of the Transvaal, the authority was expressly delegated to the Province of Transvaal by the then Governor General.[10] Local authorities were empowered to make by-laws that controlled matters related to local entrepreneurship, including issuing and cancellation of licenses and taxation. Local authorities were authorised to establish rules and procedures that governed licensing. They also registered businesses. The limitation of African entrepreneurs to sell goods that met daily needs raises the question why the Act pushed Africans into small-scale retail activities while suppressing service and manufacturing sector enterprise. This legislation devalued African skills in the face of rapid industrial development. The question can be asked as to whether in the clause of the Act there is anything recorded that relates to service enterprise or manufacturing? Was this a deliberate systematic and institutionalised action to exclude Africans from manufacturing, craft-related and service enterprise? It is not, however, the purpose of this chapter to interrogate these questions. Proceeding from these questions would limit this chapter's focus and content to the analysis of the purpose of the Act.

As informal housing grew in the urban outskirts of different urban areas in South Africa, African entrepreneurs battled over trade space. At the same time, the heightening intensity of the slum clearance scheme pushed them to municipal townships. The Urban Areas Act of 1923 officially divided municipal townships along racial groups.[11] African traders were confined to locations and whites to central business districts (CBDs) of cities and towns. The Act afforded only temporary status to African migrants and entrepreneurs in urban areas. Many urban entrepreneurs were faced with issues relating to residential permits. These issues were coupled with the fact that each entrepreneur had to comply with urban business administration conditions that required trader's application for trade. As a result, urban African entrepreneurship became fragile - traders became uncertain about their long-term residential status in urban locations. In turn, this impacted negatively on the development of their businesses. The temporary status kept African businesses small and isolated with racially designated customers.[12] African businesses did not have white, Indian or coloured clientele in segregated settlements. This official segregation became unfavourable to their growth. It also became detrimental to entrepreneurs who wanted to trade in African locations. From 1923 onwards, this obstructive attitude was adopted by white municipal authorities to aspiring African traders and this was the main source of complaints which later resulted in political action.[13] Under these adverse trade conditions, there was a need for African entrepreneurs to form an association that would represent their grievances to authorities. One of the active representative organisations that were formed was the Bantu Traders in Bloemfontein with its 123 members.[14] This association was headed by Thomas Mapikela, one of the ANC members. It adopted the name Federation of African Chamber of Commerce which later renamed NAFCOC. In this way, the demand for trade rights became an integral part of the African political struggle in urban areas.

Although African buying power was constantly increasing because of the growth of industries in urban areas, the terms of the Urban Areas Act of 1923 which declared urban areas as white only limited the growth of these enterprises. When this Act was amended into the Native Urban Areas Consolidation Act in the 1940s, African entrepreneurship was subjected to even more stringent control because more powers were given to local authorities, and legal force was felt by many African entrepreneurs all over South Africa. Local authorities '…were directed to move these Africans to areas where they were legally allowed to operate. This move affected about 160 licensed traders in Johannesburg, 121 in Cape Town and a large number in Durban'.[15] With an attempt to justify government action, the Secretary of Native Affairs wrote saying 'it was against government policy for Africans to trade in areas set aside for other groups. ...where they would obtain an exclusive monopoly'.[16] The national displacement of African traders included coffee cart operators who catered for African workers in Johannesburg. It should be noted that the policies of racial segregation in South Africa precluded African patronage from the variety of restaurants, cafes, snack bars, and feeding establishments that proliferated Johannesburg and only served the demands of the white factory or office worker.[17] Similar to the 1923 Urban Areas Act the amended Act emphasised 'lawful occupation'. This Act emphasised that the superintendent could, with the approval of the Minister, issue a permit if he was satisfied that

(a) a suitable site was available in the area set aside for ethnic group to which black belonged

(b) The applicant was fit and proper person to reside in the area

(c) The applicant was lawfully permitted to remain in the area in terms of section 10 (1) (a) or (b) of the 1945 Act

(d) If the applicant was already the registered occupier in that particular area or any other urban area, undertook that on the issue of the permit he agreed to the cancelation of the existing permit or certificate

(e) the applicant, or his wife, was not a foreign Black as defined in section 12 of the Act

(f) The applicant was financially able and willing to erect a dwelling of the required standard

(g) The applicant should be free of infectious diseases[18]

South African urban historical research has provided a clearer understanding of these developments.[19] The amended Act was intertwined with the housing policy, urban 'native administration,' tribalism and influx control and movement. This law emphasised ethnicity and the power of the superintendent. This legal measure could be best understood as the official mechanism specific to South Africa in the period of secondary industrialisation, of maintaining a high rate of capitalist exploitation through a system which guarantees a cheap and controlled labour-force.[20] It introduced problems that urban African traders faced; these problems included the lack of trade facilities, the lack of basic support services, such as water supply, sanitation and electricity. Furthermore, rent was high and competition for tenancies were fierce. Successful traders were denied opportunities to countenance their plans for expansion.[21] Above all, the granting of trade licenses became the major stumbling block and damaged the growth of the legitimate African trading class.[22]

This raised the following question: does one trace the origins of the laws that governed African entrepreneurship in the formation of segregated townships to the group areas policy or to the earlier period of segregation? The answer to this question needs further research. Historical research has revealed that long before 1923, Africans attempted to forge their own economic liberation through sharecropping, transport riding and other entrepreneurial activities.[23] In the Highveld, this economic venture was disturbed by the interference of Boer pressure groups that wanted to safeguard their economic interest against prosperous sharecroppers. The Boer agitation surfaced against African economic competition that threatened white supremacy. This was part of Afrikaner nationalism that culminated in the formation of Afrikaner Bond at the Cape in May 1883.[24] At the same time, the rural Highveld saw an unprecedented state intervention in the promotion of white farms. The state intervention was facilitated by the crisis in labour supply, and this agitated concerted action against independent farmers or sharecroppers.[25] These years were also characterised by recurrent moral panics concerning the position of the poor whites and their impoverishment. This agitation was against

African peasant prosperity and was legally enforced by the Orange Free State Act 23 of 1908, which stamped out all forms of labour tenancy. This Act played a similar role as implemented by the 1895 anti-squatting law.[26]

In short, the African occupation of land where he or she could cultivate for commercial or subsistence gain threatened the political and economic interest of the white government. For Africans, cultivation of land provided a major area of self-employment, prosperity and economic independence. This African economic self-sufficiency was disturbed by the promulgation of the 1913 Land Act. This Act stifled African self-employment enterprise that relied on land use. It also prohibited African landownership outside scheduled reserves. As a result, a set of laws were designed to discourage the economic independence of African people. It is largely in this context that subsequent legislations that controlled African entrepreneurship were designed. When these laws are examined there is indeed plenty of evidence that indicates a connection between them and the later laws that govern African entrepreneurship. The scope of this work does not, however, allow scrutiny of each law and its provision. Reading from its purpose, the Urban Areas Act of 1923 and its amended Act of 1945 indirectly reiterated the provisions of the preceding set of laws. In other words, these entrepreneurial control laws form one of many pieces of legislations enacted over the years and drawn up to push Africans to join the labour market. This directs attention to the more indirect forms that these laws played as legal tools that were used by local authorities to push aspiring African entrepreneurs to the labour market by holding trade licenses. In addition, they created segregated urban spaces in order to facilitate labour control and discourage Africans to be self-employed. These laws were, therefore, the product of South Africa's own peculiar brand of racism. It is interesting to note that white material interests appear to have weighed much more heavily on the promulgation of these laws. This was driven by the direct interest of the Afrikaners who were confronted by issues of economic, political and social problems. For the native question, immigration, profiteering, home language was central.[27] The promulgation of the 1923 Urban Areas Act and the subsequent amended Act did serve, at different times, a variety of material interests. This has been shown, for instance, that one of the earliest segregationist impulses was directed against Indians. This was often couched in the discourse of sanitation and disease, but the underlying source was more often resentment of Indian commercial competition.[28]

Freehold and business policy

In order to locate Evaton's entrepreneurship within the broader context of African entrepreneurship and laws that governed them in South Africa, it is important to establish the extent to which these laws impacted on local entrepreneurial activities. As a freehold settlement, Evaton was outside of municipal control. The study of African entrepreneurship in freehold settlements presents a certain distinct character of these areas. In the literature, for instance, Alexandra has been presented as an 'entrepreneurial community than any other on the Rand whose values and aspiration were stamped by a strong freehold property in land and private accumulation'.[29] The self-governance of the settlement made trade conditions favourable for local entrepreneurs who made the best of circumstances in a world driven by capitalism. Most of Alexandra's entrepreneurs were former sharecroppers who liquidated their rural assets and ventured into urban entrepreneurship.[30] On the other hand, Lady Selborne, which had three quarters of Pretoria's 200 000 African inhabitants in 1960, 'had fifty four licensed businessmen'.[31] From these studies, it is clear the self-governance status of freehold settlements demarcated freehold settlements from the surrounding municipal locations. In freehold settlements there were no obstacles that prevented Africans from pursuing trade and commerce. The legislation that controlled African enterprise in urban locations was not applicable to self-regulatory areas. In this context, the African entrepreneurial policy that was designed to stifle African enterprise was destined to fail in these freehold townships. This explains why some of these townships were destroyed. It is possible that the relative autonomy that these areas enjoyed, which was concomitantly attached to land ownership, impacted negatively on labour supply. In other words, these areas served as a stumbling block towards tight control of Africans. They offered a relative economic independency which denigrated the swell of the ranks of the working class. Destruction of freehold areas, for instance, was geared not only towards the creation of segregated areas, but also towards the economic subjugation of freehold residents. In this context, African entrepreneurial control could be divided into widely different areas, which were clearly different in terms of administration from one another: there were areas that were governed by municipal authorities and there were freeholds that were administered independently. As indicated, freehold areas enjoyed a relative freedom of carrying on any business in any other place than a site designated for trading or business purposes. In municipal locations, this was prohibited by local authorities. In addition, some trade activities like hawking were prohibited in municipal areas but were freely practised in freehold settlements. Freehold areas offered opportunities for local businesspeople to initiate different entrepreneurial ventures ranging from the field of transport to retailing. The question which needs to be posed on the relative autonomy that African entrepreneurship enjoyed in freehold settlements are when, why and how did local entrepreneurship become controlled by the state? The answer to this question will help us to trace the shift in local self-governance that provides a clue to the changing nature of local entrepreneurship and how the state gained control in freehold areas. As we shall see, this trace will be linked to the broader political and economic concerns of the state that struggled to achieve control over African affairs.

The evolution of trade in Evaton

The pioneer traders were often drawn from the educated residents who wanted to expand their business enterprises in Evaton. One of the first owners of a shop and butchery was Rev. Mokgothu who operated a shop before 1910.[32] His shop was responsible for feeding the developing Wilberforce Institute. It is unclear whether Mokgothu operated a fixed shop form of retailing or a home operated shop which would today be called a *spaza* in South African township language. We do not know whether he operated in the building and used equipment associated with shops. In its early period of development, as mentioned, Evaton comprised mission educated residents and former sharecroppers. These residents, such as Motshwari who was instrumental during the construction of the Wilberforce Institute in 1905, were skilled.[33] It is recorded by Dr. Nhlapo in his publication that both Mr. Motshwari and Masiza made bricks with which Mr. Matsolo built the Wilberforce as a humble structure which was a school during the week and a house of worship on Sundays.[34] This evidence reveals that personal skills shaped members of this small community to apply their attention to one thing only, for example, weaving of cloth, the making of shoes, and the shaping of iron and copper. This evidence also discloses that the construction of Wilberforce as the first community school was a collective effort that was carried in a form of reciprocity. This was evident when Rev. James Mazibuko committed himself in acquiring private postal bag in 1915. He collected the post bag from the Wilberforce Institute and delivered it to Evaton Station. The bag served the Institution, as well as the Evaton Village at large.[35] Reciprocity was perhaps enhanced by the presence of sharecroppers who valued mutuality. Among these farmers, the significance of reciprocity was noted by Tim Keegan who documented that, unlike debt-strapped white farmers who buckled first during natural disasters, networks of reciprocity that were based on mutual dependency helped sharecroppers during the time of natural and economic disaster.[36]

For instance, the iron smelter who wanted a cloth took his or her product to the butcher and traded possibly in return for hand-work. This implies that there was a significant difference in terms of the nature of home businesses that were based on specialisation. Most of these small-scale businesses were in the service sector, with the concentration of professional services. Daniel Moagi recalled that his grandfather, who came to Evaton in 1908, was a wagon wheel maker and he was active in trading with other residents. Pointing at the dilapidated structure, Daniel recounted: 'it is where he used to work'.[37] Seremi recalled that some of the elders like his father were 'jack of all trades'.[38] Due to the lack of formal records which cover this period, it is not easy to provide an accurate number of skilled residents. Furthermore, informants do not know how which residents specialised in what and how many. Their living memory does, however, inform that there were a substantial number of specialists, such as Mr. Makhene who was a brick-maker, Motuba who was a teacher and wagon maker, Mareletsi a bricklayer, Pooe the baker, Tswagong and Rapodile bricklayers and makers, Mamasile a scotch roof maker, Mr Marago a wagon maker and a crafter of wagon wheels, and many others like Sonto's grandfather, a shoe maker.[39] There were also stone masons like Meku's grandfather, leatherworkers, wood carvers, carpenters, wagon builders, teachers, clergies, iron smelters, herbalists, and so forth. In addition, women were adept with domestic related skills like sewing, cooking, butter and cheese making, to name a few.[40] Sonto's grandmother, for example, known as Gogo Ma-Mokgethi, used to collect or fetch lard from local butchers, cook it and sell the fat *umhlwehlwe*. She also used fat to make soap. On this, Sonto explained: 'I don't know how, but they made soap mixing the fat with caustic-soda, made the soap for laundry'.[41] Mrs Nkutha, the wife of Gilman Nkutha, was a basket maker and also made traditional dresses for weddings.[42] Women also made clay pots, known as *Ukhamba*, locally along with other crafts. Among these skilled residents, there was a group of skilled *Oorlams* that were officially classified as coloured in government documents. Like former sharecroppers, and the mission-educated, this group accumulated farming and artisanal skills from the white farms and missionary schools. Perhaps more revealing about this group is the archival sources, which document that the early groups of coloureds were Mr. Van Der Merwe and John Malay who looked after Easton, Adams and Company's interest. Evidence also shows that Sophia Maria Adams bought Plot 3 and 4 on Block 123 in 1905, and F. W. Francis owned Plot 8 and 9 in the Block 139 which was bought in 1910.[43] *Oorlams* were described as 'generally well clothed, civil, law abiding and skilled in farming and exceedingly useful to the farmer in dam making and in fencing'.[44] These families spent many years in mission stations and in white farms, and, perhaps because of their distinct identity, were susceptible to new ideas, Christian influence and the desire to escape from chiefly control.[45] It is possible that mission schools and the close interaction with white farmers provided these residents with skills. Before 1910, missionary schools taught African students' religious doctrine and basic academics. Africans from mission schools were increasingly advancing beyond the status of apprentice. At the same time, vocational and technical education was regarded as suitable for non-whites. In her doctoral thesis, Sheila Menjties illustrates how one of the travellers James Cameron was impressed by skills of the converts at Indaleni in 1848 when he observed that 'they are learning rough carpentry with such success as to be able to make wheelbarrows not much inferior to those of tradesmen'.[46]

This period was marked by consumer and producer coming together in every transaction. Entrepreneurial activities existed in a less recognisable and essentially historical form which bore little to the modern environment. This does not imply that earlier forms of local entrepreneurship are irrelevant and less worthy to study, but there was not that much that was happening with respect to modern entrepreneurial activities. To a large extent, our understanding of this period is hampered by the limitations and difficult nature of data sources.

Historical shift in local entrepreneurial structure

The history of local entrepreneurship presents the relationships between industrial growth that shaped urban social change, consumer mobility and corresponding shifts in the local entrepreneurial structure. This transition was also characterised by the change of the local character of Evaton from the farming peri-urban settlement into an urban township. During this period, the Provincial Secretary estimated that Evaton's population was between 30 000 to 40 000 persons and this population was likely to increase as industrial activity and the avenues for employment were increasing.[47] The combinations of these factors seem more likely to have produced a fairly recognisable new phase of entrepreneurial development in Evaton. The timing of change in local entrepreneurship can be pushed back to at least the 1930s when fixed shops, transport enterprise and other new businesses appeared in Evaton. Before the 1930s local commercial activities were primitive in nature and major changes occurred after this date. Looking at the local economic history from this perspective, the late 1930s could be perceived as the watershed. The increase of industrialisation in the late 1930s and early 1940s accelerated the town-wards movement of many rural African consumers who sought to occupy places closer to workplaces. This became worse after the Second World War. There was a large and rapid increase of movement into urban areas due partly to the growing pressure of poverty and the expansion of the industrial and commercial sector which were stimulated by the war.[48] The continued urban growth along with an expansion of the capitalist sector of the South African economy provided new opportunities for the local development of the retail and transport industry.

In Evaton, this period saw the evolution of new forms of entrepreneurial activities, such as transport, ambulances, tailors, coal-yards, hardwares, barbershops, butcheries, bakeries, brick makers, grave diggers, bricklayers, carpenters, coffin makers, money lenders, tailors, shoemakers, poultry farmers, butter makers, photographers, and small craft enterprises. These businesses were generally small, by and large single proprietorship and only catered for the local segregated African market. As a freehold area, Evaton had a white section but white residents did not use African shops and services as they had their own stores. This social arrangement reflects on segregated laws and the spatial organisation of South African society. In general, local African enterprise catered for the needs of the Evaton community. Locally, these businesses did not compete with white entrepreneurs. There were, however, few Indian shops successfully competing with local Africans and this resulted in tension between Indian and African traders. The presence of Indians is indicated by the Wilberforce financial records of the mid-1930s. In these records, it is clearly stated that the school owed Jada and Sujee some money for the hostel groceries.[49] From these records, as well as the presence of the place that is currently called *HaJada Skwereng* (Jada's Square) or which was used for meetings during the Evaton Bus Boycott, it is shown that Jada supplied the Wilberforce Institute in the 1930s.[50] The presence of Indian entrepreneurs unleashed a wave of anti-

Indian sentiment among local African traders who lobbied to the Native Commissioner for the removal of Indian traders in Evaton. In response, a Native Commissioner investigated this matter and commissioned police to further the investigation. The police reported that 'the first building visited, situated on Block 1, Portion E, Evaton Small Farms, at the corner of Adams Road and unnamed lane, nearing completion....is owned by Jada and is being let, I am informed to an Indian Mohamed'.[51] In the same letter, the native commissioner also stated that 'three stands Nos 1778 and 1780 have recently been bought by Dadabhay from Natives [but not registered in his name]...a large shop is in course of construction on one of these stands'.[52] The commissioner noted that there were some other Asiatics who occupied rooms in African-owned stands, most of whom had no visible means of livelihood. The list of these Indians was compiled by Constable Kumalo for the inspector of the Land Tenure Advisory Board in 1955.[53] Undoubtedly, these records confirm that there was a considerable infiltration of Indians into Evaton Native Township. From this evidence, it is clear that there was discrimination and prejudice levelled against Indians. It should be noted that by this time the government was struggling to keep Evaton racially segregated.

African trade in Evaton could be divided into distinct categories, namely established shop-keepers, transport operators, petty traders, skilled crafters and hawkers. Collectively, these categories formed the local commercial class. This class had demonstrated the ability to diversify, integrate and specialise in their respective trades. This was clearly reflected in the local entrepreneurial patterns of the more established entrepreneurs who constantly embarked on new economic ventures. The development of multiple entrepreneurial activities in the late 1930s can be closely identified with the innovatory process. Sergeant Pretorius's evidence that dates back to 1933 provides further information on this: 'here are eight butcher shops and each one has his own slaughter place, and nobody see to it. There are also fourteen shops, no shop hours ordinance in force, except the Sunday law'.[54] Unlike the municipality, most of the shops in Evaton were located in the residential stands not in a central area, usually laid out in square shaped shops and were small retail stores selling the same scanty stock of cigarettes and general groceries. The central business district and its attractiveness, visible in many cities and shopping malls, never existed in Evaton. For this reason, it will be misleading to link consumer perception and preference to the physical appearance of the shop. Thus, attractiveness of local shops may be associated with the personal attribute of traders. These characteristics may perhaps include the friendliness of the shop owner, and his or her sympathy when customers were in a crisis. In the context of African communities, it is likely that the issue of *abuntu* was central for attracting customers.

During this period many entrepreneurs became innovative. One of the noticeable innovations was the development of the ambulance industry. After realising that the local community lacked ambulances, Liphoko converted his taxi into an ambulance that transported sick residents to the hospital.[55] Population expansion most likely played an important role in triggering innovations. By 1938, the population growth and the development of new housing on the grazing ground led to the shortage of grazing space. This forced other residents to hire grazing space on the surrounding European farms.[56] In response William Mokwena's father saw this as an opportunity to open up a new enterprise. He went back to Heidelberg farm where he practised sharecropping and bought fodder to sell to local stock-keepers. Mokwena recalled: 'with this business he made a lot of money because people had to feed their horses and cattle'.[57] To kick start his business, Mokwena's father spent 50 pounds buying his stock, of which the transport money was 12 pounds. In return, he profited 100 pounds which amounted to more than double what he spent.[58] In Small Farms, he was the only one who sold fodder, he had no real competition. This was confirmed by a number of informants, as Mjikisi Maseko indicated, 'we had to buy fodder from Mokwena because there were no more grazing spaces'.[59] 'We had to limit our livestock because of the shortage of grazing land and Mokwena's fodder was expensive', said John Maseko.[60] His product was on high demand because of the number of livestock that people had in Evaton. The profit was enough for him to support his family and pay for housing and utilities, clothing and school fees.[61] During the early years of Evaton's development, Dwight Seremi's father manufactured coffins free of-charge as a means of contribution whenever a member of the community died. After the 1930s, however, he began to sell the coffins. This new form of economic exchange became problematic, impacting negatively on the old social relations that existed in Evaton. It restrained volunteering; civic engagement and mutual self-help by promoting paid work in the community. This resulted in the local economic behaviour which degraded the old social quality of life while introducing social fragmentation and stratification. This type of economy encouraged the local community to be employed within the formal economy while pinning down unpaid community labour. It undermined the local capacity to undertake unpaid work. In addition, it strengthened class distinction between those community members who had more materials and those who had less.

The expansion of Evaton, due to the arrival of newcomers, provided a market for many skilled residents. Mr Makhene, for instance, manufactured bricks and sold to new property owners.[62] Van Der Merwe, an *Oorlam* and a stone mason, benefitted economically by selling stones for the foundation of many houses. Stones that he designed were used to build Qupe's stone-house that still stands today.[63]

There were other individuals who specialised in baking. One of the most popular bakers was Mr. Pooe who even used an underground oven for baking. He was later joined by Mrs Nkabinde who also was known for baking delicious bread, cakes and biscuits.[64] There was also a popular herbalist, Abednigo Mkhize, who owned Muthi House, a popular landmark located on the corner of Hamilton and Boundary Road. Currently, Muthi House has been re-altered for other commercial activity, but among Evaton residents the establishment is still known as Muthi house even today. Abednigo acquired knowledge of herbs from his father who was a well-known *inyanga*[65] in the Mkhomazi District in the South Coast.[66] At the same time, there was Mr. Kgoole who used his oxen to plough for people. He would be paid in cash for his services.[67]

Some of the local enterprises that emerged in Evaton surfaced within the framework of Evaton's self-governance status. As a freehold settlement that was administered differently when compared to a municipal location, local residents were responsible for the local social services. There were no municipal establishments that carried out the digging of graves, the construction of toilets, water supply, sanitation and other public works, and any other public services. Before the 1930s, these services including the building of roads, schools and churches which were done communally without any monetary attachment. When the local economy changed some residents took advantage of this opportunity and ventured into excavating enterprises. One of the families that ventured into this enterprise were Solani Nkabinde's uncles, the Nkabinde brothers, specialised in digging wells for newcomers and graves for the deceased.[68] This entrepreneurial activity became lucrative because some new residents did not have digging skills, especially those that came from the urban Reef.

This period also saw the emergence of private dealers like R.J. Phooko who served as a middleman between the rural producers and urban market product buyers. In an exemption application, it is stated that Phooko was a partner in the Native General Agency which was operated by five natives who received stock and farm produce from natives in the countryside and sold it in the market.[69] Phooko's enterprise also specialised in writing letters for natives, possibly the uneducated, and those who needed legal letters. Phooko posed as a semi-legal expert on matters pertaining to pass laws.[70] As far as this business scheme was described by the Acting Chief Pass Officer, it was 'an unqualified success financially, therefore letter writing and representation side of the business is being exploited as much as possible, as it brings a steady income'.[71]

On the female side, Evaton women adopted entrepreneurship as one of the primary livelihood strategies to meet their household consumer demands. It is difficult to establish the number of women involved in income generating activities that involved entrepreneurship. Women in Evaton received little official attention for they were involved in informal ways of generating income. The oral testimonies indicate that some women were traders. For example, Meku, a former student of Oliver Tambo in St. Peters, Rosettenville[72], recalled that while she was a student at St Peters 'every weekend we will help '*me*' Mamakgemu who produced soap'.[73] Mamakgemu used to mix animal fats *umhlwehlwe* with caustic alkali and other concoctions to make soap. Her soap production enterprise was, however, crippled by competition between local, marginal soap producers and multinational soap manufactures like Lever Brothers who purchased local South African firms in 1911. This international soap manufacturer's commercial power was derived partly from their aggressive commitment to the new technique of advertising and marketing that was backed by travelling advertising agents.[74] During these years, Lever Brothers convinced legislators to set guidelines for the size, shape and weight of soap. This initiative outlawed many local soap manufactures, including Mamukgemu in Evaton.

Among the women entrepreneurs there were dressmakers, weavers, and broom makers. In those years, women were confined to household duties and agricultural activities, especially in rural South Africa. They never traded and were entirely dependent on their husband's remittance. In the urban areas, those who generated income independently were beer brewers, an enterprise that was illegal. In Evaton, women's' trade was very important and often enjoyed more attention than domestic activities: 'with their money, women made contributions to education, clothing and some paid *lobolo* for their sons' [75], said Mary Maseko. As entrepreneurs, local women did not conform to the missionary model and the expectation of women's roles as subservient wives and daughters. In their families, local female entrepreneurs were not conventional. They did not reflect the representation of Christian domestic ideology produced by evangelicalism in answer to industrialisation. This ideology promoted the notion of happy homes as habitats where man earn the money and his wife keeps the home and brings up the children.[76] In Evaton female entrepreneurs did not lead a purely domesticated life - they were frequently out, some employed domestic workers to help with house chores. There were therefore various income generating activities that local women were engaged in.

Perhaps Evaton represents one of the areas where a great deal of practical equality between sexes had evolved, particularly in the commercial field. Local women traded in their own rights which implied that they enjoyed the same freedom and responsibility as men. This was confirmed by Dwight Seremi who proudly remarked, 'our mothers generated more cash than our fathers'.[77] Seremi's testimony is supported by different surveys from the end of the 1920s onwards. These surveys demonstrate that the economic shortfall of many African families was partly met by what wives earned.[78] The financial contribution of married women was essential for family survival.[79] This was exemplified by Sonto Kekane's grandmother and her great grandmother. The elderly women sold brooms and clothing to the local community, as well as to the neighbouring farming community. According to Sonto 'we would walk around Evaton selling these goods, some we called 'dress and n' coat'. During the December holidays we would sell beanies, brooms and straw mats.[80] Apart from this enterprise, Sonto's granny was a money lender, locally known as *umashonisa*. Her clients were migrants who were forced by economic circumstances to borrow money for bus and train fare. It should be noted that in those years, the level of wages of migrant unskilled labour was very low, and many workers could not afford to pay rail fares. In 1942, for instance, the Interdepartmental Committee on Social, Health and Economic Condition of Urban Natives reported 'the amount required under existing conditions in Johannesburg to house, feed, and clothe a Native family of five in decency £7-14-6, many Africans workers with families receive less wages than that'.[81] Apart from money lending that was paid with a certain amount of usury interest, she was also the head of the women's society's funds and was generally considered to have given financial support to hawkers and other local female business operators.[82]

The lack of capital was the key handicap to women entrepreneurs and other residents who aspired to venture into business. African entrepreneurs had no access to overdraft facilities, and they were denied loans by white bankers. Under these conditions African entrepreneurs faced a hopelessly frustrating barrier to economic prosperity.[83] The women's financial muscle, as well as the character of the self-help scheme, did not offer a strong start-up funding as compared to financial institutions that stronger white businesses used. These constraints impacted on the size and the scope of the African enterprises which remained small.[84] With an attempt to deal with this situation, Sonto's granny introduced a credit system that catered for local women. By the end of the 1940s, this scheme made it possible for a substantial number of Evaton residents to get into business. This was confirmed by Meku who remarked, 'MaVilakazi was central; every woman who wanted cash would borrow from her'.[85] Unlike banks, to be offered credit by the scheme, applicants did not complete forms with personal details. The scheme did not operate in a formalised banking fashion. The credit security depended on the reputation of the borrower for trustworthiness. If the borrower was someone who participated in different ranges of community activities, such as helping during marriage and funeral ceremonies and other social responsibilities, she automatically qualified.[86]

Some women entrepreneurs specialised in cheese making. Other female-driven enterprises included itinerant hawking where local women specialised in farm products like chickens and eggs that were sold every weekend in the white suburbs of Johannesburg. In her testimony she recounted:

> I was still at school and my grandmother would go and fetch chickens from a farm in the west, that belonged to Mr. Van Vuuren, this would be done on Fridays, We would then slaughter the chickens and clean them, she didn't work alone, there were other ladies working with her; this one lady who has passed on too, her kids sold their place, her name was Gogo Mngomezulu, and another lady Gogo Mokgeli, she too passed, also her kids sold the place, I think it is the grand child who was left there. The Fridays were great, cause it was the one day we would get to eat meat, the chicken heads and feet, the chickens would then be packed in baskets, there was a man who had the only taxi… he would come and collect my grandmother and the other ladies, taking them to Johannesburg…. There was a garage behind the Bantu Men's Social Centre, the taxi would park there, and the

ladies would then go on in different directions to sell, my grandmother sold mostly in Lower Houghton, she had pre-placed orders and would just deliver them.[87]

Food trade became the women's domain - this could be attributed to the traditional role of mothers as food preparers in their homes. For example, Dwight Seremi's and Paul Seshabela's mother also specialised in eggs and traded in the white suburbs of Johannesburg. Oral testimonies indicate that food trade was an activity that took place in the wealthier suburbs of Johannesburg only. It could be argued that this trade was characterised by the notion of gender and constituted a major source of income in the neighbourhood. Other women entrepreneurs traded in craft. For instance, Mrs Nkutha who traded farm products also specialised in crafts that she sold to white people of Johannesburg.[88] Apart from the female hawking enterprise, other women operated culturally related enterprises, such as beer brewing, but this mostly remained the domain of the Basotho women. The Basotho women largely sold beer to Basotho male tenants and migrants who came in large numbers to Evaton over weekends.[89] Similar conditions were recorded in Alexandra where native women caused trouble over weekends.[90] The majority of female stand-owners were devout Christians and they could not brew beer. The local beer brewing enterprise was, therefore, not well received by local residents, particularly Christian stand-owners who regarded it as the source of trouble in the area. The local social order was at stake, and there was an alarming increase of crime in the area. This is seen in the testimonies of many informants. During interviews, Mokwena grumbled 'the Basotho introduced bad thing here; they used to steal from us; they stole my father's firewood'. In a similar vein, Mjikisi recollect:

When beer brewing started Evaton residents were frightened by the manner in which the BaShoeshoe were occupying their stands; there was one of the local *induna* called Palama and he started ruling. He had many criminal bodyguards who looked after him, they were dangerous, and they ended up killing each other and Ralekeke ended up killing Palama and he became the chief and Palama died.... When Evaton got spoiled it was the time when the Russians came to Evaton and the people of Evaton started to build rooms in their yards.[91]

Maseko's testimony hints at the beer brewing enterprise and the arrival of the Basotho as the source of trouble and social ills in the settlement. He describes this period as the period when the local social character changed, as the era when Evaton became dangerous. Like Maseko, Tladi Kekane describes this period as the violent historical phase that was caused by the presence of the Basotho women and men. In his testimony Tladi agreed, 'There were many parties that were held over weekends by Basotho people who turned Small Farms into little Lesotho, and they were also organised as regional factions'.[92] Drinking culture among the Basotho tenants created tension between landlords and tenants. Apart from beer brewing, other forms of illegal underground economy emerged, particularly from the Basotho migrant men who traded marijuana. As a result, local residents began to severely dislike the Basotho behaviour. This was further aggravated by the Basotho interference in the Evaton Bus Strike of the 1950s. During the strike the local resident boycotters and the Basotho anti-boycotters killed and assaulted each other, and many houses were burned down. This turned Evaton township into a hive of unrest and bitter civil strife.[93] Perhaps this is one of the factors that makes many informants embarrassed when retelling the story of the beer brewing enterprise in Evaton.

One of the most profitable businesses that emerged during this period was the transport industry. There was a vast array of informal transportation networks that emerged in Evaton. This included buses and taxis. The appearance of local informal transport came as a result of the residential segregation policies which forced African people to live far from their places of employment. It is perhaps accurate rather than misleading to assert that segregation policies that gave birth to segregated settlements were inextricably linked to the emergence of local transport enterprises in Evaton. Evaton had virtually no industries or other forms of employment. The only place where local Africans were able to find steady employment was in Johannesburg and Vereeniging. In his 1938 report, Dr. Fourie, a local health inspector, reported, 'the majority of breadwinners whose family resides in the Township are employed either on the Reef or Vereeniging'.[94] Owing to the distance of Evaton to Johannesburg and other industrial centres like Vereeniging, local residents had no choice but to use some form of transport to get to work on time. During the late 1930s, Vereeniging locality was predominantly a farming town with less job opportunities.[95] The locals who were employed in the town were poorly paid, and this level of payment made the town less attractive.[96] The city of Johannesburg, on the other hand, offered attractive and relatively decent salaries. These economic attributes attracted residents of Evaton in large numbers to Johannesburg. Apart from labour opportunities, local residents may also have been attracted by the urban lifestyle a large city like Johannesburg offered at the time.[97] As a result, Johannesburg experienced a very large daily influx of commuters going to their workplaces, and this led to a serious shortage of public transport. Local residents like Mkhwanazi, Mbhele and many others took advantage of this opportunity.

Before the 1930s, transport in the settlement mostly consisted of horse-drawn vehicles, the railway and bicycles.

After World War II, the local population exploded and there was a demand for taxis and buses.[98] This gap became an opportunity for aspiring local entrepreneurs who opened up new commercial activities of transporting residents from home to their workplaces. During this period, railway rates, food and clothing prices were high, despite the low wages earned by African workers. It was estimated to be about £20 per adult male per annum on average.[99] Furthermore, trains were very slow, overcrowded and expensive. This forced some residents who worked in Johannesburg to return home on weekends only, yet a large portion commuted on a daily basis. What intensified the situation was the Minister of Transport's announcement on 22 September 1944. The minister announced a 10% surcharge on passenger fares and railage of goods.[100] In turn, the increase of train fares was felt by train passengers of Orlando and Pimville who were 10 to 12 miles from Johannesburg. It was worse for the residents of Evaton who were 28 miles away from the city. If, for example, a weekly ticket was 2 and 6 from Orlando to Jeppestown,[101] when calculating distance, the Evaton passengers were possibly paying 50% more than Orlando residents.

At this stage, African workers occupied a lower economic status which resulted in an inability to pay rail fare with the 10% increase. With their low wages, Africans in the Union, including Evaton residents, were unable to cope with the increase. As a result, the African National Congress petitioned the Minister of Transport, in the written petition it was stated:

> For Africans to increase the 2nd and 1st class fares 10% with the 15% tax is like cutting the flesh. But to increase the third-class fares by 10% is not only cutting the flesh but also breaking the bones…We therefore most respectfully request the Honourable Minister to exclude the third-class fares from the operation of the scheme.[102]

This nature of socio-economic problem set a tone for the 1950s Bus Boycott. In this context, what needs to be asked is how local entrepreneurs responded to this situation. After realising that train fares were high and there was a serious shortage of public transport, local residents, such as J.J. Mbhele, a former independent farmer and a transport operator from Natal, James Derbyshire from Kliptown, 'a coloured man who bought property from James Kunene at the sum of 100 pounds in 1928',[103] as well as Mkhwanazi, a former Transvaal sharecropper, ventured into the transport enterprise. The opening up of transport businesses could be interpreted as twofold: a form of livelihood as well as to alleviate the shortage of transport that local residents experienced. Mkhwanazi, for instance, founded Vukaphansi Bus Services. He was a former sharecropper from Piet Retief in the Transvaal. On his arrival in Johannesburg in 1911, he opened a restaurant and a small hotel in 88 Good Street, Sophiatown. After assessing the prospects of opening a transport business in Evaton, Mkhwanazi decided to buy a property in 1938. Mary recalled 'my father was followed by his friends Zitha and Ndolela, who were already residing in Evaton'.[104] Taking an advantage of distance that residents walked between Evaton Station and Small Farms, he bought buses and operated a bus company that was called Vukaphansi Bus Company. Mkhwanazi's buses transported local people from Small Farm and Evaton east to Evaton Station.

For Mkhwanazi and J.J. Mbhele, Evaton gave them the opportunity to revive their old business activity. Mbhele, for instance, revived his old colonial transport entrepreneurial activity. Before coming to Evaton, Mbhele operated transport on a wagon which was pulled by fourteen cattle in Natal. His wagon would park at Newcastle station between twelve and one at night, waiting for the train that came from Johannesburg to Durban. He collected goods from the train which he then transported to local white shops. After delivering the goods, he would leave the wagon and take cattle to his farm where he farmed in the day. In the evening, he would once again continue with his transport enterprise.[105] In Evaton, Mbhele's taxis transported people from Evaton to West Street in Johannesburg. According to informants, he was the first person to open up Evaton/Sebokeng taxi rank which is currently operating in Westgate Station.[106] His taxi business collapsed when modern cars became the competition. According to Dwight, Mbhele's Hudson did not have windows and passengers had to cover their mouths and noses during the trip. When younger taxi operators ventured into the industry, they introduced cars. Daniel Seremi, for instance bought cars with windows, which the customers preferred. This impacted negatively on Mbhele's taxis and many passengers stopped using them.[107] Mbhele was later joined by M.S. Lephoko's and the Bakeng's. In fact, Liphoko was given capital by Mbhele, who was his cousin, to venture into the taxi industry.[108] As previously mentioned, after realising that the local community lacked ambulances, Liphoko converted his taxi into an ambulance. As a freehold area, Evaton had no hospital. The only medical assistance available was offered by the Crogman Clinic, an AME church-controlled clinic that was attached to the Wilberforce Institute. At that time the nearest hospital was in Vereeniging, but it catered mainly for whites with a very small section for Africans. Evaton residents had to use Johannesburg Native Hospital before Baragwanath opened up in 1947.

It appeared as if most of the entrepreneurs who ventured into enterprises locally had a background in business. This is illustrated by the case of Mary (nee Mkhwanazi) Maseko, the daughter of Jabula Mkhwanazi, the bus operator a shop for more than 25 years. [109] After Mkhwanazi left the bus business in 1949, he opened up a shop in his stand. Due to his age and state of health, he retired from commercial activities and gave his shop to Mary who started operating it in 1951. When Mary took over, she expanded the business and opened up a restaurant. She also smuggled western alcohol in. Mary ran her business from the 1950s to the late 1980s. A similar business background characterised Daniel Motuba's business. Motuba took over a shop from his parents. During the interview, Motuba recalled, 'while residing in Orlando, Daniel Motuba [Daniel shared the name with his father] came and established himself in Evaton'.[110] Returning to Evaton in 1947, Motuba opened up a shop. For the daily operation of the shop he relied on his wife who was also a teacher. In the early stage of business operation Motuba's wife resigned from her teaching post and administered the shop.[111] Daniel mentioned that the success of his father's enterprise relied on unpaid family labour. Perhaps one might ask how Mrs Motuba coped with traditional roles as a mother and a wife; how she conducted the roles expected of her by her family. Did family responsibilities motivate or affect her success in business? In his own words, Daniel remarked 'My father trusted my mother who was very loyal when coming to financial management.'[112] Geographically, Motuba's and Mkhwanazi's shops were well positioned. The Motuba's shop was located next to the Wilberforce Institute and it attracted Wilberforce staff and students. The Mkhwanazi's was located in Boundary Road and it attracted residents from Small Farm and the old Evaton. These shops were characteristically small and neighbourhood-oriented. They provided goods that the local community needed. In Daniel's own words,

> We were going in and out of school, I came back. I qualified as a teacher in 1965 and I went to Johannesburg to teach because there were no posts available in Evaton. I taught in Johannesburg for twenty-five years ... and came back into the same business here in Evaton. But I have decided to branch it out because we are many, we are six brothers. So, I branched it out and had the business in the

general dealing side and I did stock farming till today, I am a pig farmer now.[113]

Mary and Daniel's entrepreneurial heritage could be traced from their parents. For example, Daniel's mother was the daughter of J.J. Mbhele, a farmer and transport operator in Newcastle, Natal and Mary was the daughter of a former sharecropper. It seems, therefore, that these businesses were representative of the local business trend in Evaton at the time. This claim is supported by the Dlamini butchery. The butchery still operates today and has been taken over by each different generation in the family. It was founded by Absolom Dlamini's father who passed it to his son who continues to benefit from the wealth generated long ago by a family entrepreneur.

Perhaps the questions that needs to be asked is what consumers bought from the local shops and other shops; in which period of the year were these shops lucrative and in which times of the year did business not do well. As Evaton was not electrified,[114] one of the commodities that these shops sold fast was paraffin and candles. Wood and coal were also used but paraffin was largely used for cooking using primus stoves and for lights. A primus stove was easier to use and faster for cooking than firewood and coal and, as expressed, migrants and other local workers did not have time for coal and wood.[115] The bank has asserted that the standard explanation for the preference of paraffin in the township in the poor urban communities was that it was cost effective – 'it is cheap and readily available'.[116] Among the migrants paraffin was associated with modernity yet firewood was associated with backwardness or the past practices of rural areas.[117] Similarly, candles were mostly used for light and as a floor polish. At that time, there was a constant movement of migrants from all over the Reef who visited their 'homeboys', and girls, sisters and other relatives who resided in Evaton.[118] This constant movement benefited local businesses, for instance, weekends were very profitable. However, during the December and Easter holidays, businesses were usually quiet as many migrants returned to their homelands for the holidays. This stretched to after holidays because when they came back they would have no money to spend. In his testimony, Motuba outlined that 'our shop was well stocked, and customers got almost whatever they wanted. We used to buy in large quantities because we had enough space to store our stock'.[119] These shops handled bulk of sales of fish, poultry, fruit and vegetables, which, in other township and cities would mostly be retailed by specialised shops.

Towards local control

Special attention has been given to the growth of local entrepreneurship and the local economic changes, as well as character of consumer-demand that shaped the emergence of new local enterprises. The issue of self-governance and the business opportunity that the relative freehold autonomy created has been discussed. As a freehold area, Evaton offered unregulated opportunities for entrepreneurial activities and therefore offered opportunity to anyone with entrepreneurial initiative, or any person willing to work hard and make their fortune there. When the power of the local authorities was introduced by the amended Urban Areas Act in the 1940s, local entrepreneurship activities came under severe scrutiny for being 'unwholesome' and 'unsanitary'. This inspection focused on shops, butcheries and brickmaking.

Before 1940, the Native Commissioner did not record local entrepreneurial activities and the existing local commercial activities did not draw the attention of the Native Affairs Department. As the local socio-economic character changed, the settlement experienced a new administration system that impacted on local entrepreneurship by introducing new trade regulations.

As a thinly populated freehold settlement, the local affairs of Evaton were not supervised by municipalities. By its nature, Evaton was not a location, a 'native' village or 'native' hostel under the Native Urban Areas Act of 1923. The settlement was not defined by this Act, set apart or laid out by any local authority, nor was it under the jurisdiction of any urban location. Before 1936, Evaton was not scheduled as a 'native area', and the acquisition of properties by Africans was made lawful by the Governor General under Section 1 of the Native Land Act of 1913.[120] The status of Evaton was not even defined in Section 35 of the Native Administration Act No 38 of 1927. Since the settlement was not set apart or reserved for Africans occupation, it was open for occupation by white residents as well.

By then, the Native Affairs Department had been at the forefront of the demand for urban reform, with the power to monitor disease and to control slums. One of its major objectives was to use the provisions of the Public Health Act to condemn and prevent urban overcrowding and demolish unsanitary buildings.[121] The urbanisation of Evaton and the presence of local labour migrants who supplied labour to the surrounding industrial centres was located within this broader official framework. For example, the focus on health issues made it possible for the state to interfere in local affairs. As indicated below, in Evaton this initiative coincided with a local white public campaign for strong regulatory powers that would give the Evaton Health Committee greater control over public health.

For this study, the lobbying role of the Evaton Health Committee, the population growth and its impact on the change of local social character, provide some explanation on the development of administration processes that led to the regulation of local enterprises. These processes incorporated health issues and entrepreneurial regulations. Broadly speaking, this new development was part of the state social engineering scheme that aimed at reshaping urban areas by establishing absolute control over urban African inhabitants. This connection provides an important key to the manner in which local entrepreneurial policy was implemented in Evaton. Moreover, the uncontrollable nature of Evaton that was tailored to keep the state control at bay appeared to have hindered the state objective of keeping townships as labour resources. The consistent objective of this control was to restrict the African presence in urban areas and deny them the right to land-ownership.[122] By this time, the state was investigating possibilities of establishing local authority that would control local administrative affairs in Evaton. This was recorded in the report of the Secretary for Native Affair:

> In view, however, of the fact that the released area of Evaton…will undoubtedly become the principal residented (sic) centre and reservoir for Native Labour for the extensive industrial zone now taking shape in and around the Vereeniging District, the Department has come to the conclusion that the limited powers available under…Act No 38 of 1927…steps would have to be taken to have Ordinance No.20 of 1943 suitably amended before such control could be assumed.[123]

It is possible that the state saw the geographical location of the township and its increasing population which put the settlement under the spotlight as having a strong potential of supplying labour to the surrounding industries. This seems to suggest the belief that the Evaton urban community, like any other African urban community in South Africa, should be tightly controlled.

Control over local entrepreneurship

In the context of Evaton, the question that arises is how the policy that regulated African enterprise gained a foothold in Evaton, a settlement that was legally exempted from the 1923 Native Urban Areas Act. There are two factors that could help answer these questions. The first is the impact of the local white pressure group that organised itself under the umbrella of the Evaton Health Committee. The second is the insanitary conditions that were used by the state as a pretext to gain control over local entrepreneurship.

As a sprawling freehold settlement and one of the largest freehold settlements on the Reef, Evaton was divided into two sections, one for Africans and one for whites. In terms of administration, the white area of the settlement was under the control of the Evaton Health Committee founded in 1935 by local white residents. The responsibility of this committee was to address public health issues that affected the white community. Its jurisdiction was limited to white Evaton, but some effort was made to extend it to the African area, where there was no committee responsible for health issues. In 1939, the Native Commissioner reported that there was friction between 'Europeans and Native' inhabitants of the respective areas.[124] Although there might have been other causes of hostility, the Commissioner recorded that friction centred on grazing facilities. The trespassing of African stock was a source of much irritation to the members of the Health Committee who did not possess any grazing commonage and yet continued to believe that their area was being overrun by African-owned livestock.[125] The letter that represents this hostility was written by H.H. Baillie, the chairperson of the committee. The letter reads as follows:

> the Native is as arrogant and defiant as ever, even more so now that the 'pound' has been closed at Evaton, he continues to

invade the Whiteman's area with impunity knowing full well that neither the white or the police [will never arrest them]... The young Native has grown up in the atmosphere created by his fathers, viz trampling upon whites and openly defying them, and are also just as arrogant as their elders.[126]

H.H. Baillie and his pressure group of residents from white Evaton complained that African livestock caused a fly nuisance and unhygienic conditions, which compelled whites to lobby the central government in Pretoria for reforms that would give power to the local health committee to control the African settlement. Their aim was to gain control over local African affairs and to prevent African cattle from encroaching on their racially demarcated section.[127] However, the interim report of the Secretary of the Urbanised Areas Committee stated that 'incorporation of the Native area within the Health Committee area would not be practicable'.[128] The call for a healthy environment that later gave birth to new regulations and trade licensing originated from this health campaign. The essence of this advocacy called for the intervention of the Peri-Urban Health Board, a representative of the central government, to develop sanitary regulations and to deploy health inspectors who would make sure that residents adhered to health standards.[129] The local white health activists also protested against what they regarded as 'offensive trade', which included the slaughtering of livestock and brick making enterprises. In a 1937 letter, Baillie stated that 'natives slaughter animals in their own yards and expose large numbers of slaughterhouse waste which causes flies and bad smell'.[130] White health advocates and residents called for building an inspected public abattoir. A few years after these complaints, plans were made to set up a central abattoir in Vereeniging and implement a system of control for butcheries.[131] As the local population expanded in the 1940s, there was considerable growth of an entrepreneurial class and overtrading took place in Evaton. Many shops and butcheries emerged, some of which were located in very close proximity. This resulted in the high competition that included pricing and the manner in which shopkeepers interacted with their customers. The Native Commissioner's report stated that there were approximately 100 native general dealers and greengrocer shops.[132] At the same time, government urban control was intensifying, and it was gradually shaping up towards the reduction of the African freehold status of many African settlements into municipal controlled townships. In order to achieve this goal, public health measures were used as an excuse in Evaton, and were under intense official discussion. This is supported by voluminous correspondences, meetings and deliberations that were held by the Native Affairs Department. In one of these meetings Phillips points out that 'if control measures of the peri-urban areas and Evaton could be established and uniformity of control could be brought into being this would materially assist in removing the danger to public health'.[133] Another letter from the Secretary for Native Affairs stated that

> the Department has come to the conclusion that the limited powers available under section thirty of Act No.38 of 1927, as amended are inadequate for the effective local government of so important area...as at present constituted the Board would be unable to assume control of the settlement which forms part of released area. And steps would have to be taken to have Ordinance No. 20 of 1943 suitably amended before such control.[134]

The local control measures that were to be implemented reflected on the broader focus of the government which aimed at intensifying control of movement into urban areas. This initiative represented the preliminary phase towards the implementation of local authority in Evaton. The role of this authority was to control a frequent unregulated movement of migrants into Evaton, as well as local trade. This government's action was seen as an infringement on the rights of stand holders. As a result, Sam Rom Attorneys was commissioned by the Small Farms Stand Holders Association to oppose the implementation of local authority. In a letter addressed to the Secretary for Native Affairs, Sam Rom wrote: 'my clients now insist on writing to you direct, and to point out that they wish to form their own Advisory Board at Evaton Small Farm'.[135] A letter from the Small Farm Standholders Association to the Secretary for Native Affairs complained that:

> We are disappointed and alarmed to learn that the Small Farm Township is not supposed to fall under the local authority mentioned above but under the Peri-Urban Areas Health Board. We beg to reiterate and emphasise our joint resolution that the Small Farm Township be placed under the local authority asked for...[136]

Because of Alexandra, the Native Affairs Department was sceptical about granting administrative power to a local African resident's body to take control of the settlement without the supervisory control of a body like the Peri-Urban Areas Board, which had technical staff and an extensive experience of local government.[137] The Department concluded that 'a Native body would be financially weak and it is unlikely that they could provide Medical Officer or Engineer'.[138] In his oral testimony Sam Mokeana explains the situation as follows: 'the opposition to local authority emerged from the fact that everything including businesses were going to be controlled and many people, especially the stand holders of Evaton, did not want to work for whites, they wanted to be economically independent'.[139] From an examination of the archival sources, it is not clear whether the body of local authority was implemented or not. However, some form of control was achieved, and the Evaton Health Committee was given power in 1951 to implement regulations that governed commercial activities and other local affairs. These regulations were implemented the same year. It appeared that the laws of the Union which governed freehold areas made it difficult for a local authority body to be implemented. A memo of the Native Affairs Department stated:

> Our provisions under Section 30 of the Native Administration Act may not be adequate to meet the situations of this nature... we will have to devise some proper scheme of municipal control in Native Areas such as Evaton possible within the framework of Bantu Authorities Act (although this present difficulties)... the control of the Peri-Urban Health Board appear to be *ultra vires* and that the Department will endeavour to devise some other suitable form of urban control.[140]

This official statement leaves an unanswered question which the scope of this work does not allow further engagement in. However, the availability of trade license application letters and the entrepreneurial regulations indicate that in the 1940s there was some form of control scheme under the Peri-Urban Areas Health Board. This control body styled itself as a local authority which existed in Evaton. This implies that there was a link between the Board and the local licensing regulations.

Local entrepreneurial regulations

The implementation of the new entrepreneurial regulations in Evaton can be associated with public safety, health, morals, and welfare and the subjection of Africans to the many kinds of legal controls that intensified in the 1940s and 1950s. After the jurisdiction of the Evaton Health Committee was extended to the African section of Evaton in 1951, a set of rules and entrepreneurial regulations were implemented. These regulations were deemed to be public health regulations and were published under Part IV of the Public Health By-Laws and Regulations of the Health Committee of Evaton, published under the Administrator's Notice No.148.[141] This set of laws were approved under the provision of section 126 (1) (a) of the Local Government Ordinance, 1939, which gave the Evaton Health Committee the power to supervise the control of businesses, trade and occupation amendments.[142] The implementation of trade regulations in Evaton responded to three different socio-economic aspects. Firstly, to the white complaints about the nuisance of backyard slaughtering and brick-making pollution. Secondly, to the friction between African and Indian traders, which troubled the Native Affairs Department. Thirdly, to what was reported by the Native Affairs Department officials as overtrading. The issue of overtrading was reported by the Secretary of the Native Affairs who stated that 'there are approximately 100 Native general dealers and greengrocers...and that since the control was lifted the township has been flooded with Indian hawkers from Johannesburg and the Reef'.[143] Given the freehold conditions and autonomy that Evaton offered, local entrepreneurs came from diverse social origins and backgrounds. The commercial opportunities that the settlement offered attracted a small number of Indians who came and traded in Evaton in the 1940s and 1950s. The Indian competition, however, was not well received by local African entrepreneurs and it caused friction. According to the Native Affairs Department report, Indians owned '6 shops within the area'.[144] The Afro-Indian friction drew the attention of the Native Affairs after the local African entrepreneurs, who grouped themselves under the Evaton Native Traders, lodged a complaint with the Native Affairs Department about Indian traders.[145] After correspondence was exchanged regulatory measures intensified and a series of health inspections were conducted and trade regulations introduced in Evaton. These were set up after the local health inspector noted that the introduction of a health service was a matter of urgency. In the Native Affairs agenda, unsanitary slaughter poles were the first priority on the Health Board list. In the early 1940s, the Sanitary Board struggled for control. The Board's power, however, was extremely limited by legalities that governed the freehold settlement of Evaton. In consequence, many local butchers benefitted from this legal gap and continued to make their own slaughtering arrangements. By then the Director of Native Agriculture reported that in Evaton,

> there are 40 licensed Native butchers in the area, including three in the European Health Committee portion (and many unlicensed butchers) and these have not even a gallow with a block and tackle, let alone refrigeration and by-product facilities. Furthermore, in the Native Evaton there is no meat inspection at all.[146].

When the apartheid laws were introduced in the late 1940s, Evaton's freehold status was increasingly threatened and the Peri-Urban Board's concern over public health was felt by local butchers. Soon after the National Party took over control of government in 1948, plans were made to set up a central abattoir in Vereeniging. The strategy of the Central Meat Board emanated from a loophole that was evident in local butcheries. This initiative was accompanied by the tightening of entrepreneurial control by means of strengthened trade licensing and regulations. Oral evidence indicates that the local Native Commissioner became strict with slaughtering activities. Dlamini describes this transformation as follows: 'local police and the commissioner became strict and slaughtering was closely monitored.[147] In the late 1940s, the Deputy Director of Native

Agriculture indicated that the municipality of Vereeniging was to build a modern abattoir that would cater for the surrounding region, up to a 30-mile radius. In Evaton, this abattoir was to cater for 40 licensed butchers.[148] The chief problem that the butchers experienced was the absence of transport from the central abattoir. Despite these difficulties, the Deputy Director reported

> I strongly recommend the latter course i.e. insisting on Native butchers to obtain their meat suppliers from central abattoir at Vereeniging. The police too would prefer the course.[149]

For a few years nothing seems to have come of the Board's initiative, probably due to the unwillingness of the Vereeniging local authorities to take responsibility for finding financing for this large project because it did not then have the power to raise municipal loans.[150] This did not occur until the early 1950s when Vereeniging's municipal abattoir was opened in Leeuwkuil at a cost of R600.000. After its establishment more than 91,000 animals were slaughtered annually: 31,000 head of cattle, 3,500 calves, 33,000 sheep and 24,000 pigs.[151] The newly implemented regulations covered the keeping of animals, offensive trades, fish fryers and fishmongers, the manufacture of rag flock, storage and sale of foods, 'native' tearooms and restaurants, ice cream and similar commodities.[152] One of the local meat regulations required butchers to submit their dead animals to the authorised personnel for examination. This implied that slaughtering was now regulated by the Board and all butchers were forced to slaughter cattle in the new abattoir. The regulation stated that

> Every owner of consignee of any butcher's meat or dead animal intended for the food of man within the township, which may be conveyed or transported into the said area, shall submit the same for the purpose of examination and branding or

stamping by authorised official of the Committee may from time to time direct and such meat or dead animal shall not be delivered...until the same shall have been thus examined and branded or stamped [153]

This regulation exempted residents who slaughtered for family consumption. The newly implemented regulations were approved and promulgated in the *Provincial Gazette* and were subject to Section 5 of the Slaughtering and Meat Regulations published under Government Notice No. 2118 of 1924. These regulations granted a local committee power to oversee and administer slaughtering activities.

> All animals shall be slaughtered in the manner prescribed in the slaughter or animal Act No 26 of 1935.'...Except in a case of animals which the occupier of any premises any slaughter for his own household consumption, no person shall slaughter within the township elsewhere than at the Committee slaughter pole'...Every owner or consignee of any butcher's meat or dead animal intended for the food of men within the township, which may be conveyed or transported into the said area, shall submit the same for the purpose of examination and branding or stamping by the authorised official of the committee at such depot [154]...

Therefore, slaughtering without a committee's authorisation was prohibited. 'Any person convicted of a contravention of this regulation shall be liable...to a penalty not exceeding £25 for every animal slaughtered'.[155] These laws required local butchers to slaughter in approved places. There were fees that were attached to slaughtering,

> For slaughtering and examination of cattle over six month old each 2s.0.d

For slaughtering and examination of cattle under six months old 1s.0. d

For slaughtering and examination of pigs, each 1s, 0.d

For slaughtering and examination of sheep or goats, each 2s, 0. d[156]

The charges were payable to the committee in respect of examination and branding. The new laws had a negative impact on the growth of African butcheries, and it is possible that some private slaughterhouses went out of business. In terms of social relations, the prohibition of backyard slaughtering had a negative impact on local social relationships and the expansion of local butcheries. During the time when butchers slaughtered in their yards, they relied on local unpaid labour based on reciprocal relationships and neighbourhood networks. There were no licenses that were required; yet new regulations required anyone slaughtering animals or birds to hold a provisional or registered license. Describing the change that was brought by licensing, Thomas Mofokeng recalled:

> They will ask young boys from the neighbourhood to come and assist during butchering, they won't be paid cash, but they will be given some meat especially offals to give to their parents. This was frequently done, and boys knew that whenever they are called they will be given food.[157]

The control of slaughtering affected this kind of relationship; local boys and men who used to help during slaughtering would be offered offal and other parts of slaughtered animals for free, but after the introduction of new regulations, they had to buy what they used to get for free. In his testimony Dlamini stated, although people were selling meat, but some part of slaughtered cattle will be given to families who could not afford to buy, there were widows and elders who would be given something from the slaughtered cattle, also boys who were helping would receive some payment in the form of meat to go and cook in their homes. By the time when slaughtering became regulated, butchers sold everything because they had to cover up for slaughtering and inspection costs that the Commissioner demanded.[158]

Butchers such as Ben Moeketsi stopped practising because of the rising costs associated with butcher operations. The new expenses and tedious process of applying for licenses restrained this commercial activity and led to a decrease in the number of butcheries. The new regulations encouraged butchers who avoided the laws to break them and it was very hard for the police to monitor the situation. The Evaton Police Station was understaffed, and police dealt with different matters ranging from collecting taxes to monitoring criminal activities. This was evident in a letter that Sergeant F.H. Berhaman wrote complaining to the Director of the Native Labour:

> from time to time I am requested to undertake duties in connection with stands...I regret again I have to be relieved of the duty of valuation of stands...for several reasons. Firstly, the only means of transport is the government car which is used by myself and the clerk who collect native tax. I use the car sparingly so as not to hinder the tax collection...much of my time is spent attending to members of the public.[159]

The first problem with the regulations was the question of enforcement as butcher shops were only inspected every two years. Even if a butcher shop was caught trading non-exempt items, the fines were not large enough (£25) to deter owners from recommitting the offence. This loophole encouraged some local entrepreneurs to operate illegally and the police department arrested Jacob Mafobokoane and possibly others. The surviving sources indicate that Mafobokoane was refused a trade licence because he was convicted of failing to maintain registration for slaughtering stock and trading without a licence.[160] He was also involved in a stock theft syndicate and was suspected to be one of the receivers of stolen stock in Evaton.[161]

The persistent commercial transformation of butcheries impacted on the organisational structure of the local meat industry. Apart from the meat regulating industry, there was another set of structural factors that contributed to this change. Firstly, the expansion of the settlement reduced grazing land and residents could not keep up large numbers of cattle herds. Secondly, when entrepreneurial regulatory measures were introduced in 1951, the stock reduction regulation was introduced. These regulations impacted on the number of cattle that could be kept in each stand;

> every occupier of the erf or portion should or an erf in the town shall be entitled to keep two cattle or two horses or two mules or two donkeys or not more than five sheep or goats…the committee shall have the right to grant… to grant licenses.. . to persons wishing to keep more animals.[162]

The regulation was in line with the national stock limitation legislation of the 1950s. At the same time these regulations also prohibited local residents from keeping cows for dairy purposes.[163] This promulgation presented a drastic alteration in the dietary habits of residents. Furthermore, it contributed to poverty as local residents depended on their livestock, particularly their cattle, for their basic protein intake in the form of milk, sour milk and, less frequently, meat. It is clear that the economic transformation introduced by the state restrained local economic independence and the old organisational structure of the meat industry. This shift also impacted negatively on by-products such as hide-related entrepreneurial activities. In Evaton there were shoemakers such as Mokgethi who manufactured shoes, belts and other leather products. Edward Nxumalo recalled:

> *ntate* Mokgethi processed cow hide into shoe leather and he made shoes, he relied on skin from local butchers who gave him hide in exchange for shoes that he produced, when new laws came all this changed Mokgethi found it difficult to collect hide.[164]

The production of shoes was one of the specialities practised by a few artisans such as Mokgethi and they relied on butchers for hides. According to Dlamini, 'if I remember well Ntate Mokgethi used to come here to collect hides and at times he would drop shoes for my father. I don't know what happened to him and his business during the time of regulations'.[165]

The impact of regulations on animal keeping and the decrease of grazing land led to a lack of a local meat supply. Before the 1950s local butchers bought livestock locally. But the reduction of stock and grazing land forced them to purchase livestock from other settlements or neighbouring farms. As a result, Evaton was unable to supply and meet the demands of its own people. Dlamini remembers: 'the settlement had to rely on meat that came from other areas'.[166] Before the implementation of local regulations and licensing laws, a butchery was one of the easiest entrepreneurial activities to operate. The reason was that livestock were available in the area and butchers could slaughter without any supervision. Dlamini, who still operates a butchery, recollects: 'in what may be called the good old days, cattle were slaughtered in our yards and nobody would question you'.[167] In those years, local butchers were not willing to part with their livestock especially cattle which was still regarded as the economic backbone of the household. Local butchers clung to the belief that investment in cattle created considerable potential for socio-economic differentiation.

The introduction of new regulations came with the new technology of cold storage. The local butchers who wanted to continue operating had to adapt to totally new technologies that required every butchery shop to have modern refrigeration devices. Owing to the high cost of these facilities, it was not easy for them to maintain cold storage. Moreover, Evaton had no electricity and so storage devices could not be run. The butcher shops had to comply with inspection requirements which demanded expensive modern facilities and a building that met standards.[168] Furthermore, slaughtering fees were high, and it was not easy for local butchers to buy the necessary equipment, materials and other physical resources, including the building of a standardised butcher shop, which was costly. As a result, these regulatory measures restrained many local butchers who failed to comply with the requirements of butchery regulations. Butchers closed down their operations, and some operated illegally. Fees that were paid in the regulated slaughters depended on weight. Since animals are shaped differently, one may have more muscle or fat or bone than the next. Meat could be close trimmed or left with some fat on, so cutting differences determined quality and price. Some animals had less bone weight than others. This made a difference in the fees that butchers had to pay to the slaughter centre.

The difficulty of operating butcher shops was further aggravated by trade licence applications. Dlamini recalls that many butcheries were home-based. 'Before applying many applicants ensured their premises met the required standard which most of the applicants like my father did'.[169] Besides butchers, there were entrepreneurs who specialised in dairy products.[170] One of the well-known local dairy producers was Elias Mthimkhulu. According to his son Bheki, 'we were producing cheese and other dairy products like sour milk that was locally known as *amasi*, we had lot of *amasi* because we never had fridges and our milk got easily spoiled'.[171] New regulations that regulated dairy shops were implemented at the same time as those of the butcheries. The dairy by-law compelled dairy dealers to have proper storage with effective lights and ventilation and a drainage system.[172] The dairy shops had to be kept clean, and the storage room where milk was kept required the ceiling or inner surface of the roof and inner surface of every wall to be covered with material such as lime washing which had to be white washed twice a year.[173] The regulation required that all vessels had to be kept clean and all milk shops containing milk intended for sale were to be cleaned daily.[174] Cows that were milked were to be cleaned. It was illegal to keep milk intended for public sale in any room such as a living room, bedroom or any room in a house other than a proper storage room.[175] After the implementation of regulations, the cost of running a milk business became expensive. For instance, the cost of building storage as required by the regulations was expensive; floors had to be constructed with impervious material in order to create a channel for effectively carrying away all urine or other liquid filth to an outside concrete catch pit. Because of the expense, many milk dealers were relatively poor and operated on a small-scale. As a result, more and more milk producers left the enterprise and the local milk industry declined. The economic status of milkmen and women was clearly described by the Special Justice for Peace in a trade license application letter. He wrote: 'the applicant...use a pedal cycle, pay for the milk he buys from Mr. Cooper and then sell it by retail to residents of the location. He cannot invest a definite amount of capital in his business, as his purchase of the following day will depend on his sale'.[176]

One of the major reasons for the decline of local milk entrepreneurs in Evaton was a result of the establishment of large-scale dairy firms and the introduction of the pasteurisation technique of milk. By then the Evaton community had become a milk consuming community. According to Tsepo Khanyi, 'milk was regarded as food and a drink, milk was used for porridge in the morning, it was not only fresh milk, likewise sour milk was of importance for local residents. It was to a large extent used as a supplement to cooked food in every household'.[177] Selling milk at the doorstep in Evaton, especially in the 1940s when the practice of cattle keeping declined due to the lack of grazing land, was common. Local milk dealers were unaware of the concept of professional milk hygiene. They conducted their business in an informal way. Khanyi paints a picture on how these dealers sold their milk: 'local milkmen were cleanly dressed with white clothes and their vessels were clean, since milk was perishable, they also sold *amasi* and cream which was the by-product.[178] A justification for the elimination of local milk producers was the anxiety about public health and safety. Although the new regulations were in place, a number of local milk entrepreneurs continued to operate, though on a small-scale. These dealers undermined the new regulations which stated that 'any person licensed to carry on the trade of dairyman cow keeper, or purveyor of milk shall inform the committee without delay'.[179] Instead they continued delivering milk informally in the neighbourhoods.

The change that took place in Evaton was fundamental. The area changed from having frugal rural subsistence producers that were threatened by bad harvests to modern urban consumers. The variety of foodstuffs that were supplied to an urban population came from different local suppliers. With the local population growth, eating houses, similar to Mary Maseko's, mushroomed. These houses matched with the rising demands generated by the high population. They proved to be advantageous and they met the food demand for a burgeoning local workforce. Their growth was associated with conflict surrounding the establishment of similar enterprises in white areas, where they were regarded as noxious facilities by white urban authorities.[180] As compared to Evaton, eating houses in white areas were expensive, and white owners 'overcharged' or exploited their African patrons.[181]

As they formed part of the retail enterprise, eating houses had to comply with regulations that governed local commercial activities. According to records of the Native Commissioner, there were more 10 eating houses in Evaton.[182] The local by-laws defined them as follows: 'The term eating house shall mean any premises or place where any article of food or drink is sold or offered for sale to native'.[183] The regulations stipulated that all rooms where people ate had to receive enough light and ventilation to satisfy the inspection of the committee.[184] The floors where food and drink was consumed had to be properly cemented with concrete and cement that prevented moisture seeping in. Sufficient privies with urinals were to be provided by each eating house. The water supply had to be adequate for washing hands.[185] All the walls had to be whitewashed and be washed or redone every year.[186] If these conditions were not complied with, the authorities would serve a notice and the owner of the eating house would be subject to prosecution.

Like any other settlement, Evaton had adequate food supplying outlets that fed local residents. The bakery was one of the establishments where local residents could buy a diverse range of breads, mouth-watering pastries and cakes. In Evaton regulatory measures that aimed at the safety and quality of bread were promulgated along with other regulations. The clause of the local bakery law clearly stated that 'no person shall carry on the trade of bakers, pastry-cook confectioner or ice-cream maker unless the committee is satisfied, [and] that proper provision is made in his premises for the due observance of these conditions'.[187] Like the eating houses, bakery rooms were required to be ventilated and that there should be a proper supply of water. In the case of water supplied by shallow wells, a proper arrangement for boiling water was to be made before baking took place. Flooring had to be cemented. A similar regulation controlled different types of entrepreneurial activities ranging from tea rooms to restaurants. In part VIII of the regulations it clearly stated that 'the medical office of health or sanitary inspector may at all reasonable times enter and inspect any premises licensed as a tearoom, hotel, boarding houses, eating houses or restaurant'.[188] All these retail enterprises were regulated; it is not clear about service-related enterprises except for brick-making.

Brick-making was one of the most popular and lucrative enterprises, especially during the building boom of the late 1930s and 1940s. With the introduction of regulations and the establishment of the neighbouring Vereeniging Brick and Tile, this industry declined in Evaton. Another contribution to the collapse of this enterprise was the promulgation of new regulations which stated that:

> No person shall manufacture bricks or any other articles of clay on any brickfield or upon any other ground under the control of the committee, nor shall any person obtain or take clay or other material for any such purpose aforesaid from any such brickfield or other ground without being in possession of a licence for the purpose duly issues by the committee.[189]

Before digging material, a licensee had to go through the committee for sanitary arrangements that would satisfy the medical officer or the health inspector. If a brick maker did not comply, he would be acting illegally.

The brick-making regulations impinged directly not only on the local brick makers' pride in his craft but also on his independence, imposing control over brick-makers' work. The implementation of regulations coincided with the mechanisation of the brick-making process. This changed the local brick-makers' attitude towards the industry which was becoming difficult to operate. They were being pressured both by harsh white competition and technological innovations. Many of them looked askance at changes that threatened the security of a static and traditional arrangement of work, prices and profits. This was noted by Christina Meku who indicated that after the opening up of Vereeniging Brick and Tile, her father, Mr. Makhene, and other brick makers got frustrated by rules and regulations, as well as the restrictions that hindered them from continuing with their brick-making enterprises. The Vereeniging Brick and Tile had big machines which could make many bricks in a short period of time as compared to local brick makers.[190] The changing nature of the building industry as a whole highlighted these tensions. Thus, many brick makers surrendered to the demands of new regulations and advanced technology and were irresistibly drawn into the labour market. They abandoned their old independent economic practices and adopted new livelihoods. There was an obvious connection between the introduction of machinery, the implementation of new regulations and the growth of brick-making industries in the Vereeniging region.

The fundamental characteristic of ownership in the industry was its small-scale and risky nature. Hence, after the implementation of new regulations, many brick making enterprises suffered under the committee's control. It seems likely that the repeal of the excise tax in the 1940s and the building boom encouraged the formation of larger white-owned firms like Vereeniging Brick and Tile. The emergence of these firms replaced a small number of local long-established brick-makers who had worked within the well-defined labour context of Evaton.

Regulations and fees

The Peri-Urban Health Board set fees that were charged for each and every entrepreneurial activity.

Baker	£2.00
Boarding House where	£2.00
Accommodation is provided	£5.0.0
For more than ten persons	£1.10.0
Butcher and or fishmonger	£2.00
Greengrocer and fruiters	£1.0.0
Fresh producers	£2.0.0
Miller	£2.0.0
Restaurant	£7.10.0
Hotel	
Refreshment room or tearoom (including fruit greengrocers and ice cream	£2.0.0
	£5.0.0
Grocer	£1.10.0
Hawkers and pedlars, other than hawker	£1.0.0
	1.10.0
Peddler selling vegetable	£.10 0
	£2.0.0
Barber and hair saloon	£1.0.0
Dairy	£1.0.0.0
Bioscope	
Fishfrier	
Cobbler	
Dog Kennel	

Local Licensing

Licensing can be defined as the granting by some competent authority of the right or permission to carry on a business or do an act that otherwise would be illegal.[191]

> License may be interpreted as a nature of authority to a person to exercise an inherent right which has in public interest, been restricted or made subject to certain conditions, requirements and qualification.[192]

Licensing may at one extreme be in the nature of a special privilege and at another extreme a right which can be exercised simply by payment of prescribed fees.[193] In Evaton licensing was used from the early 1940s to regulate and control local economic activities ranging from brick-making to butcheries. The goals of local licensing, including prohibition, regulation, administration, and revenue, were mixed and sometimes confused. The overall justification for licensing was to promote public interest by ensuring healthy and safe delivery and generally the public good and general welfare. Trade licensing in South Africa was based on numerous statutes, ordinances and by-laws. The local licensing laws in Evaton were based on the Evaton Health Committee regulations and the national laws that governed businesses. In this settlement, licensing involved two separate components. Firstly, it determined the granting of permission to local entrepreneurs to operate commercial activities. Secondly, it determined permission that stipulated the circumstances under which permission could be granted for the issue of licenses. Permission was then the gist of licensing and the Licensing Board was responsible for carrying out licensing responsibility. Its Board enjoyed the power to grant or deny, renew or refuse to be renewed, withdrawn through suspension, withdrawn temporarily through suspension or withdrawn altogether.[194]

It was not simply routine public registration but rather licensing provided a means of requiring the payment of a tax, and a means of conditioning certain private activities in the public interest. It also demanded the requirement of entry into entrepreneurship. In the context of Evaton, licensing prevented local commercial activities, such as illegal trade, from developing into a nuisance. The official justification of local licensing was that it prohibited nuisance activities for the benefit of the local communities.[195] This was the case with local slaughter-houses which were deemed to be health hazards. It was the same with brick making and the air pollution that the industry caused. In Evaton, licensing was associated with inspection which was an effective device employed by the local Health Committee to ensure that the physical facilities provided by the licensee were up to standard and that certain consumer goods were delivered properly to the consumers. Licensing, therefore, ensured that communities were served honestly, fairly and satisfactorily.

It is, therefore, important for this section to interrogate the procedures and the legal requirements for the issuing of licenses in Evaton. The issuing of licenses in Evaton was governed by the Rural Licensing Board. There were a number of government departments that were involved in the process. The application for a license was officially circulated within the Police Department which was under the authority of Special Justice of the Peace, the Department of Labour and the office of the Native Commissioner. Each office had to assess the application and give its recommendation report to the Licensing Board. The police had to assess the social background and criminal records of the applicant and submit a recommendation to the Chief Native Commissioner and the approval of the Minister would then be sought. In the case of renewals, the Chief Native Commissioner delegated the authority to approve.[196] The issuing of trade licenses in Small Farms which was by then new was in the hands of the Licensing Board without the intervention of the Department.[197]

In the case of Jim Joubert's application for license, the local police vouched for his good character and could say nothing negative about him.[198] From the records it appears that the Department of Native Labour evaluated work and business experience and educational background. For the application to be assessed and approved, educational, criminal, work experience and financial status were evaluated by these departments. The Native Affairs Department also assessed the geographical location of the proposed business and its proximity to a similar commercial establishment in the vicinity. If an applicant was illiterate, that is, he or she could not read and write, the application was turned down. Responding to Jim Joubert's application, the Special Justice for Peace wrote, 'Applicant has had no schooling, cannot read and write and the only official language he speaks is Afrikaans. He will not be able to comply with Section 134 Act 24 1936 and has no intention of keeping books'.[199] The issue of geographical proximity was noted in Josiah Moagi's application letter where the Additional Native Commissioner, I.P. O'Driscoll, pointed out, 'In view of the fact that the applicant has no educational or any experience of business, and there is a butchery nearby, I am unable to recommend the application'.[200] Moagi's proposed butchery was to be located ¾'s of a mile away from Mabasa's butchery.[201] The issue of capital also inhibited entry to the entrepreneurial world during the application process. Responding to John Ntsene's application, O'Driscoll wrote, 'The applicant's meagre capital, it is doubtful whether either venture could be successfully conducted'.[202]

It was the same with John Mtsweni who was refused a license because of the location of his proposed butchery. The Secretary of Native Affairs wrote to Mtsweni, 'I have the honour to inform you that this application was refused as it was considered that there are sufficient...butchers in the Evaton Township'.[203] Unlike other applicants who never challenged the decision of the Licensing Board, Mtsweni challenged the refusal which he regarded as unfair. Before he applied for a license, Mtsweni carefully explored different business activities and potential locations as well as categories within which his business fell. In order for him to obtain a licence, he also followed the required procedure during his application. He was aware what was required and what his trading space should look like. 'Before applying many applicants ensured their premises met the required standard which most of the applicants like my father did'.[204] As he met all these requirements before applying, Mtsweni felt that the decision of the Secretary of Native Affairs was unfair; he then challenged it with the help of legal experts who petitioned the Secretary. B. Pencharz, his attorney, wrote

> With regard to the first paragraph of your letter under reply, we would point out that in 1942, the writer interviewed the late Col Denys Reitz who was then the Minister of Native Affairs in regards to the very point raised by you, and as a result of such interview, the writer was informed that in future your Department would regard each case on its merits and would not take up the attitude that there were already sufficient licenses.
>
> With regard to the second paragraph of your letter under reply, we are informed by the applicant that he will have a commencing capital of £150.0.0 which we think should be sufficient for his purpose, and that he will obtain the service of a bookkeeper at the minimum sum of £1 .0.0.[205]

The Secretary of Native Affairs responded

> In reply to your letter... I have the honour to inform you that in view of the content paragraph thereof, the Department is prepared to reconsider the application...it will be necessary for the view of the Rural Licensing Board to be obtained, and I shall be

glad if you will request Mtsweni to make a formal application to the Board and advise me of the result thereof.[206]

The outcome of the attorney's petition helped Mtsweni receive a license which the Minister approved. The provision of the Proclamation No 104 of 1933 (amended in 1952) provided that no business should be established within two miles of the similar trading site already occupied. This rule was successfully challenged by Mtsweni who won the case. The issue of licensing procedure was also challenged by a group of local entrepreneurs who belonged to the Evaton Native Traders Association, which laid a complaint before the Native Affairs Department about the delay in granting trading licenses.[207] In response to this grievance, the Department acknowledged that the procedure for dealing with licences was cumbersome and varied according to the situation of the trading site.[208] Attempting to solve this problem, the Department felt that the application procedure was complicated and needed to be simplified. The Native Commissioner recommended that, 'In order to simplify the procedure in the Released Area, we recommend that the Chief Native Commissioner be given delegate authority to approve of the new licenses in the Released Area, as well as renewals, in terms of Section 24 of the Native Trust and Land Act, 1936'.[209]

It is clear from the surviving sources that most trade license applicants were not educated. For economic reasons, most of these applicants did not have a formal education that satisfied the screening process of the Rural Licensing Board – the economic status of their parents did not enable them to access formal education, which was expensive at the time. Along with other requirements, education became one of the critical resources for acquiring trade licenses. Their desire to venture into entrepreneurship was motivated by a number of reasons that were beyond their control. One of these motives was low wages which has already been presented. This implies that they were motivated by financial rewards, such as increasing income at the time when income inequality was rising in the South African labour market. Apart from that, they wanted to create jobs for themselves in order to be independent and enjoy self-actualisation.

It is then important to interrogate the effect which entrepreneurial restructuring had on individuals and how it stimulated illegal dealings. From the local entrepreneurs' point of view, the laws that governed local enterprises, especially business registration and taxation systems, were overly complex and difficult to understand. Mokwena recalled:

> we could not understand what the government wanted, and it was not easy to get licenses, we would have enough money for opening up business, then they would require education, you will have education then they would say no you don't have experience it was really frustrating.[210]

Local entrepreneurs were often subjected to lengthy and costly delays in clearances and the approval process. A survey of license application sources demonstrates that lack of capital was the greatest problem facing aspiring entrepreneurs. In the case of Katy and Richard Ntshika's application, I.P. O'Driscoll, the Additional Native Commissioner, responded to their application as follows, '... neither of the applicants have any experience, and they have only £11 capital, and in view of the Special Justice of the Peace's Evaton remarks, I do not recommend the application'.[211] The requirement of experience meant that the founders should have worked in the industry or operated the business before. Certainly, experience had a huge positive effect when entrepreneurs had it, but it was unreasonable for the Board not to give a chance to those who had the desire to take entrepreneurial risks to prove themselves. Perhaps experience was used as a justification to discourage those who desired to venture into entrepreneurship.

It is, therefore, clear that local entrepreneurship was marked by different strategies that aimed at hindering or rather discouraging aspirant entrepreneurs from entering into entrepreneurship, as in the case of J. Leburu, who before applying for a butcher's license in 1946 worked as an agent for African Life Insurance Company in Johannesburg and as a block man in a butchery in Pimville for 4 years, with STD 7'.[212] His application was turned down on the basis that there was a nearby butcher, owned by Isaac Moeketsi, next to his proposed business premises which was approximately 500 yards away.[213] In the opinion of the Special Justice of the Peace, there were sufficient butcheries in Evaton to fulfil the needs of the population.[214] He was also refused on the fact that he had only £35 to finance his business.[215] License application requirements were tricky, and Licensing Board officials were aware that it was difficult for Africans to meet all the requirements. These tactics legitimised the denial of licenses, while officials overlooked business integrity and good character. The question of business integrity and good character is arguable considering there is no evidence whether business applicants really were competent or not.

Most licenses were associated with daily fresh products such as milk; vegetable and mineral water, appear to have been granted by the Rural Licensing Board. At a more general level, these businesses seem to have been committed to the healthy well-being of local residents. They provided critical opportunities to increase access to healthy foods, including fresh fruits and vegetables. It could be argued that the promotion of healthy food was in line with the national policy on health and labour. It is difficult to establish whether the role of the Rural Licensing Boards in promoting healthy shops was compelling when considering that much of the discussion about the position of Africans within South African society revolved around problems of health. During this period, the health problem rhetoric became the central justification for implementing a system of urban segregation.[216] The promotion of these stores and health were multifaceted. On the one hand, it served as a means to undo African economic progress which had already been made in Evaton. On the other hand, it aimed to control local enterprises and benefit from local revenues while promoting a healthy workforce.

Arguing from the health perspective, a better understanding of how these enterprises created a demand for healthy and less healthy purchasing patterns appears to have been part of the toolkit of the Peri-Urban Health advocates and officials. These health measures appear to have been evoked to foster specific sets of political and economic interests in South Africa and were part of the language of legitimation. This is reflected in Jim Joubert's[217] application letters for a fresh produce licence. I.P. O'Driscoll, the Additional Native Commissioner, wrote:

> The application is recommended, notwithstanding his meagre capital and lack of education and experience as no great measure of these qualifications is required to conduct a business of Fresh Produce Dealer, and it is thought desirable that the use of fresh fruit and vegetable be encouraged amongst residents of Evaton Native Township.[218]

It should be noted that the central government incorporated Evaton as part of the local industrial labour pool and the Board was concerned with local economic regeneration against a wider backdrop of a changing manufacturing economy in the 1940s. This prompted the Board to put its emphasis on the promotion of a healthy local workforce which included elements of physiology, infectious diseases, hygiene and health promotion and nutrition.

Conclusion

The chapter has shown that African entrepreneurship in Evaton was free from government legislation until the 1940s. The emergence of a wide range of control measures resulted from the population explosion that placed Evaton in the spotlight. These measures were introduced through health parlance that was used by the Peri-Urban Health Board as an excuse for the implementation of trade licenses. It is possible that with the new entrepreneurial policy shops arose from the change that was introduced by the National Party and white pressure groups. This is evident in the tone of the letters that were sent by the Evaton Health Committee to the Native Affairs Department. The newly introduced by-laws impacted negatively on butcheries which formed important local entrepreneurial activity.

Notes

[1] L. Kuper, *African Bourgeoisie*.

[2] P. Morris, *A History of Black Housing in South Africa*, Johannesburg, South African Foundation, 1981.

[3] Ibid, p. 36.

[4] D Van Tonder, 'First Win the War, The Clear the Slums, The Genesis of the Western Removal Scheme, 1940-1949,' Unpublished paper presented at the History Workshop, University of the Witwatersrand, 1990.

[5] R. Sternberg and S. Wennerkers, The Effect of Business Regulations on Nascent and Young Business Entrepreneurship, *Small Business Economics*, 2007 *(28)*.

[6] M. Swanson, Urban Origins of Separate Development, *African Studies*, 1976.

[7] Native Urban Area Act of 1923, Government Printers UG 22, 1923.

[8] Wits Historical Papers, A letter from the Secretary for Bantu Administration and Development to Messrs. Broomberg Graaf and Karb, SAIRR collection, AD 843 RJ file F1, 18 December 1961.

[9] Wits Historical Papers, A letter from Director of Native Affairs to Dr Xuma, Xuma Papers AD 843, ABX 440706, 6 July 1944.

[10] Ibid

[11] M. Swanson, Urban Origins.

[12] S.M.S. Keeble, The expansion of Black Business.

[13] A. Cobley, *Class and Consciousness*.

[14] Ibid

[15] Ibid, p. 38

[16] Correspondence between the Director of the Institute of Race Relations and the Secretary for Native Affairs, 14 December 1955, AD 843 RJ Records of the South African Institute of Race Relations papers, Historical Papers, University of the Witwatersrand.

[17] C.M. Rogerson, Feeding the common people of Johannesburg.

[18] The Act quoted from S.M.S. Keeble, The expansion of Black Business.

[19] M. W. Swanson, 'The Rise of Multiracial Durban: Urban History and Race Policy in South Africa, 1830-1930' unpublished Ph.D. thesis, Harvard University, 1964. T. R. H. Davenport, 'African townsmen? South African (Natives) Urban Areas Legislation Through the Years', *African Affairs*, 68 1969 'The triumph of Colonel Stallard', *South African Historical Journal*, 1970, *The Beginnings of Urban Segregation in South Africa* Grahamstown, 1971. 4 See, for instance, P. Mayer, *Townsmen or Tribesmen* Cape Town, 1963, B. A. Pauw, *The Second Generation* Cape Town, 1963.

[20] H. Wolpe 'Capitalism and cheap labour in South Africa: From Segregation to Apartheid' *Economy and Society*, 1(4):425-456, 1972.

[21] A. Cobley, *Class and Consciousness*.

[22] Ibid

[23] T. Keegan, 'Crisis and Catharsis in the Development of Capitalism, S. Meintjies, Edendale 1850-1906: A case study of rural transformation and class formation, N. Etherington, 'African Economic Experiments in Colonial Natal 1845-1880.

[24] T.H.R Davenport, *The Afrikaner Bond: The History of South African Political Party, 1880-1911*, Cape Town, Oxford University Press, 1966.

[25] T. Keegan, *Rural Transformation.*

[26] Ibid

[27] D. O' Meara, *Volks-kapitalisme: Class Capital and Ideology in the Development of Afrikaner nationalism 1934-1948*, Cambridge, Cambridge University Press, 1983.

[28] P. Maylam, 'Explaining the Apartheid City: 20 Years of South African Urban Historiography,' *Journal of Southern African Studies*, Vol 21, No.1 1995.

[29] P. Bonner and N. Nieftagodien, *Alexandra*, p, 31.

[30] Ibid, p. 5.

[31] T. Lodge Political Organization in Pretoria's African Township in B. Bozzoli (ed) *Class Community and Conflict: South African Perspective*, Johannesburg, Ravan Press, 1987.

[32] J. Nhlapo *Wilberforce Institute*, Boitshoko Institute,1949.

[33] J. Nhlapo *Wilberforce Institute*, Boitshoko Institute,1949.

[34] Ibid

[35] Ibid

[36] T Keegan, *Rural Transformation* pp. 18-25.

[37] Interview with Daniel Moagi, conducted by Vusi Kumalo, Evaton, 21 May 2011.

[38] Interview with Dwight Deremi, conducted by Vusi Kumalo, Evaton, 16 May 2011.

[39] Interview with William Mokoena, conducted by Vusi Kumalo, Evaton, 17 May 2011.

[40] Interview with Dwight Seremi, conducted by Vusi Kumalo, Evaton, 16 May 2011.

[41] Interview with Sonto Kekane, conducted by Vusi Kumalo, Evaton, 16 May 2011.

[42] Interview with Thembi Tshabangu conducted by Vusi Kumalo, Evaton, 18 May 2011.

[43] National Archive of South Africa, Notes on Information Gleaned through telephone enquiries, Evaton Location, NTS 361/364, undated.

⁴⁴ Native Labour, *Friend* 26 February 1892. See C. Murray, 'Land of the Barolong: Annexation and Alienation, unpublished paper.

⁴⁵ T. Keegan, *Rural Transformation*.

⁴⁶ S. Menjties, 'Edendale 1850-1906.

⁴⁷ National Archive of South Africa, The Report of the Native Commissioner on Evaton, TPB 1305, 1938.

⁴⁸ P. Morris, *A History of Black Housing in South Africa, Johannesburg*, South Africa Foundation, 1981.

⁴⁹ Wits Historical Papers, Wilberforce Institute Financial Statement, A B Xuma Papers, AD 843, 1932-1933.

⁵⁰ Ibid

⁵¹ National Archive of South Africa, A letter from the Native Commissioner to the Chief Native Commissioner GNLB, 273, 22 November 1955.

⁵² Ibid

⁵³ Ibid

⁵⁴ National Archive of South Africa, A letter from Sergeant Pretorious to the Magistrate of Vereeniging, Enforcement of Dog Tax at Evaton Township, NTS 361/362, 16 May 1933.

⁵⁵ Interview with Daniel Motuba, conducted by Vusi Kumalo, 29 March 2011.

⁵⁶National Archive of South Africa, A letter from Secretary of Native Affairs to the Provincial Secretary, NTS 361/364, 12 August 1946.

⁵⁷ Interview with William Mokwena, conducted by Vusi Kumalo Evaton, December 2010.

⁵⁸ Ibid

⁵⁹ Interview with Mjikisi Maseko conducted by Vusi Kumalo, Evaton, 11 May 2011.

⁶⁰ Interview with John Maseko, conducted by Vusi Kumalo, Evaton, 13 June 2010.

⁶¹ Interview with William Mokwena, conducted by Vusi Kumalo, Evaton, 12 May 2011.

⁶²Interview with Dwight Seremi, conducted by Vusi Kumalo, Evaton, 11 May 2011.

[63] Interview with David Qupe, conducted by Vusi Kumalo, Evaton, 23 June 2011.

[64] Interview with Solani Nkabinde, conducted by Vusi Kumalo, Evaton, 23 May 2011.

[65] *Inyanga* is a man or women who has an extensive knowledge of African herbs that heal different kinds of diseases.

[66] Interview with Johannes Buthelezi, conducted by Vusi Kumalo, Evaton 21 June 2011.

[67] Interview with James Nkosi, conducted by Vusi Kumalo, Evaton, 28 May 2013.

[68] Interview with Solani Nkabinde, conducted by Vusi Kumalo, 28 May 2013.

[69] South African National Archives, A letter from R T Luther to the Secretary for Native Affairs dated, GNLB 273/ 3, April 1917.

[70] National Archive of South Africa, A letter from the Acting Chief Pass Officer to the Director of Native Labour, GNLB 273 160/17/030. Undated.

[71] Ibid

[72] It is common in African communities for elderly women to be addressed by youngster as *me* in SeSotho or *mamu* in IsiZulu.

[73] Interview with Christina Meku, conducted by Vusi Kumalo, Evaton, 27 June 2011.

[74] T. Burke, *Lifebouy Men, Lux Women: Commodification, Consumption and Cleanliness in Modern Zimbabwe*, London, Leicester University, 1996.

[75] Interview with Mary Maseko, conducted by Vusi Kumalo, Evaton, 20 May 2012.

[76] D. Gaitskell, 'Housewives, Maids or Mothers: Some contradistinctions of Domesticity for Christian Woman,' *Journal of African History*, 24, 1983.

[77] Interview with Dwight Seremi, conducted by Vusi Kumalo, Evaton, 12 July 2011.

[78] Johannesburg Joint Council for European quoted in D. Gaitskell, 'Housewives, Maids or Mothers.

[79] Ibid

[80] Interview with Sonto Kekane, conducted by Vusi Kumalo, Evaton, 13 May 2011.

[81] Quoted in the African National Congress Deputation on Increased Railroad, Wits Historical Papers Xuma Papers, ABX 441002, 1944.

[82] Interview with Sonto Kekane, conducted by Vusi Kumalo, Evaton, 13 May 2011.

[83] G. Hart, *Some Socio Economic Aspects,* R. B. Savage, *A Study of Bantu Retail.*

[84] Ibid

[85] Interview with Christina Meku, conducted by Vusi Kumalo, Evaton, 27 June 2011.

[86] Interview with Sonto Kekane, conducted by Vusi Kumalo, Evaton, 13 May 2011.

[87] Interview with Christina Meku, conducted by Vusi Kumalo, Evaton, 27 June 2011.

[88] Interview with Mafika Nkutha, conducted by Vusi Kumalo, Evaton, 13 April 2009.

[89] Interview with Tladi Kekane, conducted by Vusi Kumalo, Evaton, 7 July 2010.

[90] P. Bonner and N. Nieftagodien, *Alexandra.*

[91] Interview with Mjikisi Maseko, conducted by Vusi Kumalo, Evaton, 12 April 2009.

[92] Interview with Tladi Kekane, conducted by Vusi Kumalo, 7 July 2010, De Deur.

[93] E. Mphahlele, The Evaton Riots, unpublished paper, www.disa.ukzn.ac.za/webpages/DC/asjan57.11/asjan57. 11pdf

[94] National Archive of South Africa, Report of the Inspection at Evaton Native Township, NTS 361/364, 9 September 1938.

[95] R. Leigh, *Vereeniging History,* Vereeniging, 1968.

[96] Interview with Mjikisi Maseko, conducted by Vusi Kumalo, 28 May 2013.

[97] Ibid

[98] Native Commissioner's Report on Transport, Pretoria, Government Printers, 1943.

[99] Wits Historical Papers, ANC Deputation on Increased Rail Fares, Xuma Collection, ABX 441002, 2 October 1944.

[100] Wits Historical Papers, ANC Deputation on Increased Rail Fares, Xuma Collection, ABX 441002, 2 October 1944.

[101] Ibid

[102] Ibid

[103] National Archive of South Africa, A letter from McCrobet and De Villiers Attorneys to the Secretary for Native Affairs, NTS 376 252/56, 16 February 1930.

[104] Interview with Mary Maseko, conducted by Vusi Khumalo, Evaton, 28 July 2010.

[105] Ibid

[106] Interview with Dwight Seremi, Daniel Motuba, Paul Seshabela conducted by Vusi Khumalo, Evaton, 31 July 2010.

[107] Interview with Dwight Seremi, conducted by Vusi Kumalo, Evaton, 20 July 2009.

[108] Interview with Daniel Motuba, conducted by Vusi Kumalo, Evaton, 21 May 2010.

[109] Ibid

[110] Interview with Daniel Motuba, conducted by Vusi Kumalo, August 2011.

[111] ibid

[112] Ibid

[113] Ibid

[114] At that time electricity was confined largely to white areas, all African townships lacked electricity while white suburbs enjoyed the benefits of electricity. This was not compatible to a country in which coal resources were almost unlimited. Effort was made to bring coal in the form of electric light and power to African townships to brighten homes, for cooking, heating washing and refrigeration.

[115] Interview with Mary Maseko, conducted by Vusi Khumalo, 20 May 2010.

[116] L. Bank, The Social Life of Paraffin: Gender, Domesticity and the Politics of Value in Southern African Township (ed) M. McAllister, *Culture and the Commonplace: Anthropological Essays in Honour of David Hammond-Tooke*, Wits University Press, 1997.

[117] Ibid

[118] Interview with Tladi Kekane, conducted by Vusi Khumalo.

[119] Motuba interview

[120] National Archive of South Africa, A letter from S. P Bunting Attorneys Notary and Conveyances written to the Secretary for Native Affairs, NTS 361/364, 28 September 1931.

[121] S. Parnel, 'Creating Racial Privilege: The Origins of South African Public Health and Town Planning Legislation,' *Journal of South African Studies*, Vol. 19, 1993, pp, 417-488.

[122] S. Parnel, Creating Racial Privilege: The Origins of South African Public Health and Town Planning Legislation, *Journal of South African Studies*, Vol 19, 1993, pp, 417-488.

[123] National Archive of South Africa, Evaton Native Township and Evaton Small Farms: Released Area No.8 Transvaal, NTS 361/364, 13 June 1946.

[124] National Archive of South Africa, Interim Report No.7 in respect of Evaton, District of Vereeniging, in the Province of Transvaal, NTS 361/362, undated.

[125] National Archive of South Africa
Report of the inspection at Evaton Native Township on NTS 361/364 National Archive of South Africa, 9 September 1938.

[126] National Archive of South Africa, A letter from H.H Baillie to the Native Commissioner, TALG, 7 /15562, 12 April 1934.

[127] Ibid

[128] Interim Report No. 7 in respect of Evaton, District Vereeniging in the Province of the Transvaal, 11 March 1939, NTS 361/364 national Archive of South Africa.

[129] Ibid

[130] National Archive of South Africa, A letter from Baillie to the Native Commissioner, TALG 7/15571, 17 January 1937.

[131] National Archive of South Africa, Peri Urban Health Inspection, NTS 361/364, 3 May 1943.

[132] National Archive of South Africa, The Native Commissioner Report, NTS 361/364, 12 May 1941.

[133] National Archive of South Africa, A report of the Native Commissioner reporting to the Honourable the Minister of Native Affairs, NTS 361/364, 27 May 1947.

[134] National Archive of South Africa, A letter to the Provincial Secretary from the Secretary for Native Affairs, NTS 361/364, 18 June 1946.

[135] National Archive of South Africa, A letter from Sam Rom Attorneys to the Secretary for Native Affairs, NTS 361/364, 6 December 1945.

[136] National Archive of South Africa, A letter from the Standholders of Small Farm to the Secretary for Native Affairs, NTS 361/364, 12 May 1947.

[137] National Archive of South Africa, Notes of Discussion with Dr. Maule Clark on Health Conditions at Evaton Native Township, NTS, 361/364, 17 April 1947.

[138] Ibid

[139] Interview with Sam Mokoena, conducted by Vusi Kumalo, 12 February 2013, Evaton.

[140] National Archive of South Africa, Native Affairs Memo on Question of Local Authority for Evaton Native Affairs, NTS 361/364, 11 June 1953.

[141] National Archives of South Africa, Evaton Health Committee, Public Health By-Laws and Regulations Amendment, TALG 13/155562, 21 February 1951.

[142] Ibid

[143] National Archive of South Africa, The Report of the Acting Secretary to the Minister of Native Affairs, NTS 361/364, 27 May 1947.

[144] Ibid

[145] Ibid

[146] National Archive of South Africa, The Report of the Director of Native Agriculture on Evaton Native Slaughter Facilities, NTS 361/364, undated'

[147] Interview with Absolom Dlamini conducted by Vusi Khumalo, Evaton, 25 July 2011.

[148] National Archive of South Africa, The Report of the Deputy Director of Native Affairs entitled 'the future' NTS 361-364, undated.

[149] Ibid

[150] National Archive of South Africa, The Report of the Deputy Director of Native Affairs NTS 361-364, undated.

[151] National Archive of South Africa, Evaton Health Regulations, NTS 361/364, undated.

[152] Ibid

[153] National Archive of South Africa, Evaton Health Committee: Regulations and By-Law - General

[154] National Archive of South Africa, Evaton Health Committee: Regulations and By-Law2 - General

[155] National Archive of South Africa, Evaton Health Committee: Regulations and By-Law - General, TALG 7/15562, 1944.

[156] Ibid

[157] Interview with Thomas Mofokeng, conducted by Vusi Kumalo, 20 July 2012, Evaton.

[158] Interview with Absolom Dlamini, conducted by Vusi Kumalo, Evaton 12 May 2011.

[159] National Archive of South Africa, A letter from Sergeant F.H Brehrmann, to the Director of Native Labour, NTS 361/362, 12 September 1943.

[160] Ibid

[161] National Archive of South Africa, A letter from the Assistant Native Commissioner to the Native Commissioner NTS 1247 1385/162, 9 October 1951.

[162] National Archive of South Africa, A letter from H.H Baillie to the Native Commissioner NTS 1247 1385/162, 27 May 1929.

[163] Ibid

[164] National Archive of South Africa, Evaton Health Committee, Regulation for the Supervision, Regulation and control of Businesses, Trade and Occupation Amendments. TALG 13/155552, 1944.

[165] Interview with Absolom Dlamini, conducted by Vusi Kumalo, 2 July 2011, Evaton.

[166] Ibid

[167] Ibid

[168] Ibid

[169] Interview with Absolom Dlamini, conducted by Vusi Kumalo, 3 July 2011.

[170] Ibid

[171] Interview with Bheki Mthimkhulu, conducted by Vusi Kumalo, 12 May 2012, Sebokeng.

[172] National Archive of South Africa, Evaton Health Committee, Regulation for the Supervision, Regulation and control of Businesses, Trade and Occupation Amendments. TALG 13/155552, 1944.

[173] Ibid

[174] ibid

[175] Ibid

[176] National Archive of South Africa, A letter of trade license application by Jim Joubert, 29 March 1946, NTS 1244, 1323/162, undated.

[177] Interview with Thabang Khanyi, conducted by Vusi Kumalo, 12 May 2010, Evaton.

[178] Ibid

[179] National Archive of South Africa, Evaton Health Committee, Regulation for the Supervision, Regulation and control of Businesses, Trade and Occupation Amendments. TALG 13/155552, 1944.

[180] C Rogerson, Feeding the common people of Johannesburg, *Journal of Historical Geography* Vol 12, issue 1, pp 56-73.

[181] Ibid, p,58

[182] National Archive of South Africa, A letter from the Native Commissioner to Peri Urban Health Board, NTS 361/364, 23 May 1945.

[183] National Archive of South Africa, Evaton Health Committee, Regulation for the Supervision, Regulation and control of Business: Trade and Occupation amendments, TALG 13/155552, 1944.

[184] Ibid

[185] National Archive of South Africa, Evaton Health Committee, Regulation for the Supervision, Regulation and control of Business: Trade and Occupation amendments, TALG 13/155552, 1944.

[186] Ibid

[187] Ibid

[188] Ibid

[189] National Archive of South Africa, Evaton Health Committee, Executive Committee, 27 August 1954, TALG 13/155552.

[190] Interview with Christina Meku, conducted by Vusi Kumalo, 20 July 2011, Evaton.

[191] Report of the Commission of Inquiry into Trade Licensing and Allied Problem, Government Publisher, Union of South Africa U G 2, 1961.

[192] Ibid, p. 2

[193] Ibid

[194] Report of the Commission of Inquiry into Trade Licensing and Allied Problem, Government Publisher, Union of South Africa U G 2, 1961'

[195] Ibid

[196] National Archive of South Africa, Report of the Native Affairs Commissioner on Evatton Township, NTS 361/364, 27 May 1947.

[197] Ibid

[198] National Archive of South Africa, A letter of trade license application for Jim Joubert, NTS 1244 1330/162.

[199] Ibid

[200] National Archive of South Africa, A letter written by the Additional Native Commissioner in response to the trade license application of Josiah Moagi, NTS 1312/162, 12 April 1946.

[201] Ibid

[202] National Archive of South Africa, A letter written by the Additional Native Commissioners for the General Dealer application of John Ntsene NTS 361/364, 25 August 1946.

[203] National Archives of South Africa, Application for Butchery for John Mtsweni, NTS 1244, 1309/162, 6 September 1946.

[204] Interview with Absolom Dlamini, conducted by Vusi Kumalo, 20 July 2011, Evaton.

[205] National Archive of South Africa, Application for Butchery for John Mtsweni, NTS 1244 1309/162, 27 November 1946.

[206] National Archives of South Africa, Application for Butchery for John Mtsweni, NTS 1244

[207] National Archive of South Africa, Report of the Native Affairs Commissioner on Evaton Township, NTS 361/364, 27 May 1947.

208 Ibid

209 Ibid

210 Interview with William Mokwena, conducted by Vusi Kumalo, 12 July 2012, Evaton.

211 National Archive of South Africa, Application for Trade License of Katy and Richard Ntshika, NTS 25 August 1946.

212 National Archives of South Africa, Application for Trade License of J. Leburu NTS 1310/162, 13 August 1946.

213 Ibid

214 Ibid

215 ibid

216 M Swanson, The Sanitation Syndrome: Bubonic Plague and Urban Segregation in the Cape Colony, 1900- 1909. *Journal of African History*. 18(3): 1977, p. 387-410.

217 We should not be confused by the surname of Joubert as referring to a white resident, it was stated in previous chapters that there were groups of Oorlams in Evaton who were officially classified as coloureds. These coloureds had white surnames that they acquired.

218 National Archive of South Africa, Application for Trade License of Jim Joubert, NTS 1244 1330/162, 14 October 1946.

Chapter 4

Conclusion

This historical study was motivated largely by the fact that Africans were deprived of economic and political autonomy by successive white governments. This deprivation lies in the complex and inter-connected processes of dispossession experienced by Africans, first of their land and second of economic independence.[1] This study has drawn attention to a number of significant reactions to the processes of dispossession, displacement and economic subjugation. Firstly, it illustrated how property ownership influenced local community formation, and how it worked against the backdrop of the land restrictions faced by Africans. Secondly, it shed light on how displaced and broken rural communities reshaped themselves in a new space where they enjoyed relative autonomy. Thirdly, it captured how the complex processes of internal community formation were shaped by government decrees that combined internal structuring and development, giving Evaton its distinct character. Economically, Africans were increasingly losing their economic independence and becoming proletarianised. This study was thus also concerned with illustrating the struggles of a group of Africans for economic independence within a particular locality. This was explained through analysing the economic developments that discussed matters such as subsistence economy to the rise of entrepreneurship. This was also captured through the examination of one group of people, defined by their presence in Evaton, from the time they departed from their various farming areas to establish various entrepreneurial activities.

This study did not only present the connection between local entrepreneurs and the notion of economic independence in

Evaton in the first half of the twentieth century. It offered insights into the relationship between freehold settlements and the fulfilment of personal desires restricted by discriminating laws. It has shown how Evaton was seen by different categories of Africans as a space where they could escape certain state restrictions. It also captures how the locality provided opportunities for basic economic and educational advancement. Evaton offered new opportunities that Africans were denied by the state. In addition to entrepreneurship, the establishment of the Wilberforce Institute by the AME Church reflected the desire by Africans for autonomous and African-controlled education. The other was the establishment of independent churches which reacted against religious domination. In these churches, Africans were inspired to preach without authorisation and surveillance from white missionaries. Most importantly, it was self-governance that Evaton enjoyed. The settlement provided relative autonomy and an attractive urban destination for the regulated migration of African workers. It also allowed stand-holders to create social relationships by forming supportive community groups, self-help and mutual aid. This generated internal community solidarity and local networks that cut across ethnic lines. These social networks were clearly reflected in independent churches.

In the late 1930s and 1940s, when the area experienced a spurt in population growth, the local economic activity was transformed. This quickened the pace of urbanisation that emerged along with new economic activities. It gave residents an opportunity to grow economically by investing in businesses. Some residents turned from subsistence farming to become entrepreneurs. As a freehold settlement, Evaton may be perceived as the social space that provided commercial opportunities away from white urban towns and locations. The freehold status and its relaxed laws attracted urban entrepreneurs who could not grow economically in other urban locations. Importantly, African women enjoyed considerable independence in Evaton. This was displayed by their role in business. Local women were involved in income-generating activities in a form of entrepreneurship. During these years, African women in urban areas of South Africa dominated the beer brewing enterprises. Other women were not economically active but rather assisted their families through the physically demanding work of maintaining a subsistence economy in the reserves. Others were active in doing washing for whites. Unlike the large group of African women who engaged in the illicit beer brewing activity, local women were hawkers who traded food products and crafts in urban Johannesburg. For the Christians in Evaton, the beer brewing activity was the most disliked activity partly because of the social disorder that local migrant tenant Basotho women caused through this enterprise. This shed light on how local women played an important role in feeding Johannesburg, a topic which has received little attention from historians. This also provides an insight on the connection between Evaton and Johannesburg and the relative role of food consumption and production. This implies that local women formed a chain of food suppliers to the growing city of Johannesburg. The research has explained how purported health concerns impacted on business regulatory measures, and particularly in butcheries. It has also shown how new regulations contributed to the demise of butcheries and shops. Interestingly, though not distinct to Evaton, the study connects entrepreneurial regulatory measures and the manner in which the government came to assert its control over Evaton. This investigation compared two different periods, the era before and after 1940. These two periods presented two different administration approaches. Firstly, the period when the Native Commissioners had a limited role in local affairs. Secondly, the subsequent era when virtually every aspect of Evatonian's lives was subjected to the intrusion of clerks, bureaucrats and administrators of one sort or another. In the period before the 1940s, Evaton presented a different entrepreneurial environment that was free of regulations, and unlimited trade opportunities. For the local entrepreneurial community, freehold tenure implied that they were permanent residents rather than temporary visitors in urban areas. They traded freely in their own spaces. They could build any type of structure without application to building authorities. There were no regulations that regulated what to trade and how.

In the 1940s, the changing political and economic conditions in South Africa ushered in a new set of dynamics for Evaton entrepreneurs. These conditions impacted on the freehold status that precluded the national government to gain total control over the local economy. Given the relative independence that Evaton enterprises displayed, local entrepreneurship demonstrated a strong commercial character that attributed prospects for bright future growth and commercial development. The interference of the central government in the administration of local affairs presented, however, a turning point in the history of the local economy. New regulations and licenses were implemented and restrained local economic independence and the freehold status of the area. The settlement status was degraded into a municipality-controlled township, local commercial activities that prevented residents from working in white industries declined and the culture of labour market dependence emerged.

Notes

---

[1] C. Murray, 'Land of the Barolong: Annexation and Alienation,' unpublished seminar paper, University of London, 1984.

Bibliography

Books and articles

Ballard, C. (1991). 'The Repercussions of Rinderpest: Cattle Plague and Peasant Decline in Colonial Natal,' *International Journal of African Historical Studies*, Vol. 19, 1986

Baines, G. (1990). Origins of Urban Segregation: Local Government and the Residence of Africans in Port Elizabeth 1845-1865, *South African Historical Journal*, Vol 22

Balandier, G. (1970). *Sociology of Black Africa* London

Bank, L. (1991). Beyond the Bovine Mystique: Entrepreneurship, Class and Identity, A seminar paper that was presented in the Institute for African Studies, University of the Witwatersrand

Berger, I. (2001). An African American 'Mother of the Nation' : Madie Hall Xuma in South Africa, 1940-1963, *Journal of African Studies, Vol 27*

Beinart, W. Delius, P and Trapido, S. (1984). *Putting the Plough on the Ground: Accumulation and Dispossession in Rural South Africa 1850-1930*, Johannesburg, Ravan Press, 1986

Bergh. J and H Feinberg, (2004) 'Trusteeship and Black Land Ownership During the Nineteenth and the Twentieth Century,' *Kleio, 36: 1, 170-193*

Bonner, P. (1988). Desirable or Undesirable Sotho women? Liquor, Prostitution and the Migration of Sotho Women to the Rand 1920-1945. A seminar paper that was delivered in African Studies Institute, University of the Witwatersrand

------------- (1982). The Transvaal Native Congress 1917-190: Radicalisation of the Black Petty Bourgeoisie on the Rand *in S Marks and R Rathbone (ed)Industrialisation and Social Change in South Africa: African Class Formation, Culture and Consciousness 1870-1930*. New York, Longman Group

---------- (1995). 'African Urbanisation on the Rand Between the 1930 and 1960: its Social Character and Political Consequences', *Journal of Southern African Studies*, Vol 21 No.1, p 115-129

---------- (1990). An Evil Empire: The Russian on the Reef 1947-1957, A paper presented to the 5th History Workshop, at the University of the Witwatersrand

Bonner, P. and Nieftagodien, N. (2009). *Alexandra: A History*, Johannesburg, Wits University Press

Bonner, P. and Segal, L. (1998) *Soweto, A History*, Cape Town, Maskew Miller Longman

Bordner, J. (1989). Power and Memory in Oral History workers and Managers in Studerbaker, *The Journal of American History* Vol. 75 No.4 1989 pp. 1201-1221

Bradford, H. (1984). Mass Movement and the Petty Bourgeoisie: The Social Origins of the ICU leadership, 1924-19, *The Journal of African History*, Vol. 25, No 3, 1984

Braun, L. F. (2008). *The Cadastre and the Colony: Surveying territory and legibility in the Creation of South Africa* 1860-1913 Ann Arbor, Pro Quest, 2008

Burns, C, (2004) 'Controlling Birth 1920-1960' *Southern African Historical Journal*, Vol 50, 2004, pp, 170-198

Campbell, J. T. (1987). T D Mweli Skota and the making and unmaking of a Black elite, A seminar paper that was delivered at History Workshop, University of the Witwatersrand

---------- (1993). Social Origins of African Methodism in the Orange Free State, African Studies Seminar Paper presented at the University of the Witwatersrand.

---------- (1998). *The Songs of Zion The African Methodist Church in the United States and South Africa*, Chapel Hill, University of North Caroline Press

Carruthers, J. Urban Land Claim in South Africa: The Case of Lady Selborne Township, African Historical Review, Vol 22, 2000

Chanock, M. (2001). *The Making of South African Legal Culture: Fear, Favour, and Prejudice*, Cambridge, Cambridge University Press

Chakalson, M. (1986). The Road to Sharpeville, A Seminar Paper presented in the Institute for African Studies at the University of the Witwatersrand

Christopher, A. J. (1987). Apartheid Planning in South Africa, The Case of Port Elizabeth, *Geographical Journal*, Vol 153, No.2, pp 195 -204

Claasen, J. W (1995). Independents made Dependents. *Journal of Theology for Southern Africa*, 95:15-34.

Cochrane, J.R. (1987). Servants *of Power: the role of the English-speaking churches in South Africa 1903-1930* Johannesburg: Ravan.

Cobley, A. (1990). Class *and consciousness: the Black petty bourgeoisie in South Africa, 1924 to 1950*, New York, Greenwood

Curtin, D. P. (1965). *The Image of Africa: British Ideas and Action, 1780 -1850,* London

Cuthbertson, G. (1987). 'Missionary Imperialism and Colonial Warfare: London Missionary Society attitudes to the South African War, 1899-1902.' *South African Historical Journal*, 19:93-114.

Cuthbertson, G. (1995). "Cave of Adullam": Missionary Reaction to Ethiopianism at Lovedale, 1898-1902. *Missionalia* 19, no.1, April: 57-64.

Davenport, T. R. H (1991). *South Africa: A Modern History,* London, McMillan Press

Davenport, H.R (1966). *The Afrikaner Bond: The History of South African Political Party, 1880-1911*, Cape Town, Oxford University Press

Delius, P. and Trapido, S. (1983) 'Inboekseling and Oorlams: The Creation and Transformation of Servile Class, in B. Bozzoli (ed), *In Town and Countryside in the Transvaal: Capitalist Penetration and Popular Response*, Johannesburg, Ravan Press

Delius, P. (1984). *The Land Belong to Us: The Pedi Polity, the Boers and the British in the Nineteenth Century Transvaal*, Berkeley, University of California Press

Denis, P. (2003). 'Oral history in a wounded country in Draper, J. A. (ed) *Orality and Colonialism in Southern Africa*, Pietermaritzburg, Cluster Publications

Du Plessis, W. (1996). 'Historical Overview: Evolution of Land Tenure and Administration System in South Africa' International Conference Paper, Orlando, Florida

Elias, C. M. (1983). An Historical Review of the Supply of Housing for Urban Africans in the Cape Peninsula 1900-1982, unpublished paper, University of Stellenbosch, Department of Sociology, Occasional Paper 7, May 1983

Etherington, N. (1978), African Economic Experiments in Colonial Natal 1845-1880, *African Economic History*, No. 5

Field, S. (2001). *Lost Communities Living Memories: Remembering Forced Removals in the Cape,* Cape Town, David Phillip Publishers

Feinburg, H (1993). 'The 1913 Land Act in South Africa: Politics, Race and Segregation in the early 20th Century, '*International Journal of African Historical Studies*, Vol 26 No.1 pp 65-109

Gaitskell, D. (1983) 'Housewives, Maids or Mothers: Some contradistinctions of Domesticity for Christian Woman,' *Journal of African History*, Vol. 24

Galbraith, G. S. and Galbraith, D.M. (2007). An empirical note of entrepreneurial activity, intrinsic religiosity and economic growth, *Journal of Enterprising Communities: People and Places in Global Economy*, Vol, 1, No. 2

Gish S.D, (2000). A.B Xuma, *African, American, South Africa*, New York, New York University Press,

Gwala, N *(1989)* Political Violence and Struggle for Control in Pietermaritzburg, *Journal of Southern African Studies, Vol, 15, No. 3*

Guy, J. (1979). *The destruction of the Zulu Kingdom: The Civil War in Zululand, 1879-1884,* London Longman Publishers, 1979

Hart, G. (1972). *Some Economic Aspects of African Entrepreneurship: with particular reference to Transkei and Ciskei*, Institute of Social and Economic Research, Grahamstown Rhodes University

Hart, D. and G. Pirie, (1984). The Sight and Soul of Sophiatown, *Geographical Review,* Vol. 74, 1984

Harries, P. 'A Forgotten Corner of the Transvaal: Reconstruction the History of a Relocated Community through Oral Testimony and Song' in B. Bozzolli (ed) *Class Community and Conflict: South African Perspective.*

Horrell, M. (1960). *The Survey of the Race Relations In South Africa 1954-1970,* Johannesburg, South African Institute of Race Relations

Howarth, D. (1994). The Ideologies and Strategies of Resistance in Post-Sharpeville South Africa: Thoughts on Anthony Marx's Lessons of Struggle, *Africa Today,* Vol 41, pp. 21

Hughes, H. (2011). *First President: A life of John L Dube, founding president of the ANC*, Johannesburg, Jacana Media

Jalloh, A. (2003). 'Reconstruction Modern African Business History,' in T. Falola and C Jennings (ed) *Africanizing Knowledge: African Studies Across the Discipline*, Texas, Transaction Books

Joyce, P. '*(1995)*. The End of Social History,' *Social History, Vol, 20, No.1*

Katz, M. (1990). Undeserving Poor: *From the War on Poverty to the War on Welfare,* New York

Keegan, T. (1985). Crisis and Catharsis in the Development of Capitalism in South African Agriculture, *African Affairs,* 84

Keegan, T. (1987). *Lowdown to Highveld Rural Transformation in industrializing South Africa, The Southern Highveld to 1914* McMillan Press, London

Kuckertz, H. (1985). 'Organizing Labour Force on Mpondoland: A New Perspective on Work Parties,' *Journal of African International Institute,* Vol. 55

Kuper, L. (1965). *An African Bourgeoisie: race, class and politics in South Africa* New Haven, Yale University Press

Krige, E. and J. D. Krige. (1943). *The Realm of a Rain-Queen: A Study of the Pattern of Lovedu Society.* London: Oxford University Press

Lambert, J. (1999). 'African reasons for purchasing land in Natal in the late 19th, early 20th centuries,' *African Historical Review,* Vol. 31.1

La Hausse, P. (1990). The Cows of Nongoloza: Youth Crime and Amaliata in Durban 1900-1936, *Journal of Southern African Studies,* Volume 16, pp. 79-111

Landman, C. (1996). Christina Nku and the St John: Hundred Years Later, *Studia Historiae Ecclesiasticae Vol. 32 1-32*

Lambert, J. (1999). 'African reasons for purchasing land in Natal in the late 19th, early 20th centuries,' *African Historical Review,* Vol. 31.1

Letsoalo, E. (1987). Land Reform in South Africa, Green Paper on South African Land Policy, published in 1996

Lodge, T. (1987). Political Organisations in Pretoria's African Township, 1940-1963 in B Bozzoli (ed) *Class community and Conflict: South African Perspective,* Johannesburg, Ravan Press

Lodge, T. (1987). Political Organization in Pretoria's African Township in B. Bozzoli (ed) *Class Community and Conflict: South African Perspective,* Johannesburg, Ravan Press

Lulat. Y. G-m. (2008). *United States Relations with South Africa: A Critical Overview from the colonial period to present,* New York, Peter Lang

Mahoney, M (1999). 'The Millennium comes to Mapumulo: Popular Christianity in Rural Natal' 1866-1906, *Journal of Southern Africa Studies*, Vol. 25 No 3, pp. 375-391

Matsitela, T. (1982). The Life Story of Nkgono Mma-Pooe Aspect of sharecropping and proletarianisation in the Northern Orange Free State 1890-1930 in Marks, S. et al (ed) *Industrialization and Social Change in South Africa: African class formation, culture and consciousness 1870-1930*, London, Longman Publishers

Mayer, P. (1961). Xhosa *in Town: Studies of the Bantu-speaking population of East London*, Cape Town, Oxford University Press

Maylam, P (1983) 'African Squatters in Durban, 1935-1950, *Canadian Journal of African Studies* 17, 413-28

------------- 'Explaining the Apartheid City: 20 Years of South African Urban Historiography,' *Journal of Southern African Studies*, Vol 21, No.1 1995

Manson, A. (1998). 'Christopher Bethel and the Securing of the Bechuanaland Frontier, 1878-1884" *in Journal of Southern African Studies*, Volume 24, Number 3

Mancoe, J. (1934), *The Bloemfontein Bantu and Coloured People's Directory*, Bloemfontein, AC White P and P Printer

Marks, S. and Rathborne, R. (1982). *Industrialization and Social Change in South Africa: African class formation, culture and consciousness 1870-1930*, London, Longman Publishers

Marks, S. (1986). The *Ambiguities of Dependence in South Africa*. Johannesburg Ravan Press

Mathews, Z.K (1981). Let *My People Go Cape Town*, David Phillip Publishers

Mbiti, J. (1970). African *Religions and Philosophies*, New York, Doubleday and Company.

Meintjes, J, (1971). *Sandile: The Fall of the Xhosa Nation*, Cape Town, Molobi, V. (undated) The AICS and the Theological Training with Special Reference to the St John Apostolic

Church of Ma Nku, Research Institute for Theology and Religion

Murray, C. (1984) 'Land of the Barolong : Annexation and Alienation, unpublished seminar paper, University of London

Mphahlele, E (1959). *Down 2nd Avenue*, London, Faber and Faber

Mweli Skota, T.D. (1932). The *African Yearly Register*, Johannesburg: R.L. Esson and Co. Ltd

-------------------- (1965). *The African Who's Who*, Johannesburg: Central News Agency

Nieuwenhuysen, J. P. (1962). Iron and Steel – Future Industry for Border Area, *South African Journal of Economics*, Vol. 30

Nhlapo, J. (1949). *Wilberforce Institute*, Boitshoko Institute

Newman, R. (1983). 'Archbishop Daniel William Alexandra and the African Orthodox Church,' *The international Journal of Historical Studies*, Vol.16, No 4

Novak, W. J. (1993). Public Economy and the Well-Ordered Economy: Law and Economic Regulations in 19th Century America, *Law and Social Inquiry*, Vol.18, No. 1, p 1-32

O'Meara, (1983) D. *Volks-kapitalisme: Class Capital and Ideology in the Development of Afrikaner nationalism 1934-1948*, Cambridge, Cambridge University Press

Parker, P. and Mokhesi-Parker, J. (1998). *In the Shadow of Sharpeville: Apartheid and Criminal Justice*, New York, New York University Press

Parnell, S. M. (1987). Johannesburg Backyard: the slum of Doornfontein, Bertram and Prospect Township. History Workshop, University of the Witwatersrand

-------------- (1993). Creating Racial Privilege: The Origins of South African Public Health and Town Planning Legislation, *Journal of South African Studies*, Vol. 19, pp. 417-488

Peiries, J. (1987). The legend of Fenner-Solomon, Lawyer in Stockenstrom District in B. Bozzolli (ed) *Class Community and Conflict: South African Perspective*, Johannesburg, Ravan Press

Phillips, R.E. (1938). *Bantu in the City*, Alice, Lovedale Press

Plaatjie, S. (1996) *Native Life in South Africa*, Johannesburg, Ravan Press

Portelli, A. (1998). What makes oral history different? Robert Perks and Alistair Thompson (ed) *The Oral History Readers*, London

Posel, D. (1991). *The Making of Apartheid 1948-1961: Conflict and Compromise*, Oxford Clarendon Press

Pohlandt-McCormick, H (2000). 'I Saw a Nightmare . . .': Violence and the Construction of Memory,' *History and Theory*, Vol. 39

Peires, J (1976). *A History of the Xhosa 1700-1835*. Grahamstown, Rhodes University Press

Savage, R.B. (1966). *A Study of Bantu Retail Traders in Certain Areas of the Eastern Cape Institute of Social and Economic Research*, Grahamstown Rhodes University

R. Sternberg, R and Wennerkers, S (2007). The Effect of Business Regulations on Nascent and Young Business Entrepreneurship, *Small Business Economics, (28)*

Sunkler B. G. (1964). *Bantu prophets in South Africa*. London: Oxford University Press,

Reyburn, L. (1960). African *Traders: Their position and problems in Johannesburg South Western Township*, South African Institute of Race Relations

Rich, P. (1978). 'Ministering to the White Man's Needs: the Development of Urban Segregation in South Africa, 1913-1923', History Workshop Conference Paper, University of the Witwatersrand

Rich, P. (1989). 'Managing Black Leadership: The Joint Councils, Urban Trading and Political Conflict in the Orange Free State, 1925-1942;' in P. Bonner et al, (ed) Holding *Their Ground: Class Locality and Culture in 19th and 20th Century*, Ravan Press, Johannesburg

Rogerson, C (1986). Feeding the common people of Johannesburg, *Journal of Historical Geography* Vol 12, issue 1, pp 56-73

Saunders, C and C.W. de Kiewiet (1986), A History of South Africa and Economic History in Africa, Vol, 13, 323- 330

Seeking, J. (2000). The Rise and Fall of the Weberian Analysis of Class between 1949 and the early 1970s, Working Paper for Centre for Social Science Research, University of Cape Town

Shepperson, G (1953). 'Ethiopianism and African Nationalism', *Phylon,* Vol. 14.No.1 1940-1956, pp. 9-18

Swanson, M. (1977). The Sanitation Syndrome: Bubonic Plague and Urban Segregation in the Cape Colony, 1900- 1909. *Journal of African History.* 18(3): pp. 387-410

--------------(1976). Urban Origins of Separate Development, *African Studies,*

Sundkler, G.M. (1961). *Bantu prophets in South Africa.* London, International African Institute

Southall, R. (1980). African Capitalism in Contemporary South Africa, *Journal of Southern African Studies*, Vol. 7, No. 1

Trapido, S. (1986). Putting the Plough on the Soil, in Beinart, W, Delius, P and Trapido, S (ed) *Putting the Plough on the Soil*, Johannesburg, Ravan Press

Trotter, H. (undated). Truma and Memory: The Impact of Apartheid Era Forced Removals on Coloured Identity in Cape Town, unpublished paper Yale University

Thomas, A. (2001). 'It changed Everybody's lives: The Simon Town Group Areas Act Removals, in S. Field (ed) *Lost Communities Living Memories: Remembering Forced Removals in the Cape,* Cape Town, David Phillip Publishers

Thompson, A. (1998). 'Anzac Memories: putting popular memory theory into practise in Australia' in R, Perks and A Thomson (eds) *The Oral History Reader*, New York Routlegde.

Tonkin, E. (1992). *Narrating our Past: The Social construction of Oral History*. Australia, Cambridge University Press

Tosh. J, (1991). The *pursuit of history: aim methods and new directions in the study of modern history*, London, Longman publishers, 1991,

Van Onselen, C. (1996). *The Seed is Mine: The Life of Kas Maine A South African sharecropper 1894-1985*, Cape Town, David Phillip.

D Van Tonder, (1990). 'First Win the War, The Clear the Slums, The Genesis of the Western Removal Scheme, 1940-1949,' Unpublished paper presented at the History Workshop, University of the Witwatersrand

Visser, W. (2004). Trends in South African Historiography and the Present State of Historical Research, Paper presented at the Nordic Africa Institute, Uppsala, Sweden

Walshe. A P, (1969). 'The origins of African Political Consciousness in South Africa,' *Journal of Modern African Studies*, Vol. 7 No. 4, pp. 583-610

White, A. J. and White, L. G, (1953). *Dawn in Bantuland: An African Experiment or An Account of Missionary Experiences and Observation in South Africa*, Christopher Publishing House, Boston

Wilson, M and Mafeje A, (1963). *Langa*, Oxford University Press, Cape Town

Wolpe, H (1972). 'Capitalism and cheap labour in South Africa: From Segregation to Apartheid' *Economy and Society*, 1(4): pp. 425-456, 1972

Theses

Bear, A. (1998). Urbanisation and Settlement growth in the Pietermaritzburg, Durban Region, Unpublished MSc Thesis, University of Natal

D J Childs, (2009). The Black Church and the American Education: The African Methodist Episcopal Church Educating for Liberation, unpublished PhD Thesis, University of Miami

Cripps, E.A. (2012). Provisioning Johannesburg, Unpublished MA thesis, University of South Africa

Edward, I. (1989). Mkhumbane Our Home African Shanty Town Society, unpublished PhD Thesis, Durban, University of Natal, 1989

Fast, H. (1995). 'Pondoks, Houses and Hostels: A History of Nyanga, 1946-1970, with a Special Focus on Housing.' PhD Thesis, University of Cape Town, Cape Town

Field. S (1996). 'The Power of Exclusion: Moving Memories from Windermere to the Cape Flats, 1920-1990. PhD Thesis, University of Essex, Colchester

French, J. (1980). Mpanza, J and Sofasonke Party 1980, M.A. Dissertation Johannesburg, University of the Witwatersrand.

Glaser, C. (1990). 'Anti-Social Bandits, Juvenile Delinquency and the Tsotsi Gang Subculture on the Witwatersrand, 1935-1960,' Masters Thesis, University of the Witwatersrand

Lucas, J. (1995). Space, Society and Culture: Housing and Local Level Politics in a Section of Alexandra Township, 1991-1992, Master's Thesis, University of the Witwatersrand, Johannesburg

Kagan, N. (1978). African Settlements in the Johannesburg Area 1903-1923. Master's Thesis University of Witwatersrand, Johannesburg

Keeble, S. (1980). The Expansion of the Black Business into the South African Economy with Specific Reference to the Initiatives of the National African Federated Chamber of Commerce in the 1970s, Unpublished MA Thesis, University of the Witwatersrand, 1980

Mentjes, S. (1988). 'Edendale 1850-1906. A Case Study of Rural Transformation and Class Formation in an African Mission in Natal, PhD Thesis, University of London,

M. Ngcaba, The Decline of Rural Agriculture in the Rural Transkei: The Case of Mission Location in Butterworth, Unpublished Masters Thesis, Rhodes University, 2002

Ramoroka, M. D. (2009). 'The History of the Barolong in the District of Mafikeng: A study of the Intra Batswana Ethnicity and Political Culture from 1852-1950,' Unpublished PhD Thesis, University of Zululand

Rogerson, C (1983). The Casual Poor of Johannesburg, South Africa: the Rise and Fall of Coffee-Cart Trading. Ph.D. Thesis, Queen's University, Ontario, Canada

Tommasselli, R. (1983). The Indian Flower sellers of Johannesburg, Unpublished MA Thesis, University of the Witwatersrand,

Interviews

Interview with Alf Kumalo, conducted by Vusi Kumalo, 15 January 2011, Evaton

Interview with Tladi Kekane, conducted by Vusi Kumalo, 16 July 2009, Evaton

Interview with Lily Nondala and Moagi, conducted by Vusi Kumalo, 12 May 2011, Evaton

Interview with Joshua Vilakazi, conducted by Vusi Kumalo, 20 May 2012, Vereeniging

Interview with John Dandala, conducted by Vusi Kumalo, 20 October 2011, De Duer

Interview with Mjikisi Maseko, conducted by Vusi Kumalo 30 September 2009, Evaton

Interview with Mandla Maseko, conducted by Vusi Kumalo, 13 January 2010, Evaton

Interview with Lily Nondala, conducted by Vusi Kumalo 19 September 2010, Evaton

Interview with Mamokiti Seloane, conducted by Vusi Kumalo, 21 May 2012, Sebokeng

Interview with Mohlalepule Moloi, conducted by Vusi Kumalo, 23 July 2012, Phiri

Interview with Mjikisi Maseko, conducted by Vusi Kumalo, 29 December 2011, Evaton

Interview with Tladi Kekane, conducted by Vusi Kumalo, 7 July 2010, De Deur

Interview with Mjikisi Maseko, conducted by Vusi Kumalo, 29 December 2011, Evaton

Interview with Steven Shabe, conducted by Vusi Kumalo, 28 June 2012, Evaton

Interview with Sphiwe Tshabalala, conducted by Vusi Kumalo, 15 May 2009, Evaton

Interview with Dudu Nkabinde, conducted by Vusi Kumalo, 27 September 2010

Interview with Mjikisi Maseko, conducted by Vusi Kumalo, 29 December 2011, Evaton

Interview with Amos Masilela, conducted by Vusi Kumalo, 21 July 2012, Evaton

Interview with Lily Nondala, conducted by Vusi Kumalo, Evaton. 12 October; 2011

Interview with Sphiwe Tshabalala, conducted by Vusi Kumalo, 15 May 2009, Evaton

Interview with Skatane Moloi, conducted by Vusi Kumalo, 20 September 2012, Sharpeville

Interview with Lord McCamel, conducted by Vusi Kumalo, 23 November 2003, interviews for Evaton Regeneration Project

Interview with Jackson Mokwena, conducted by Vusi Kumalo, 12 June 2012, Evaton

Interview with Abram Mogale, conducted by Vusi Kumalo, 30 June 2012, Evaton

Interview with Jackson Mokwena, conducted by Vusi Kumalo 12 June 2012, Evaton

Interview with A K Mokale, conducted by Thamsanqa Flatela in Evaton on behalf of the Wits African Studies Institute 12 May 1982

Interview with Paul Seshabela, conducted by Vusi Kumalo, 10 September 2010, Evaton

Interview with Mjikisi Maseko, conducted by Vusi Kumalo, 11 June 2011, Evaton

Interview with Lucy Dlamini, conducted by Vusi Kumalo, 12 March 2010, Evaton

Interview with Absolom Dlamini, conducted by Vusi Kumalo, 12 March 2010, Evaton

Interview with Absolom Dlamini, conducted by Vusi Kumalo, 12 March 2010, Evaton

Interview with Lucy Dlamini, conducted by Vusi Kumalo, 12 March 2010, Evaton

Interview with Absolom Dlamini conducted by Vusi Kumalo, 12 March 2010, Evaton

Interview with Daniel Motuba, conducted by Vusi Kumalo, 25 May 2011, Evaton

Interview with Ben Tsotetsi, conducted by Vusi Kumalo, 12 May 2011, Evaton

Interview with Enoch Madonsela, conducted by Vusi Kumalo, 13 August 2012, Evaton

Interview with Daniel Motuba, conducted by Vusi Kumalo, 25 May 2011, Evaton

Interview with Jacob Sibeko , conducted by Vusi Kumalo, 23 May 2011, Evaton

Interview with Dumisa Qupe, conducted by Vusi Kumalo, 12 May 2011, Evaton

Interview with John Manana, conducted by Vusi Kumalo, 12 May 2012, Evaton

Interview with Mjikisi Maseko, conducted by Vusi Kumalo, 14 May 2010, Evaton

Interview with Tsepo Khanyi, conducted by Vusi Kumalo, , 3 July 2009, Evaton

Interview with Sonto Kekane, conducted by Vusi Kumalo, 4 July 2010, Evaton

Interview with Jacob Mofokeng, conducted by Vusi Kumalo, 9 June 2011, Evaton

Interview with James Mogale, conducted by Vusi Kumalo, 18 July 2011, Evaton

Interview with Dwight Seremi, conducted by Vusi Kumalo, 13 June 2011, Evaton

Interview with David Qupe, conducted by Vusi Kumalo, 21 July 2011. Evaton

Interview with Amos Moagi, conducted by Vusi Kumalo, 23 July 2010, Sebokeng

Interview with Aubrey Mofokeng, conducted by Vusi Kumalo, 15 May 2011, Evaton

Interview with Thembi Nkutha, conducted by Vusi Kumalo, 23 September 2011, Evaton

Interview with Paul Seshabela, conducted by Vusi Kumalo, 12 July 2010, Evaton

Interview with Paul Seshabela, conducted by Vusi Kumalo, September 2010, Evaton

Interview with Sonto Kekane, conducted by Vusi Kumalo, 4 July 2010, Evaton

Interview with Oupa Motuba, conducted by Vusi Kumalo, 7 January 2012

Interview with Merriam Pooe, conducted by Vusi Kumalo, 1 June 2012

Interview with Manuel Pheku, conducted by Vusi Kumalo, 2 July 2010, Evaton

Interview with William Ndlovu, conducted by Vusi Kumalo, 23 November 2011, Evaton

Interview with Paul Nkosi, conducted by Vusi Kumalo, 2 May 2011, Evaton

Interview with Abel Nkosi, conducted by Vusi Kumalo, 25 November 2010, Evaton

Interview with Bheki Mthimkhulu, conducted by Vusi Kumalo, 12 May 2012, Sebokeng

Online resources

Duncan G. A. Pull up Good Tree and Push it outside: The Rev Tsewu dispute with the Free Church of Scotland Mission, http://ngtt.up.ac.za

Bergh, J. and Feinberg, H. 'Trusteeship and Black Landownership in the Transvaal during and the Nineteenth and Twentieth Centuries', http//reference. Sabinet.co.za/webx/access/electronic-journal/kleio/kleio-v3a8pdf

Information on Vaal Triangle www.vaaltriangle.info.co.za/history/vereeniging/chapter_14/56.htm , p. 5

Slater, H. 'The Changing Pattern of Economic Relations in Rural Natal', http:// sas – space. ac.uk/3657/1

E. Mphahlele, The Evaton Riots, unpublished paper, www.disa.ukzn. ac.za/webpages/DC/asjan57.11/asjan57.11pdf

Primary sources

Digital Innovation South Africa, University of KwaZulu Natal Sanibona ILAM CR3735 Wilberforce Institute Singers, 1940

Documentation Centre for African Studies, University of South Africa, Urban Trade Regulations, Leo Kuper's Papers, FI 5854 Roll 1 Microfilm

Historical Papers, University of the Witwatersrand, Discussion notes of the Western Areas Scheme, Church and Society, SACC Collection, AC 623, 12.3.1, 1942

Historical Papers, University of the Witwatersrand, Minutes of the meeting between the Johannesburg African Chamber of Commerce and the Deputy Minister of Bantu Administration and Development, Records of the South African Institute of Race Relations papers, AD 1715, 18 November 1963

Historical Papers, University of the Witwatersrand, A letter from the Quintin Whyte to the Editor of Cape Times, Records of the South African Institute of Race Relations papers AD 1715, 11 April 1963

Historical Papers, Wilberforce Institute Financial Statement, A B Xuma Papers, AD 843, 1932-1933

Historical Papers, University of the Witwatersrand, A letter written by Eva Morake to Dr A.B. Xuma, Xuma Papers, 10 March 1937

Historical Papers, University of the Witwatersrand, Crogman Clinic Committee minutes, Xuma Papers, AD 843, 1945

Historical Papers, University of the Witwatersrand, Correspondence between the Director of the Institute of Race Relations and the Secretary for Native Affairs, RJ Records of the South African Institute of Race Relations papers, AD 1715

Historical Papers, University of the Witwatersrand Crogman Clinic Committee, Xuma, Papers AD 843, 1945

Historical Papers, University of the Witwatersrand A letter from Quintin Whyte to the members of the African Traders Action Committee, AD 1715, Records of the South African Institute of Race Relation papers, 5 April 1959

Historical Papers, University of the Witwatersrand A letter from Mr E. H Change to the Principal of Wilberforce Institute 7 March 1936, Xuma Papers, AD 834

Historical Papers, University of the Witwatersrand, An application letter for employment as a teacher from Tema J Motshumi to Dr Xuma, , AD 834, 20 February 1934

Historical Papers, University of the Witwatersrand, A letter from Mr H.M Burrough to the Transvaal Education Department, Xuma Papers, AD 834, 1937

Historical Papers, University of the Witwatersrand, A letter from Opperman to Dr Xuma on the increase of the student roll dated AB Xuma Papers, AD 834, 17 July 1938

National Archive of South Africa, A letter from Hope Baillie to the Acting Entomologist Mr Gunn, File BNS 1/8/ 116/ 4197, 25 July 1909

National Archive of South Africa, A letter from the Native Commissioner to the Secretary of Native Affairs on Evaton Administration matters, File NTS 361/364, 27 July 1930

National Archive of South Africa, A letter from the Native Commissioner to the Secretary of Native Affairs on Evaton Administration matters, NTS 361/364, 31 July 1930

National Archive of South Africa, A letter from Hope Baillie to the Acting Entomologist Mr Gunn, BNS 1/8/ 116/ 4197, 25 July 1909

National Archives of South Africa A letter from Easton, Adams and Company to the Director of Native Labour, File NTS 361/364, 9 November 1936

National Archives of South Africa, A letter from the Director of Native Labour to the Secretary for Native Affairs, NTS 361/362, September 1947

National Archive of South Africa, A letter from J. B. Malindisa to the Native Commissioner NTS 361/364, 28 August 1939

National Archives of South Africa, A letter written by Easton Adams Company to the Secretary Health Committee, NTS 361-364, 21 March 1936

National Archive of South Africa, A letter from Bunting to the Native Commissioner, 361/364, 1936

National Archives of South Africa A letter written by Easton Adams Company to the Secretary Health Committee, 21 March 1936, File NTS 361-364, 20 November 1916

National Archives of South Africa, A letter from the Secretary for Native Affairs to the Secretary for Justice, File JUS 240 3/881/6, 20 November 1916

National Archives of South Africa, A letter written to the Secretary of Native Affairs from the Native Commissioner, File, NTS 361/364 14 October 1915

National Archive of South Africa, A Letter from Macrobert and De Villiers Attorneys to the Secretary for Native Affairs, File, NTS 376 252/26, 16 January 1930

National Archive of South Africa, A letter written to the Secretary of Native Affairs from the Native Commissioner, NTS 361/364, 14 October 1915

National Archives of South Africa, A letter from J De Roos to the Secretary of Native Affairs JUS 240 3/881/16, 1 December 1916

National Archive of South Africa, A Letter from Macrobert and De Villiers Attorneys to the Secretary for Native Affairs dated NTS 376 252/26, 16 January 1930

National Archive of South Africa, A letter from J B Malindisa to the Native Commissioner NTS 361/364, 28 August 1939

National Archives of South Africa, A letter from the Secretary for Native Affairs to the Secretary for Justice 20 November 1916, 20 November 1916, JUS 240 3/881/6

National Archive of South Africa, A letter from the Assistant Native Commissioner to the Native Commissioner, File, NTS 1247 1385/16, 29 October 1951

National Archive of South Africa, A letter from the Assistant Native Commissioner to the Native Commissioner, NTS 1247 1385/1629, October 1951

National Archive of South Africa, A letter from the Native Commissioner to the Secretary of Native Affairs on Evaton Administration matters NTS 361/364, 27 July 1930

National Archive of South Africa, AA letter from Baillie to the Native Commissioner, File TALG 7/15571,

National Archive of South Africa, A letter from the Standholders of Small Farm to the Secretary for Native Affairs, File NTS 361/364, (undated)

National Archive of South Africa, A letter from Sam Rom Attorneys to the Secretary for Native Affairs, NTS 361/364, 6 December 1945

National Archive of South Africa, A letter from Sam Rom Attorneys to the Secretary for Native Affairs, NTS 361/364, 6 December 1945,

National Archive of South Africa, A letter from the Native Commissioner to the Secretary of Native Affairs on Evaton Administration matters NTS 361/364, 31 July 1930

National Archive of South Africa, A letter from Hope Baillie to the Acting Entomologist Mr Gunn dated, BNS 1/8/ 116/ 4197, 25 July 1909

National Archive of South Africa, A letter from the Secretary for Native Affairs to the Native Affairs Department NTS 361/364, 13 October 1944

National Archives of South Africa, A letter from J De Roos to the Secretary of Native Affairs, JUS 240 3/881/16, 1 December 1916

National Archives of South Africa, A letter from R. T. Luther to the Secretary for Native Affairs, GNLB 273, 3 April 1917

A letter from McCrobet and De Villiers Attorneys to the Secretary for Native Affairs dated 16 February 1930 NTS 376 252/56 National Archive of South Africa

National Archive of South Africa, A letter written by the Additional Native Commissioner in response to the trade license application of Josiah Moagi, NTS 1312/162

National Archive of South Africa A letter from Sergeant Pretorious to the Magistrate of Vereeniging, Enforcement of Dog Tax at Evaton Township, NTS 361/362, A letter from S. P Bunting Attorneys Notary and Conveyances written to the Secretary for Native Affairs, 28 September 1931, NTS 361/364, National Archive of South Africa,16 May 1933, Trade License Application for Jim Joubert, 29 March 1946, NTS 361/364 NTS 1244, 1323/162

National Archive of South Africa, A letter written to the Secretary of Native Affairs from the Native Commissioner 14 October 1915 NTS 361/364

National Archive of South Africa, A letter written by the Secretary for Native Affairs to Moagi on his application for mortgage bond 12 November 1941, NTS 361/ 364

National Archive of South Africa, Director of Native Agriculture's report on slaughter facilities NTS 361/364

National Archives of South Africa, A letter from R. T. Luther to the Secretary for Native Affairs dated 3 April 1917, GNLB 273

National Archives of South Africa, A letter from the Acting Chief Pass Officer to the Director of Native Labour GNLB 273 160/17/030

National Archives of South Africa, A letter from R. T. Luther to the Secretary for Native Affairs dated 3 April 1917, GNLB 273

National Archives of South Africa, A letter from the Acting Chief Pass Officer to the Director of Native Labour GNLB 273 160/17/030

National Archives of South Africa, A letter from S.P Bunting to the Secretary for Native Affairs, 28 September 1931 NTS 361/364, South African Native National Archives

National Archives of South Africa, Trade License Application for J Leburu NTS 1310/162, 13 August 1946

National Archives of South Africa, Trade License Application for Katy and Richard Ntshika, NTS 1305/162, 25 August 1946

National Archive of South Africa, Trade Licence Application for John Mtsweni, NTS 1244 1309/162, 27 November 1946

National Archive of South Africa, Report of the Native Affairs Commissioner on Evaton Township, 27 May 1947, NTS 361/364,

National Archive of South Africa, A report of the Native Commissioner reporting to the Honourable the Minister of Native Affairs,, 27 May 1947, NTS 361/364

National Archive of South Africa, The Report of the Deputy Director of Native Affairs entitled 'the future' undated NTS 361-364,

National Archive of South Africa, The Report of the Director of Native Agriculture on Evaton Native Slaughter Facilities, undated, NTS 361-364

National Archive of South Africa, The Report of the Acting Secretary to the Minister of Native Affairs, 27 May 1947, NTS 361/364

National Archive of South Africa, A Report of the Deputy Chief Health Inspector on Local Health Condition, 27 May 1940, NTS 361-364

National Archive of South Africa Report of the Native Affair Commission, NTS 361/364, 1939

National Archive of South Africa, The Report of the Secretary for Native Affairs, 15 September 1935, URU Vol, 524. Ref 3/881/16, A Report of the Deputy Chief Health

National Archive of South Africa, Inspector on Local Health Condition,17 May 1946, NTS 361-364

National Archive of South Africa, The Native Commissioner Report, 12 May 1941, NTS 361/364

National Archives of South Africa Untitled document from the Secretary of Native Affairs NTS 361/364

National Archive of South Africa, Peri Urban Health Inspectors Report. NTS 361/364, 3 May 1943

National Archive of South Africa, Report of the Native Affairs Commissioner on Evatton Township, , NTS 361/364, 27 May 1947

National Archives of South Africa Pass Officer report on his visit to Wilberforce Primary Section, 1919 NTS 373/56 5, December, 1935

National Archives of South Africa, A report from the Secretary of Native Affairs, SNA 287, NA 2870, 1905

National Archive of South Africa, A Letter from Macrobert and De Villiers Attorneys to the Secretary for Native Affairs NTS 376 252/26, 16 January 1930

National Archive of South Africa, Interim Report No. 7 in respect of Evaton, District Vereeniging in the Province of the Transvaal, , NTS 361/364, 11 March 1939

National Archive of South Africa, Native Affairs Memo on Question of Local Authority for Evaton Native Affairs, 11 June 1953, NTS 361/364

National Archive of South Africa, Interim Report No. 7 in respect of Evaton, District Vereeniging in the Province of the Transvaal, , NTS 361/364, 11 March 1939

National Archive of South Africa, Notes of Discussion with Dr. Maule Clark on Health Conditions at Evaton Native Township, , 361/364, 17 April 1947

National Archive of South Africa, The Health conditions report that was presented by Dr Clark to the Secretary for Native Affairs, , NTS 361/364, 12 May 1939

National Archive of South Africa, The Report of the Inspector of Urban Locations on Evaton Township, NTS 361/364, 1 September 1938

National Archive of South Africa, Evaton Health Committee, Regulation for the Supervision, Regulation and control of Businesses, Trade and Occupation Amendments. TALG 13/155552, 1947

National Archive of South Africa, Evaton Health Committee, Executive Committee, TALG 13/155552 27 August 1954

National Archives of South Africa, A Report of the Secretary of Peri Urban Health Board, NTS 361/364, 12 August 1956

National Archive of South Africa, The Discussion with Dr Maule Clark, Deputy Chief Health Inspector at Pretoria on the conditions at Evaton Native Township, NTS 361/ 364, 17 April 1947

The Office of the Surveyor General, Pretoria, Deeds of Transfer 9427/1905 9428/ 1905

Government Publication

Native Urban Areas Act, Act No. 21 of 1923, Union of South Africa, Pretoria, Government Printers 1923

Native Economic Commission, Sol Plaatjie testimony in Economic Commission, 1932, UG. 22 Pretoria, Government Printers

Occupation of Church, School and Mission Sites in Native Areas, prepared by Union Department of Native Affairs, Government Printing and Stationary Office, Pretoria, 1918

Official Yearbook of the Union of South Africa, 1960, p 535, Pretoria, *Government* Printers

Report of the Commission of Inquiry into Trade Licensing and Allied Problem, Government Publisher, Union of South Africa U G 2, 1961

Report of the Commission of Inquiry into Shop hours to the honourable administrator of Transvaal on shop hours, Pretoria, Government Printers, 1968

Newspapers and Magazines

The Rand Daily Mail, 20 June 1933
The Black Sash Magazine, 1983, p. 25
Native Labour, *Friend* 26 February 1892.